To the Great
Crew at De Gustibus...
You are the Best!
not my handwriting!
_____ Amos

Thank you very much to Arlene, Bobbi and
Florence for your help who made this demonstration
atractive and fun! Keep the calories down from now on!

Arlene —
    Wow, was the _____ ! I
want you to know how grateful I am
that you considered me to give a class.
I enjoyed every minute (then collapsed
on my bed as soon as I got home!).
    I really loved working with — and
was so impressed by _____ — your staff.

The best places to
be in New York...
...with Arlene

To
Dear Arlene
and to all
the girls that
made it so
easy.
    Thank you
Con affetto
Nadia

Dear Arlene,
    I just wanted to thank
you again for inviting me
on the De Gustibus program.
Your arrangements + organisation were excellent and
it was a great pleasure to
work with you.
    Please do drop by any
time you are in Paris.
    All best wishes for the
continuing success of the
series

Dear Arlene —
    Just a note to
thank you for your
assistance with the
Cooking Class. It was
Vas without a doubt
our best experience
with the New York
Trip. Your team is
tops and you run
a great operation
    Best _____

Dear All —
Thanks for treating
us so well! You
have spoiled us for
all our other classes
Emmy, Mark, Parke

What a wonderful time;
I enjoyed the time; to no ends
Sincerely
Edna Lewis

Arlene,

Thanks for having me at De Gustibus. Your staff was fantastic; so helpful + friendly and it was amazing to see + experience what you've worked so hard to build + grow. The place feels of 1,000 good times.

I'll be back hopefully on a book tour w/ books in hand?!!

Happy Holidays!

[signature]

It was nice to be here.

[signatures]

Arlene –

Thank you for having us at De Gustibus. You are always so wonderful to speak to – you instill such energy and creativity in your classes. We enjoyed it very much – and the KNIVES ARE FABULOUS!

David Page and Barbara Shinn
(Home Restaurant)

To the Wonderful Staff at De Gustibus,

Many Thanks for such a Wonderful Team Effort. You Made it so Easy to Have Fun And Enjoy my Classes At your School.

All My Best for a Wonderful Holiday!

Sincerely,
[signature]
@ 5/15

P.S. Looking forward to seeing everyone @ 5/15

Wow! What an extraordinary time. I can't thank every one enough for all the support and hard work. Things are wonderful working end with a team such as De Gustibus' an easy one, or well. Congratulations your faithfully observed award.

James Bond

Dear Arlene,

Had a wonderful and challenging time at De Gustibus. Thanks for all your help and support. Your staff was great.

Best –
Jane

Best Wishes to all my new friends.

Dear Arlene –

A belated but sincere thanks for having Joe and me at De Gustibus. My highest compliments to you and your terrific staff. We felt very welcome and your efforts on behalf of our book were greatly appreciated. Any time you want us back, we'll be there?!. And thanks so much for accommodating my mother and her friends — very generous.

All Best,

David Lynch

COOKING AT
DE GUSTIBUS

De Gustibus COOKING SCHOOL

De Gustibus at Ma[...]

THE GREAT C[...]

We dine in restaurants and cook at home. The p[...]
cooks in restaurants and dines at home.

The simple fact is: both **we** and **they** are home co[...]
Which is why a spirit of warmth and authenticity p[...]
De Gustibus cooking classes. It's an assemblage [...]
world's foremost culinary talents— who also prep[...]
wholesome, unpretentious, delicious food for frie[...]
Same as we do.

So, you'll get cooking tips and techniques, recipe[...]
best **home cooks** ever.

Take Master Chef Jacques Pepin. He learned "ea[...]
stringiest chicken neck or a drop of precious fish[...]

Jim Dodge, one of the new breed of American b[...]
Barely adds sugar. Puts six bananas in banana [...]
distractions. Simple. Real. Down-to-earth.

And Maestro Giuliano Bugialli dares to say: "It[...]
discover **real** Italian food . . . follow a truck driv[...]

Or, follow De Gustibus' world-renowned chefs [...]
selected by Maison Louis Jadot, **you'll** become [...]

All classes will be held in our professionally-eq[...]
Enrollment is limited, so please register now. Fo[...]

COOKING AT
DE GUSTIBUS

Celebrating 25 Years

of Culinary Innovation

Arlene Feltman Sailhac

STEWART, TABORI & CHANG

NEW YORK

With deepest love, I dedicate this book first to my father, Stanley Kessler, who is always with me in spirit.
I can't quite believe that he won't be in the Boca Raton bookstore asking,
"Doesn't everyone want to buy my daughter's book?"

And to my mother, Adelaide, for her courage and independence and for
taking me back to my youth by asking daily, "Have you finished the book yet?"

And, of course, to my son, Todd Feltman, and my husband, Alain Sailhac—
could anyone have two stronger supporters?

Text copyright © 2005 Arlene Feltman Sailhac

Recipe credits and acknowledgments appear on page 6

Food photographs copyright © 2005 Ellen Silverman

Published in 2005 by
Stewart, Tabori & Chang
115 West 18th Street
New York, NY 10011
www.abramsbooks.com

Library of Congress Cataloging-in-Publication Data
Feltman-Sailhac, Arlene.
Cooking at De Gustibus at Macy's : celebrating twenty-five years of culinary innovation / Arlene Feltman Sailhac.
p. cm.
Includes index.
ISBN 1-58479-459-3
1. Cookery. I. De Gustibus (Cooking school) II. Title.

TX714.F45 2005
641.5--dc22
2005018800

Designed by Jessi Rymill and Galen Smith
Graphic Production by Kim Tyner

The text of this book was composed in Clarendon, Sabon, and Trade Gothic.

Printed in China

10 9 8 7 6 5 4 3 2 1

First Printing

Stewart, Tabori & Chang is a subsidiary of
LA MARTINIÈRE

Page 2 (clockwise from top left): *Tyler Florence and me with the De Gustibus team; Paul Prudhomme; Jacques Pépin; Giuliano Bugialli; Nobu Matsuhisa; Giuliano Bugialli, Jane Asche, and Alain Sailhac; James Beard; Craig Kominiak and Julia Child.*

CONTENTS

CREDITS

p. 26: From *Craig Claiborne's: A Feast Made for Laughter* by Craig Claiborne, copyright © 1982 by Craig Claiborne. Used with permission of Doubleday, a division of Random House, Inc.

p. 28: From *The Wolfgang Puck Cookbook* by Wolfgang Puck, copyright © 1986 by Wolfgang Puck. Used by permission of Random House, Inc.

p. 29: From *The Foods and Wines of Spain* by Penelope Casas, copyright © 1982 by Penelope Casas. Used by permission of Alfred A. Knopf, a division of Random House, Inc.

p. 31: From *The Classic Italian Cookbook* by Marcella Hazan, copyright © 1976 by Marcella Hazan. Used by permission of Random House, Inc.

p. 37: From *Chez Panisse Pasta, Pizza and Calzone* by Alice Waters, copyright © 1984 by Tango Rose, Inc. Used by permission of Random House, Inc.

p. 40: Recipe created by Madeleine Kamman. All rights reserved.

p. 47: From *The Prudhomme Family Cookbook* by Paul Prudhomme, copyright © 1987 by Paul Prudhomme. Reprinted by permission of HarperCollins Publishers, Inc.

p. 63: Copyright © 2000 Susan Feniger and Mary Sue Milliken. All rights reserved.

p. 68: Charlie Palmer and Judith Choate.

p. 88: From *Cooking with Daniel Boulud* by Daniel Boulud, copyright © 1993 by Daniel Boulud. Used by permission of Random House, Inc.

p. 95: From *The Italian Baker* by Carol Field, copyright © 1985 by Carol Field. Reprinted by permission of HarperCollins Publishers, Inc.

p. 114: From *Moosewood Cookbook* by Mollie Katzen.

p. 116: Excerpted from *China Moon Cookbook*. Copyright © 1992 by Barbara Tropp. Used by permission of Workman Publishing Co., Inc., New York. All rights reserved.

p. 123: Adapted from *The Splendid Table: Recipes from Emilia-Romagna, the Heartland of Northern Italian Food* (New York: William Morrow). Copyright © 1992 by Lynne Rossetto Kasper. Used by permission of the author. All rights reserved.

p. 126: Reprinted with permission from *Fog City Diner* by Cindy Pawlcyn. Copyright © 1993 by Cindy Pawlcyn, Ten Speed Press, Berkeley, CA. www.tenspeed.com.

p. 142: Reprinted with permission of Simon & Schuster Adult Publishing Group from *The Figs Cookbook* by Todd English and Sally Sampson. Copyright © 1998 by Todd English and Sally Sampson.

p. 144: From *Four-Star Desserts* by Emily Luchetti, HarperCollins Publishers, Inc., 1996. Used by permission of the author.

p. 164: From *Adventures in Jewish Cooking* by Jeffrey Nathan, copyright © 2002 by Jeffrey Nathan. Used by permission of Clarkson Potter/Publishers, a division of Random House, Inc.

p. 178: From *Mario Batali Simple Italian Food* by Mario Batali, copyright © 1998 by Mario Batali. Used by permission of Clarkson Potter/Publishers, a division of Random House, Inc.

p. 188: From *Not Afraid of Flavor: Recipes from Magnolia Grill* by Ben and Karen Barker. Photographs by Ann Parks Hawthorne. Copyright © 2000 by Ben and Karen Barker. Used by permission of the University of North Carolina Press. http://www.uncpress.unc.edu/.

p. 190: From *The Last Course* by Claudia Fleming, copyright © 2001 by Claudia Fleming. Used by permission of Random House, Inc.

p. 216: From *The Zuni Café Cookbook* by Judy Rodgers. Copyright © 2002 by Judy Rodgers. Used by permission of W. W. Norton & Company, Inc.

ACKNOWLEDGMENTS

After twenty-five years, I could fill this entire book with the names of people who need to be thanked. There are countless reasons why, but the main one is their dedication to the creation of the finest dining in the world, which has made these twenty-five years speed by. Since I don't have the room to name everyone individually, I would like to first deeply thank the seven hundred and fifty chefs, cooking teachers, authors, and other experts for sharing their knowledge, their love, and their food in the many De Gustibus classes. It has been an inspiration and a privilege to have you join us in our search for the finest culinary experience. I can honestly say that, without each of you, De Gustibus at Macy's could not exist.

And from there, many, many thanks must go to:

My extremely loyal clients—words can never express what your dedication has meant to me and to the De Gustibus classroom.

Cathleen Burke and all of the people at the Kobrand Corporation who have, over the years, enlightened our audience with an unbelievable array of the finest international wines and created an everlasting bond through their appreciation of the pairing of great food and fine wine.

Jane Asche, for being with De Gustibus for the past twenty-two years—your loyal support and devotion to our work has made my job so much easier.

Amaral Milbredt, who has been the consummate professional, allowing us to orchestrate a truly proficient kitchen under every conceivable circumstance.

Judith Choate, my wonderful and reassuring writer, sounding board, food maven, and good friend.

Judith Weber, my faithful agent, who went beyond the call of duty reading my manuscript and offering sage advice.

Leslie Stoker, the brilliant publisher of Stewart, Tabori & Chang and Galen Smith of the same, who did a masterful job of taking twenty-five years of collateral material and turning it into the yearbook I imagined.

Jessi Rymill, for all of her artistic help.

Leda Scheintaub, for her terrific recipe testing.

Ellen Silverman, for her fine food photography.

And, of course, all of the people at Macy's Herald Square who believed in my idea of creating a world-class cooking school in the store.

From the Beginning

There probably has not been a day during the past twenty-five years that I have not been thinking about or planning for a De Gustibus event. "What does the audience really want to see and learn about?" "What is the hot topic—the hotter chef?" "What are the trends pointing toward?" "What chefs should we book for next season?" "What can we do to keep the kitchen assistants excited?" "What do we need to add to the kitchen to meet the demands of the experimental young chefs?" "How do I balance the classes that we need to do in a way that will accommodate the busy schedules of the chefs and the audience?" And you know what? I've enjoyed every moment of these years—the planning, the execution, the friendships, the growth of my own knowledge about the culinary arts, the near-disasters, the laughs, the losses, the excitement. Like a mother with a tribe of unruly children, I wouldn't have missed one day of it.

My life was not always this exciting. Growing up, I was always first to the table, and in our house there were two table rules: more is better; and eat fast so you can get seconds before someone else empties the dish. I had a grandmother who believed in using only high-quality seasonal ingredients and cooked with great style, but in my house we had ordinary meals with no fancy dishes served. I was, however, fascinated with cookbooks and loved to watch the first televised cooking shows, featuring such early culinary luminaries as Dione Lucas. I fancied a career in the hospitality industry, but my parents insisted that I get a teaching degree so that I could always support myself. In the end, their insistence turned out to be fortuitous for me.

I dutifully went off to college and graduate school and became a certified speech pathologist. I immediately went to work, then got married, entertained a lot, and worked as a speech pathologist while living in many different places, includ-

ing Brussels, Belgium, where I had my first major food epiphany.

In 1975 I returned to New York and landed a job supervising the speech clinic at City College. It was during this period that I met and struck up a friendship with Doris Weisberg, a professor in the department. We took the Convent Avenue bus together daily and spent most of our travel time talking about food, our mutual passion. Doris had attended some short-lived lectures at Hunter College featuring food professionals discussing all areas of cuisine. When we realized that there was nothing comparable in New York City, we decided to adapt a program similar to the one at Hunter. We boldly asked Perla Meyers, Jacques Pépin, Giuliano Bugialli, and Paula Wolfert each to give a talk about their careers and particular interest in food. I can assure you that ignorance is truly bliss! They all said yes, as they were based in New York City and, although they traveled around the country teaching, there were very few places in New York where they could talk about their specialties.

After we had our lineup, we realized that we had no facility in which to feature them. Since we had no budget, no audience, and no expertise, it wasn't easy to find a spot. After much looking, however, we settled on CAMI Hall, the annex to Carnegie Hall. It had a large stage and an auditorium—and that was it. Well, it may have had a sound system—I don't remember.

Perla was the first guest. She said, "I'm not going to speak for three hours, I need to cook." So she brought an assistant, an electric frying pan, a chicken breast, some garlic, and butter. And even salt and pepper! She talked and talked, and all we heard was the assistant chopping garlic in the background. So began De Gustibus!

We continued at CAMI Hall for another season, but when Jacques Pépin began his class carving tiny olives, onions, and lemons into little animals to be used for garnishing and nobody could see or hear, we thought we had better change our venue. Besides, Jacques told us, "I don't want to be on a stage. I need to be near the people," and we realized that if we were going to continue to attract leading culinary personalities and an audience, we would have to provide a little bit more.

During this time, Doris and I were still working at the college. Although it was a bit exhausting, we believed so strongly in what we were doing that we decided to search for a bigger and better space and continue with our classes. We found TOMI Hall (the Theatre Opera Music Institute), where theatrical performances were held every night but Monday—which suited us just fine!

Having a little more self-confidence by now, we invited Julia Child, Marcella Hazan, Diana Kennedy, and, again, Jacques Pépin—this time to really cook for a crowd. The theater changed its scenery every week, so we never knew if there would be an avant-garde abstract or a rural farmhouse as the backdrop for our chefs. I have to admit that some of the guest chefs didn't find this as amusing as we did.

As we began to get more into the cooking part of the presentations rather than the lecturing, we needed water, electricity for our portable stoves, mirrors, kitchen equipment, and, of course, some type of refrigeration. There was absolutely nothing kitchenlike about the theater, so Doris and I became culinary sherpas. We would pack up the items from the featured chef's shopping list and haul them to the theater. After the demonstration we would hand out plastic utensils and the audience would come up to the stage to sample a bite of the chef's presentation. People seemed to have a good time, but being young and eager, we believed that we could do better.

Along came Perla again. She told us that she had designed a cooking school on the eighth floor of Macy's Herald Square that she was no longer using and that it was probably available. Macy's was offering some cooking classes but did not have the personnel to run a real school. Doris and I met with the head of special events, Ruth Schwartz, who was also passionate about food and who thought that we could make a great freelance project of the school. Now the fun really began!

De Gustibus now had a proper kitchen and an almost-private space—we were partitioned off from the selling floor but had a door and some very nice chairs for the audience. We "fattened" the program, adding some more high-profile chefs who would present many different types of food as well as prepare enough to give a sample of everything that they cooked to our guests. I threw myself into the program, but Doris decided that her calling was really academia, so I bought the school and became the sole proprietor. On my own and a bit scared, I soldiered forth.

For years, people had eaten their four-star meals on their laps, picnic-style. Some of the regulars brought their own boxes with which they would create laptop tables on which they could dine in style. We called them, with fondness, "the box people."

It was my goal to present the world's best cooking talents to avocational cooks just like me who wanted to learn as much as they could about the proper way to cook without going to a professional cooking school. I tried to invite all of the

9

chefs who I felt could help educate us, but I have to say I did not foresee that many of these chefs would become the rock stars of the food world. I started with such exceptional personalities as André Soltner, Martha Stewart, Wolfgang Puck, and Paul Prudhomme. Emeril Lagasse taught his first class when he had just been made the executive chef at Commander's Palace. Alain Ducasse came when he was thinking of opening a restaurant in Pittsburgh. Daniel Boulud was the souschef at the Polo Room in the Westbury Hotel in New York City. My husband-to-be, Alain Sailhac, was executive chef at Le Cirque, where the most sophisticated diners in the world ate nightly. Then came along the young turks—the Americans Larry Forgione, Charlie Palmer, and Alfred Portale among them. What a lineup we had.

As the De Gustibus audience became more and more knowledgeable and the chefs more creative, I knew that I had to improve the facilities. The classes were still sharing space with Macy's puppet theater, so at Christmas and Easter we had to pack up all of our equipment, wheel out the stove, and totally close down to make room for the elves and bunnies to move in. As luck would have it, Macy's decided that Santa was going to be a virtual reality and we had to vacate the De Gustibus home of seventeen years.

We were shifted to a very welcoming, at-long-last private spot, in which a state-of-the-art demonstration kitchen was re-created. Miele appliances constructed a spectacular kitchen, and we were able to obtain fine china and glassware on which to feature the four-star meals being prepared. We furnished the space with long tables and comfortable chairs for the audience. From our original six classes per year, we went to one hundred and twenty classes annually, including hands-on, on-location classes in restaurant kitchens where the students are instructed by the restaurant's chef as they prepare the meal of the day, as well as summer culinary excursions abroad. I have hosted all but two of the classes over the past twenty-five years—for one of them I was too ill to stand and crack the jokes that the classes had gotten used to, and for the other I was getting married to my very special chef, Alain Sailhac.

I have tasted all of the meals that have been prepared in the De Gustibus classroom throughout these wonderful years. I can honestly say that I have never had a bad one! They have all excited my palate and urged me to continue my quest for learning. Unfortunately, I would have needed an encyclopedia-sized book to share them all with you. So, for this book, I will go on just a little gastronomic trip through time so that we can see some of the seminal moments in the history of De Gustibus. At first I thought some of the recipes would be dated, but in fact I found even the oldest ones to be just as timely today as they were when they were first presented. I have tried to select those recipes and those chefs who made a special mark on the periods I featured here.

As you might have already guessed, I think that De Gustibus is a very privileged place to be. I have enjoyed the meals of more than seven hundred of the world's best cooks, some of them four-star chefs, some of them brilliant food writers, and all of them friends. At De Gustibus we have seen ingredients used long before they became widely available, tasted the finest foods available, and watched intently as meals were prepared with singular commitment and great love. I have learned something new almost every day and still eagerly look forward to each class. The world of food has never been brighter or more thought-provoking, and I am looking forward to another twenty-five years of culinary pleasure. I very much hope that you enjoy looking backward through our history.

—Arlene Feltman Sailhac, September 2005

De Gustibus non est disputandum
(Of taste there is no dispute)

Right (clockwise from top left): *Alain Sailhac and me; Barbie Teplitz and Betti Zucker with customers; Wolfgang Puck; Rocco DiSpirito; Julia Child and me with De Gustibus chefs and staff; Jean-Louis Palladin; André Soltner.*

DE GUSTIBUS

The Great
Cooks
reveal their
secrets

1980 to 1985

The Senior Class

When my own passion led me to organize cooking classes in New York, I had absolutely no idea that a culture of cuisine was in its embryonic stage. I simply thought that there might be other home cooks who would enjoy learning more about cooking and food by taking classes with recognized professionals. Although I had heard about culinary adventures in other cities, at that time there were no cooking classes of the type that I envisioned in New York City. It seemed like an opportune time to do something with my own personal enthusiasm for the *art culinaire*.

Our first press bite came from Suzanne Hamlin in the New York *Daily News*, who led off her article as follows: "Two women, university professors by trade, food fans by avocation, have organized a series of talks which they have tagged 'De Gustibus' or, in full Latin, '*de gustibus non est disputandum*'—of taste there is no dispute." She continued, "The featured food personalities promise a full evening." In fact, these first classes *were* more lecture than demonstration, and I had no thought that they could evolve into actual teaching classes giving center stage to four-star meals prepared in a theater setting in one of the world's great department stores and accompanied by incomparable wines presented by all of the world's great chefs and food personalities.

In the beginning most of the De Gustibus classes featured cooking teachers, cookbook authors, or food writers, since chefs were not yet the headliners that they would become. Julia Child, THE STAR in 1980, was the most well-known of our prominent guests due to her nationally distributed Public Broadcasting System television series. The others were cookbook authors or food personalities with very defined interests: Giuliano Bugialli and Marcella Hazan, both writers and teachers, focused on the foods of their native Italy; Jacques Pépin was just beginning to meld American ingenuity into the French classics of his homeland; British ex-pat Diana Kennedy was becoming a recognized authority on classic Mexican cooking; Paula Wolfert had just begun her long-term concentration on the foods of the Mediterranean; and Perla Meyers seemed to have an inkling of the future with her spotlight on cooking with seasonal ingredients. We were just beginning to see a broadening interest in a myriad of cuisines as they were incorporated into American culinary traditions, and all of these cooks and teachers would have an impact on the future of American food.

Our first featured restaurant chef was Michel Fitoussi in 1981. He had caught the attention of the New York press as well as restaurant goers with his unprecedented and (then-considered) outrageously expensive $50.00 prix fixe menu at the Palace Restaurant, which featured such exotica as gold leaf–covered foods. This put us all on notice that we were in the midst of a revolution into over-the-top restaurant experiences which went hand in hand with equally over-the-top entertaining in public places led by catering companies such as Glorious Foods. Wall Street was booming, wallets were flush, and the culinary world reaped the benefits. As the restaurant scene flourished, so did the chefs. For the first time in history, the next five years would find American chefs competing with Hollywood stars for tabloid attention.

Preceding pages (clockwise from top left):
Madeleine Kamman; Dieter Schorner; James Beard and me; Alice Waters; Perla Meyers; André Soltner; Larry Forgione; Paul Prudhomme; De Gustibus audience; illustration of Julia Child; Alain Sailhac.
Right: *Craig Claiborne.*

> From *The Restaurant Reporter*:
> "Those well-organized and **appetite-inspiring lectures** on cooking are under way again. As usual, the outfit behind them, De Gustibus, shows **superb taste in speakers** who will work in a well-laid-out facility."

14

1980–1985

Andree Abramoff
Len Allison
Elizabeth Andoh
Lee Bailey
Jean Banchet
Lidia Bastianich
James Beard
Simone Beck
Rose Levy Beranbaum
Antoine Bouterin
Gerard Boyer
Flo Braker
Giuliano Bugialli
Marian Burros
Jane Butel
Anna Theresa Callen
Penelope Casas
Michel Chabran
Julia Child
Craig Claiborne
John Clancy
Bernard Clayton
Marion Cunningham
Ariane Daguin
Julie Dannenbaum
Abe De La Houssaye

Michel Fitoussi
Larry Forgione
Pierre Franey
André Gerin
Ed Giobbi
Richard Grausman
Gael Green

Jacques Maximin
Perla Meyers
Maurice Moore-Betty
Judith Olney
Jean-Louis Palladin
Guy Pascal
Jacques Pépin

The very first time that **Jean-Jacques Rachou,** the chef-owner of the influential French restaurant **La Côte Basque** in New York City, was scheduled to teach a class at De Gustibus, he decided that he would rather serve lunch than do a demonstration. He brought a fully prepared **four-course lunch** for eighty people up on the passenger elevators, but no raw ingredients. Luckily, this was when Macy's still had a marketplace, so we all ran down to buy raw chicken, vegetables, and so forth so he could, at the least, give some demonstration of how he had prepared our magnificent lunch. Being the consummate pro, he pulled it off beautifully. The letter of agreement between chefs and De Gustibus was totally revised after that experience!

In an invitation to Perla Meyers, dated December 29, 1980, I wrote, "We have made **several changes** from our first series. First, we are in a smaller theater with inclined seating so **everyone can see.** We also have an overhead mirror. Most important, however, our events are five cooking demonstrations revolving around a central theme."

Christian Delouvrier
Alain Ducasse
Florence Fabricant

Bert Greene
Marcella Hazan
Libby Hillman
Christopher Idone
Yan Jacquot
Madhur Jaffrey
Judith Jones
Barbara Kafka
Madeleine Kamman
Diana Kennedy
Albert Kumin
Jean Paul Lacombe
Emeril Lagasse
Karen Lee
Gaston Lenôtre
Edna Lewis
Florence Lin
Sheila Lukins
Copland Marks
Lydie Marshall
Zarela Martinez

Paul Prudhomme
Wolfgang Puck
Jean-Jacques Rachou
Felipe Rojas-Lombardi
Anne Rosenzweig
Michel Rostang
Julie Sahni
Alain Sailhac
Richard Sax
Francine Scherer
Dieter Schorner
André Soltner
Marlene Sorosky
Martha Stewart
Jeremiah Tower
Alice Waters
Barry Wine with
    Noel Commis
Paula Wolfert
Eileen Yin-Fei Lo

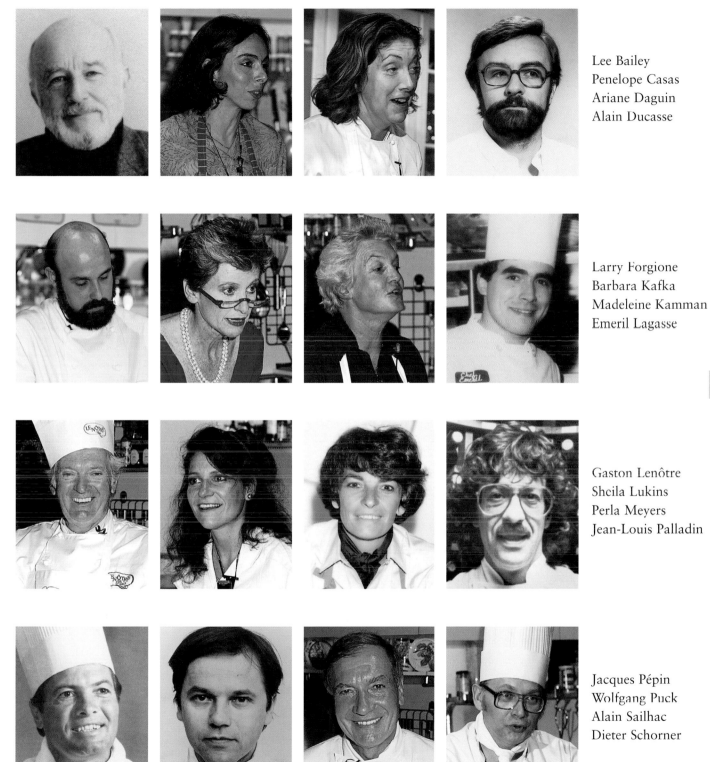

Lee Bailey
Penelope Casas
Ariane Daguin
Alain Ducasse

Larry Forgione
Barbara Kafka
Madeleine Kamman
Emeril Lagasse

Gaston Lenôtre
Sheila Lukins
Perla Meyers
Jean-Louis Palladin

Jacques Pépin
Wolfgang Puck
Alain Sailhac
Dieter Schorner

Daniel Boulud
Alain Ducasse
Thomas Keller
Emeril Lagasse
Wolfgang Puck
Jean-Georges Vongerichten

AN AMERICAN PLACE
CHEZ PANISSE
THE FOUR SEASONS
THE FRENCH LAUNDRY
JAMS
LA CÔTE BASQUE
LE CIRQUE
LE FRANÇAIS
LUTÈCE
NOBU
THE RIVER CAFE
SPAGO
STARS
THE QUILTED GIRAFFE
YUCA

25 YEARS OF

STANDING
ALONE

JULIA CHILD

MOST INFLUENTIAL
RESTAURANTS

MOST POPULAR CUISINE
THROUGHOUT THE YEARS

FRENCH

MOST HEROIC CHEF

ANDRÉ SOLTNER

He was scheduled for an operation to remove kidney stones the morning of his class and was in terrible pain but said, "I cannot cancel with so many people involved."

FROM THE AUDIENCE TO THE STAGE

SARA MOULTON, *who was and still is the head of the test kitchen for Gourmet magazine, used to take classes at De Gustibus as part of the magazine's enrichment program. She subsequently became a television superstar and one of our best-loved teachers.*

Superlatives

1980 to 2005

MOST LONG-STANDING DE GUSTIBUS TEACHER

GIULIANO BUGIALLI, *who has taught to sold-out classes for every one of our twenty-five years.*

ON THE MENU

APPETIZERS, SOUPS, AND SALADS

Watercress and Scallop Salad
Perla Meyers—1981

Petites Homards de Maine en Court Bouillon
(Elegant Lobster Soup)
Alain Sailhac—1983

Terrine de Foie Gras au Sauternes
Ariane Daguin—1985

Buffalo Chicken Wings
Craig Claiborne—1983

Radicchio and Arugula Salad
with Hot Goat Cheese and Herbs
Wolfgang Puck—1983

Ensalada de Anguilas
(Baby Eel Salad)
Penelope Casas—1983

Flaked Parsley Salad
with Black Olives and Pecorino Cheese
Paula Wolfert—1985

SAUCES AND SIDES

Tomato Sauce I
Marcella Hazan—1980

Eggplant in the Neapolitan Style
Giuliano Bugialli—1981

Baked Apples with Morels for James Beard
Larry Forgione—1983

Gingered Cranberry Relish
Sheila Lukins—1983

PASTA AND GRAINS

Squash and Nasturtium Blossom Pasta
Alice Waters—1984

Liang Mien Huang
(Two-Sides Browned Noodles)
Florence Lin—1981

MEAT, GAME, AND POULTRY

Aiguillettes d'Agneau à la Bateliere
(Thin Strips of Lamb in the Style of the Barge People)
Madeleine Kamman—1984

Poularde en Papillon Fermière
(Butterflied Roast Chicken)
Julia Child—1980

Poulet au Vinaigre
(Chicken in Vinegar Sauce)
Jacques Pépin—1980

FISH AND SHELLFISH

Shrimp Étouffée
Paul Prudhomme—1983

BREAD AND DESSERTS

Brioche Nanterre or *Parisienne*
(French Brioche)
Bernard Clayton—1984

De Gustibus Lemon Tart
Albert Kumin—1984

Crème Brûlée
Dieter Schorner—1982

WATERCRESS AND SCALLOP SALAD
1981
PERLA MEYERS, *Cookbook Author, Teacher*

Perla was one of the first teachers at De Gustibus. Although invited to lecture, she said, "talking is not enough," so she brought an electric frying pan to CAMI Hall (the annex of Carnegie Hall, our first venue), and while she talked, her assistant sautéed chicken breasts and garlic in the pan sitting on the stage floor. Perla also introduced us to the kitchen at Macy's, for which we are eternally grateful. Beyond all of this, Perla has been a pioneer in the promotion of seasonal cooking and is one of our most respected teachers.

For many years in America, watercress was used almost exclusively as a garnish. In this recipe Perla showed how this inexpensive peppery green created a much more interesting salad than iceberg lettuce, which many people were still using as a basic salad green. With her focus on healthful, seasonal cooking, Perla was way ahead of the pack.

---

2 large bunches fresh watercress

½ pound bay scallops (see Note)

2 cups vegetable stock

¼ cup crème fraîche

2 tablespoons Dijon mustard

¼ cup walnut oil

2 tablespoons red wine vinegar

Coarse salt and freshly ground pepper to taste

2 tablespoons minced fresh chives or scallion greens

Bay scallops are tiny, very sweet, and usually expensive East Coast scallops. On the West Coast, small calico scallops are often sold as bay scallops.

Trim the watercress, discarding the tough stems. Place the watercress in cold water to cover and, using your hands, gently mix to remove any dirt. Drain well and rinse again in cold water. Dry well in paper towels or in a salad spinner.

Place the scallops in a salad bowl, cover with damp paper towel, and refrigerate.

Place the vegetable stock in a small saucepan over medium heat and bring to a simmer. Add the scallops, lower the heat, and cook, without boiling, for about 3 minutes, or until the scallops are opaque. Do not overcook the scallops or they will be tough.

Transfer the scallops and cooking liquid from the pan to a bowl, and immediately place it in an ice-water bath to chill the scallops quickly. Once chilled, the scallops can be refrigerated in their cooking liquid until ready to serve.

Combine the crème fraîche and mustard in a small bowl. Whisk in the oil and vinegar, then season with salt and pepper to taste. Add the chives, taste, and if necessary season again with salt and pepper.

Drain the scallops and pat them dry.

Remove the watercress from the refrigerator and toss in the scallops. Drizzle the dressing over the top and toss to coat lightly. Add a large grinding of pepper and serve immediately.

Serves 4

PETITES HOMARDS DE MAINE EN COURT BOUILLON
(ELEGANT LOBSTER SOUP)
1983

ALAIN SAILHAC, *Chef, Executive Dean at The French Culinary Institute*

Le Cirque Restaurant, owned by Sirio Maccioni, was the place to be seen in the roaring eighties. But unlike many other hot spots, the food was more than equal to the scene. Alain Sailhac (now my husband) brought three stars to the table as he veered toward the light side of the classic French cuisine in which he had been trained. His style greatly influenced many of the young American chefs who were climbing the stairway to the stars during the heyday of the big spender.

With this recipe, Alain showed the class that a very elegant soup could be prepared ahead of time so that home cooks could present a restaurant-quality dish at a dinner party. It was also the first time that we had seen *pousse Pierre* used, and Alain suggested that its delicate sea flavor would also work well as an accent to grilled or roasted fish.

I am always amazed to watch Alain cooking professionally in front of the class, as it gives me the opportunity to understand his culinary artistry, which I never see at home. Believe it or not, he can even make the process of pâté making seem sexy as he gently smooths the top. He is a spectacular chef and an even greater husband!

Head of 1 red snapper

Four 1-pound lobsters

1 stalk celery, well washed, peeled, and cut crosswise into thin slices

4 ounces (about 2 medium) carrots, peeled and thinly sliced crosswise

4 ounces (about 1 medium) onion, peeled and chopped

Coarse salt and freshly ground pepper to taste

1 large ripe tomato, peeled, cored, seeds and membrane removed, and finely diced

2 tablespoons coarsely chopped fresh flat-leaf parsley

4 ounces *pousse Pierre*, blanched (see sidebar)

2 tablespoons coarsely chopped fresh dill

To make the bouillon, place the snapper head in a bowl with cold water to cover. Allow to soak for 15 minutes.

Place the lobsters in a stockpot with at least 8 quarts of water. Bring to a boil and boil for 3 minutes. Remove from the heat and drain well, reserving half of the lobster cooking water. Set the lobsters aside to cool slightly. Return the reserved lobster cooking water to a large saucepan.

Drain the snapper head and cut it into four pieces. Add the pieces to the lobster cooking water. Place over medium-high heat and bring to a boil. Lower the heat and simmer for 30 minutes or until reduced by half, skimming off the foam and particles that rise to the surface.

Strain the reduced fish stock through a fine sieve into a clean saucepan. Add the celery, carrots, and onion and return to medium-high heat. Bring just to a boil and immediately lower the heat. Cook at a bare simmer for 30 minutes. Remove from the heat and season with salt and pepper to taste. Again, strain the stock into a clean saucepan and place over low heat to keep warm. Taste and, if necessary, add salt and pepper to taste. (The recipe can be made up to this point and the stock cooled in an ice-water bath, placed in a storage container, covered, and refrigerated for 1 day or frozen for up to 3 months.)

To make the soup, preheat the oven to 200°F.

Shell the lobsters, carefully keeping the body and claw meat intact. Using a sharp knife, cut the bodies crosswise into very thin slices.

Place an equal portion of the sliced lobster meat in each of four shallow soup bowls. Place the bowls in the warm oven for just 30 seconds to warm slightly.

Remove the soup bowls from the oven and ladle the hot bouillon over the lobster. Add an equal portion of the tomato, parsley, *pousse Pierre*, and dill to each bowl. Place two lobster claws on top and serve immediately.

Serves 4

Pousse Pierre, also known as samphire or perce-pierre, is a type of edible European beach plant often used as a salad component or a garnish. In France it infuses considerable flavor into the meat of sheep that are raised on salt marshes or near the sea. The richly flavored lamb or mutton is then marketed as *pré-salé*. In America it is sold seasonally in fine fish markets. It may be replaced with another edible beach plant or seaweed such as sea bean, which is a different type of samphire found along both the Atlantic and Pacific coasts of the United States.

TERRINE DE FOIE GRAS AU SAUTERNES

1985

ARIANE DAGUIN, *Specialty Food Entrepreneur, D'Artagnan*

Ariane Daguin, the daughter of one of the great French chefs, André Daguin, came to America to learn about our food business and, instead, taught us a thing or two. With her partner, George Faison, Ariane founded D'Artagnan, now America's leading specialty meat purveyor, supplying restaurants and home cooks with raw and prepared foie gras, wild game from Europe and the British Isles, and other imported luxuries. They were the first purveyors in America to bring New York State foie gras to the marketplace. In this class Ariane taught us how to prepare a foie gras terrine that, up until this time, had only been available canned, imported from France. It was absolutely delicious!

1 very fresh grade-A foie gras

Coarse salt

1 bottle fine-quality Sauternes

Freshly ground white pepper

¼ cup all-purpose flour

Although **foie gras** translates as "goose liver," it can be the enlarged liver of either a goose or a duck. It comes in three grades, A, B, and C, with A being the highest quality—a creamy texture, minimal veining, and absolutely free of any blemishes. In 2004 foie gras made big news when protesters against the force-feeding of fowl (the technique used to produce huge livers) caused the state of California to outlaw the production of foie gras there by 2010. We hope that this law will be overturned.

Place the foie gras in a nonreactive container. Generously season all sides with coarse salt. Pour 8 ounces of the Sauternes into another container and set it aside. Pour the remaining Sauternes over the foie gras, cover, and refrigerate for 8 hours or overnight.

Preheat the oven to 220°F. Line a 2-inch-deep baking pan with newspaper. Set aside. Bring a large pot of water to a boil over high heat. Remove the foie gras from the soaking liquid and place it in the boiling water for 2 minutes. Immediately remove the liver and pat it dry. Taste a tiny bit to check for saltiness. If needed, season with additional salt and a bit of freshly ground white pepper. The entire liver, including any space between the lobes, should be seasoned.

Tightly fit the seasoned foie gras into a standard 3 × 5 × 9-inch terrine mold with a lid. Pour the reserved Sauternes over the foie gras.

Combine the flour with just enough cold water to make a very thick paste. Using a pastry brush, generously coat the edge of the terrine and its lid with the flour paste. Place the lid on the terrine and push down to make sure there is an even fit.

Set the terrine in the newspaper-lined baking pan, add enough water to come at least halfway up the sides of the pan, and place the pan in the preheated oven. Bake for 40 minutes, or until the internal temperature reaches 120°F on an instant-read thermometer. Remove the terrine from the oven. Uncover and either place the lid upside down on top of the terrine or cover the foie gras with a piece of wax paper and place a heavy can or pan on top to weigh down and compress the foie gras as it cools.

After 2 hours, check to see that the fat has risen to the top and is entirely covering the foie gras. If not, press down more firmly and let rest for another hour.

Cover the entire terrine with plastic film and refrigerate for 2 days before serving with slices of toasted country bread and the best bottle of Sauternes you can afford.

Makes 1 terrine

BUFFALO CHICKEN WINGS
1983
CRAIG CLAIBORNE, *Food Writer*

Restaurant critic for *The New York Times* and leading authority on American food, Craig Claiborne introduced the world to American culinary treasures as well as introducing Americans to many as-yet-undiscovered ethnic foods. In this class he talked about the move by young American chefs from "continental" or French cuisine to regional cooking.

This snack food or appetizer went on to become one of the most widespread finger foods eaten in the United States. Wings are now served in almost every bar in the country and are often featured in wing-eating contests matched with local brews. In class we were all stunned by Craig's precision—he measured and remeasured, even for the simplest recipe.

4 pounds (about 24) large chicken wings, well washed and dried

Coarse salt and freshly ground pepper to taste

4 cups vegetable oil

¼ cup (½ stick) unsalted butter

2 to 5 tablespoons Frank's Louisiana Red Hot Sauce, to taste

1 tablespoon white vinegar

2 cups Blue Cheese Dressing (recipe follows)

1 bunch celery stalks separated, trimmed, well washed, dried, and cut into 4-inch sticks

Cut off and discard the small tip of each wing. Cut the main wing bone and the second wing bone at the joint. Sprinkle with salt and pepper to taste.

Heat the oil in a deep-fat fryer with a basket or a deep heavy-bottomed saucepan over medium-high heat. When the oil is hot but not smoking, add the wings, a few at a time, and fry for about 10 minutes, or until golden brown and crisp. Remove the wings from the oil and place on paper towels to drain. Continue frying and draining wings until all of the wings are cooked.

Place the butter in a small sauté pan over medium heat. When melted, add the hot sauce to taste along with the vinegar.

Place the hot wings on a serving platter and drizzle with the seasoned butter. Serve immediately with Blue Cheese Dressing and celery sticks on the side.

Serves 4 to 6

BLUE CHEESE DRESSING

1 cup mayonnaise, preferably homemade

½ cup sour cream

¼ cup crumbled Maytag blue cheese (see Note)

2 tablespoons finely minced onion

1 tablespoon finely chopped fresh flat-leaf parsley

1 tablespoon fresh lemon juice

1 tablespoon white vinegar

Salt and freshly ground pepper to taste

Cayenne to taste

Combine the mayonnaise, sour cream, and blue cheese in a small mixing bowl. Stir in the onion and parsley and when well blended, stir in the lemon juice and vinegar. Season with salt, pepper, and cayenne to taste.

Cover with plastic film and refrigerate for at least 1 hour to allow the flavors to blend before serving.

Note: During this period, regional, artisanal American cheeses had begun to chip away at the stronghold that imported cheeses had on the fine cheese market. Maytag blue from Iowa was a consistent award winner and was recommended time after time in the De Gustibus classroom.

RADICCHIO AND ARUGULA SALAD
WITH HOT GOAT CHEESE AND HERBS
1983

WOLFGANG PUCK, *Chef/Owner, Spago, Chinois, Granita, Postrio, Lupo, Wolf,*
Wolfgang Puck Express, Cookbook Author

One of the most influential chefs of his generation through his restaurants Spago and Chinois on Main, Wolfgang Puck has been credited with elevating pizza to haute cuisine. As a tribute to his enthusiasm and passion, it is said that only "Wolfie" could put smoked salmon and goat cheese on pizza and get people to pay for it. His warm goat cheese salad was the seminal recipe for the multitude of warm goat cheese salads that are still being featured in restaurants all over the world. He is a favorite at De Gustibus as he can prep, cook, and entertain without missing a beat!

One 8-ounce fresh goat cheese log, cut crosswise into 4 equal slices

½ cup extra-virgin olive oil

1 teaspoon fresh thyme leaves

4 small (about 4-ounce) heads radicchio, pulled into leaves, well washed, and dried

½ pound arugula (or mâche), trimmed to the leaves, well washed, and dried

Mustard Vinaigrette (recipe follows)

Place the goat cheese slices in a single layer in a small, shallow bowl. Add the oil and thyme and turn each piece to coat well. Cover with plastic film and refrigerate for 8 hours, turning once.

Place the radicchio and arugula in a salad bowl. Add just enough of the Mustard Vinaigrette to coat lightly and toss to combine. Place an equal portion of the dressed greens on each of four salad plates.

Remove the goat cheese from the refrigerator. Uncover.

Spoon about 2 tablespoons of the thyme-scented oil into a small sauté pan over low heat. When just hot, add the slices of goat cheese and heat for 1 minute on each side.

Using a slotted spoon, transfer a slice of warm goat cheese to each salad and serve immediately.

Serves 4

MUSTARD VINAIGRETTE

1 large egg yolk, at room temperature

1 teaspoon Dijon mustard

1 teaspoon minced fresh tarragon

⅛ teaspoon fine salt, or to taste

Pinch freshly ground pepper

1 cup olive or almond oil

Combine the egg yolk, mustard, tarragon, salt, and pepper in a small nonreactive bowl, whisking to blend well.

Whisk in the oil in a slow steady stream until all of the oil is incorporated and the vinaigrette is well emulsified. (The vinaigrette may be made up to a day in advance and stored, covered and refrigerated.)

Note: This dressing was created before there was any concern in this country about eating raw egg yolks. Today, for safety, we would suggest that you use farm-fresh eggs that have been well washed or that you microwave the raw yolk for about 5 seconds.

Wolfgang decided to introduce us to his line of frozen **pizzas**. He brought 200 frozen pizzas for us to bake so that the class could try all of the varieties. Needless to say, this was a class that went overtime.

ENSALADA DE ANGUILAS
(BABY EEL SALAD)
1983
PENELOPE CASAS, *Cookbook Author*

Penelope Casas was an early proponent of the Mediterranean diet. Her specialty was the foods of Spain, and in this recipe she used baby eels, which would take many, many years to make their way onto restaurant menus. More than twenty years later, this delicacy is not often seen except in a few urban tapas bars, bistros, and trattorias.

In is interesting to note that Penelope was a proponent of tapas—or what, for a time, came to be known as grazing, long before the Spanish-food craze of recent years.

¼ pound fresh uncooked baby eels, rinsed (see Note)

2 cloves garlic, peeled and crushed

½ dried red chili, seeds removed and crushed

2½ tablespoons Spanish extra-virgin olive oil

1½ teaspoons red wine vinegar

1 teaspoon minced fresh flat-leaf parsley

Coarse salt and freshly ground pepper to taste

1 medium head leafy lettuce, pulled apart, trimmed, well washed, and dried

Dry the eels very well and place them in a bowl.

Combine the garlic, chili, oil, vinegar, and parsley in a small bowl, whisking to blend. Pour the dressing over the eels and toss to coat. Season with salt and pepper to taste. (At this point, the eels may be covered and refrigerated for up to 6 hours. Remove them from the refrigerator and let them stand at room temperature for 20 minutes before serving.)

Line a small serving platter with the lettuce leaves. Spoon the seasoned eels into the center of the platter and serve.

Note: Since it is almost impossible to find baby eels (except in some Asian markets), Penelope suggests that you use the frozen ones which, according to her, will work even better than fresh in the States as "American eels are just too skinny" to be any good. Frozen baby eels are available from LaTienda.com.

Serves 4

FLAKED PARSLEY SALAD
WITH BLACK OLIVES AND PECORINO CHEESE
1985

PAULA WOLFERT, *Cookbook Author, Teacher*

Long before anyone was talking about the Mediterranean diet, Paula Wolfert was traveling, tasting, and promoting this ancient yet very contemporary, healthy way of eating. This is a classic example of very ordinary ingredients combined in an unusual but accessible way to make a light and savory salad. Who would have thought that the everyday diner parsley garnish could be turned into such a beautifully orchestrated dish?

It was Paula's exploration of the foods of the Mediterranean that introduced American chefs to many "new-to-them" traditional methods of preparation and untried ingredients. I would hazard a guess that the increased restaurant use of exotic spices and herbs, yogurt, pomegranates, dried beans, couscous, and bulgur has been due to Paula's writings. Her books are still frequently used as reference guides.

2 large bunches very fresh curly-leaf parsley, well washed and dried

24 Kalamata or niçoise olives, pitted and thinly sliced

3 teaspoons finely minced shallots

3 tablespoons olive oil

3 tablespoons Worcestershire sauce

4 teaspoons cider vinegar or rice wine vinegar

Coarse salt and freshly ground pepper to taste

3 tablespoons freshly grated Pecorino-Romano cheese

Remove the stems from the parsley. Tear each parsley leaf into tiny bits. Place the parsley bits in a nonreactive bowl. (You should have about 4 cups of parsley.) Add the olives and shallots and toss to combine.

Drizzle on the olive oil, followed by the Worcestershire sauce and vinegar. Season with salt and pepper to taste and toss to combine.

Mound the parsley salad onto a chilled serving platter. Sprinkle with the cheese and serve immediately.

Serves 4

Paula Wolfert was the first cook to introduce us to **preserved lemons,** a Middle Eastern kitchen staple, and for a long period, she was the only one using them. By early 2000, however, preserved lemons were found in all types of restaurants all over the world. Now, even many of the De Gustibus home cooks prepare them and keep them on hand to add a hint of the Middle East to their recipes. Many chefs now use them as a standard garnish for grilled fish.

To make preserved lemons, Paula told us to cut 2 lemons into 8 wedges each, toss them with ⅓ cup coarse salt, and place the salted lemons in a glass container with a noncorrosive lid. Add ½ cup lemon juice, cover, and store at room temperature for 7 days, shaking the container from time to time to evenly distribute the salted juice. After 7 days, add enough olive oil to cover the lemons completely and store, covered and refrigerated, for up to 6 months.

TOMATO SAUCE I

1980

MARCELLA HAZAN, *Cookbook Author, Teacher*

In America Marcella Hazan is to Italian cooking what Julia Child was to French. She introduced the country to the flavors and techniques of traditional Italian cooking through her cookbooks, and for those American cooks lucky enough to travel, her cooking school in Venice, Italy. In her De Gustibus class, Marcella was insistent upon our understanding that cooking was not just about recipes but about knowing ingredients and then preparing them with love.

This is a classic example of Marcella's devotion to simplicity. Many, many American chefs now embrace this philosophy after years of extravagance on the plate. From her first De Gustibus class, Marcella stressed the importance of "less is more."

2 pounds fresh, ripe plum tomatoes (see Note)

½ cup (1 stick) unsalted butter

1 medium yellow onion, peeled and halved

1½ teaspoons coarse salt, plus more to taste

¼ teaspoon sugar

Wash the tomatoes well and pat dry. Core them and cut them in half lengthwise.

Place the tomatoes in a heavy-bottomed saucepan over medium heat and bring to a simmer. Cover and simmer for 10 minutes.

Remove the pan from the heat, transfer the tomatoes to a food mill, and press them back into the saucepan. Add the butter along with the onion halves, salt, and sugar and place over medium heat. Bring to a simmer. Lower the heat and cook at a low simmer for 45 minutes. Taste and, if necessary, adjust the seasoning with additional salt.

Remove from the heat. Remove and discard the onion halves and serve the sauce over pasta.

Note: If fully ripe plum tomatoes are not available, they may be replaced with 2 cups of canned plum tomatoes with their juice. If using canned tomatoes, begin with puréeing them through the food mill and proceed as above.

Serves 6

31

EGGPLANT IN THE NEAPOLITAN STYLE
1981
GIULIANO BUGIALLI, *Cookbook Author, Teacher*

Giuliano Bugialli has, without a doubt, given the most classes throughout our twenty-five years. His classes are always sold out and, no matter the weather, everyone turns up. Because he is such a strict taskmaster in the old-school sense, we always learn something new and alluring about classic Italian cooking. With this recipe we were introduced to the traditional Italian combination of eggplant and anchovies—a far reach from the Eggplant Parmesan to which we were accustomed.

In all of Giuliano's classes, he likes to prepare and cook everything from scratch, with only the vegetables prepped beforehand. He feels that it is important that we get the full measure of four courses being prepared in their entirety—including fresh pasta! He has given a whole new meaning to the phrase "simple home cooking."

When De Gustibus began, Italian cooking was in its infancy in the United States, with just the bastardized versions of southern Italian cooking on most menus. Today, because of the influence of the Italian traditionalists such as Giuliano, fine Italian food is the number one favorite throughout the country.

---

6 medium-size thin eggplants

About ½ cup coarse salt, plus more to taste

2 cups vegetable oil

¾ cup olive oil

About 1½ cups unbleached all-purpose flour

3 whole canned anchovies in salt or 6 anchovy filets in oil, well drained

Leaves from 15 sprigs fresh flat-leaf parsley

2 cloves garlic, peeled

2 tablespoons red wine vinegar

Salt and freshly ground pepper to taste

Using a small sharp knife, carefully remove the peel from the eggplants. Cut the eggplants into 1½-inch cubes. Spread the cubes out over a large platter or baking tray and sprinkle with about ½ cup of the salt, tossing to coat each cube. Set aside for 30 minutes.

Transfer the salted cubes to a colander and rinse under cold running water. Shake off excess water and pat dry with paper towels.

Line a baking tray with a double layer of paper towels. Set aside.

Combine the vegetable oil with ¼ cup of the olive oil in a deep-fat fryer fitted with a basket placed over medium-high heat. Bring the oil to 375°F on an instant-read thermometer.

While the oil is heating, place the eggplant in a colander, about a handful at a time, sprinkle with flour, and toss to coat lightly, allowing the excess flour to fall through the holes of the colander.

When the oil has reached the proper temperature, begin adding the floured eggplant, fifteen cubes at a time. Using a slotted spoon, nudge the eggplant cubes so that they turn often, browning them well on each side.

When the cubes are golden brown, transfer them to the prepared baking sheet to drain, and continue browning until all of the eggplant has been fried.

While the eggplant is frying, begin the sauce. If using anchovies packed in salt, rinse and filet them under cold running water. Set aside.

Using a sharp chef's knife, chop the parsley and garlic together on a cutting board until very finely minced but not mushy.

Heat the remaining ½ cup of olive oil in a heavy-bottomed saucepan over low heat. When warm, add the anchovies and, using a fork, mash them into the oil. Stir in the vinegar and cook, without stirring, for about 2 minutes, or just until the vinegar begins to evaporate. Season with salt and pepper to taste.

The eggplant should, by now, be fried and drained. Transfer the drained eggplant to a serving platter. Pour the anchovy sauce over the top. Sprinkle the parsley/garlic mixture over all and toss to combine. Serve immediately.

Serves 8

BAKED APPLES WITH MORELS FOR JAMES BEARD
1983

LARRY FORGIONE, *Chef/Owner, An American Place, Cookbook Author*

Larry Forgione is now known as the premier traditional American chef, following in the footsteps of his mentor, James Beard. His New York City restaurants as well as his specialty food company, American Spoon Foods, have, throughout our twenty-five years, brought the very best of America's heartland to the table. As the father of American cooking, Larry Forgione forged the way for a whole generation of young chefs, allowing the newcomers to broaden the regional American dining experience.

In this recipe we were introduced to wild American mushrooms, once quite rare in the kitchen unless you were able to hunt them yourself. Now most specialty food stores carry an assortment of wild mushrooms throughout the year.

4 medium baking apples, well washed

4 cups water

¼ cup white wine

¼ cup fresh lemon juice

2 tablespoons unsalted butter, at room temperature

½ teaspoon chopped shallots

12 ounces wild mushrooms, preferably agricus augustus, chanterelles, or boletus, wiped clean, trimmed of stems and any dark pieces, and cut into ½-inch pieces (see Note)

Coarse salt and freshly ground pepper to taste

1½ cups Wild American Morel Sauce (recipe follows)

½ cup homemade veal or chicken stock (see Note)

¼ cup fresh white bread crumbs

2 tablespoons chopped fresh flat-leaf parsley

Preheat the oven to 400°F.

Using a paring knife, carefully cut into each apple, at the stem end, through the core to make a funnel-shaped opening. Carefully cut out most of the apple flesh to make a large funnel-shaped opening, leaving a ½- to ¾-inch-thick shell.

Combine the water, wine, and lemon juice in a nonreactive saucepan just large enough to hold the apples.

Place the apples in the liquid in the saucepan, making sure that the water mixture covers them. (If not, add just enough additional water to cover.) Place over medium-high heat and bring to a boil. Lower the heat and simmer for about 5 minutes, or until the apples are poached but still quite firm.

Using a slotted spoon, transfer the apples to a double layer of paper towels to drain, cut sides down.

While the apples are poaching, begin making the filling: Place the butter in a heavy sauté pan over medium heat, warming until it begins to foam. Immediately add the shallots, followed by the mushrooms, and cook, stirring frequently, for about 5 minutes, or until the shallots and mushrooms have softened. Season lightly with salt and pepper.

Pour off any excess butter, then stir in ½ cup of the Wild American Morel Sauce. Bring to a simmer and cook, stirring occasionally, for about 10 minutes, or until the sauce has thickened. Remove from the heat and set aside.

Place the apples, cut sides up, in a baking pan just large enough to hold them without crowding. Season the openings with salt and pepper to taste, then fill each apple with an equal portion of the reserved mushroom mixture.

Pour the stock into the pan. Sprinkle the top of each apple with the bread crumbs and place in the preheated oven.

Bake, uncovered, for about 10 minutes, or until the filling is very hot and the bread crumbs are golden.

While the apples are baking, place the remaining morel sauce in a small saucepan over medium heat and cook for about 4 minutes, or until hot.

Remove the apples from the oven. Place on a serving dish and sprinkle with parsley. Serve with the sauce passed on the side.

Serves 4

WILD AMERICAN MOREL SAUCE

½ cup (1 stick) plus 2 tablespoons unsalted butter, at room temperature

1 medium carrot, peeled, trimmed, and chopped

1 small rib celery, well washed, peeled, and chopped

¼ cup chopped onion

2 tablespoons chopped shallots

1 small clove garlic, peeled and minced

Mushroom trimmings from main recipe

1 cup brandy

½ cup port wine

½ cup dry white vermouth

5 cups homemade rich veal or chicken stock (see Note)

1 ounce dried whole American morels, tied in a cheesecloth bag

Coarse salt and freshly ground pepper to taste

Place 2 tablespoons of the butter in a large saucepan over medium heat. When hot, add the carrot, celery, onion, shallots, garlic, and mushroom trimmings and sauté for about 5 minutes, or until the vegetables have softened. Scrape the vegetables into a fine sieve and press lightly with a spatula to remove excess butter.

Return the vegetables to the saucepan over medium-high heat. Add the brandy, port, and vermouth and cook, scraping the bottom and sides of the pan with a wooden spoon to deglaze the pan of all the browned bits. Bring to a boil and boil for about 15 minutes, or until the liquid is reduced to ½ cup.

Add the stock and morels tied in a cheesecloth bag. Season with salt and pepper to taste and bring to a simmer. Simmer, uncovered, for about 1 hour, or until the sauce has reduced by half. Remove the cheesecloth bag and set it aside to allow the morels to cool. Strain the sauce through a fine sieve into a clean 2-quart saucepan, discarding the solids.

When the morels are cool enough to handle, open the bag and cut them into thin slices. Add the sliced morels to the reduced sauce. Place over medium heat and bring to a simmer. Simmer for about 10 minutes to thicken a bit.

Cut the remaining ½ cup of room-temperature butter into small pieces and whisk it into the hot sauce. Do not complete this step if you're not using the sauce immediately. (If not using immediately, cool in an ice bath, transfer to a container, cover, and refrigerate for up to 3 days or freeze for up to 3 months. When ready to use, reheat the sauce in a small saucepan over medium heat and, when hot, whisk in the ½ cup of butter as above.)

Note: Save all of the mushroom trimmings from the apple filling, as they are used to make the Wild American Morel Sauce.

Since so much of the flavor in the sauce will come from the stock, we recommend using a rich, homemade stock. If this is not possible, use the finest-quality unsalted stock available. Some specialty food stores now carry excellent house-made stocks, which we also recommend over canned stock or broths.

GINGERED CRANBERRY RELISH
1983
SHEILA LUKINS, *Entrepreneur, Cookbook Author*

Sheila Lukins is truly a legend in her own time. Her company, The Silver Palate, was born in the late seventies on Manhattan's Upper West Side as a small storefront catering endeavor, and was a pioneer in the development of elegant ready-to-eat food as a replacement for home cooking for two-career families. For the first time, New Yorkers could purchase a well-prepared meal that simply required heating to make a wonderful dinner. The prepared and packaged food industry and high-end branding of prepared foods blossomed from the work of Sheila and her partner Julee Russo. With *The Silver Palate Cookbook,* one of the best-selling cookbooks in publishing history, they made cooking and entertaining seem easy and fun. And, in doing so, they introduced many new ingredients to the casual kitchen—dried cherries, for example, about which Sheila could never stop talking. Her favorite cherries are featured in this cranberry relish recipe, which I still make every Thanksgiving!

3 cups unsweetened dried Michigan cherries (see Note)

2 cups fresh cranberries

2 cups sugar

½ cup coarsely chopped crystallized ginger

1¼ cups freshly squeezed orange juice

¾ cup water

2 tablespoons freshly grated lemon zest (optional)

Combine the cherries, cranberries, sugar, and ginger in a medium, heavy-bottomed nonreactive saucepan over medium heat. Stir in the juice, water, and zest and bring to a simmer.

Simmer, stirring occasionally and skimming off any foam that rises to the surface, for about 10 minutes, or until the cranberries pop and the flavors have blended.

Remove from the heat and scrape into a nonreactive container. Set aside to cool before covering and refrigerating until ready to use. This relish will keep, covered and refrigerated, for a week.

Note: If you can't find unsweetened dried Michigan cherries, use sweetened ones, but cut the amount of sugar to about 1 cup.

Makes about 4 cups

SQUASH AND NASTURTIUM BLOSSOM PASTA

1984

ALICE WATERS, *Chef/Owner, Chez Panisse, Cookbook Author*

Here is California cooking at its Chez Panisse best. Alice Waters, known as the mother of New American cooking, made her first appearance at De Gustibus in 1984 in celebration of the best that California had to offer. All of the herbs, full of blooms, were sent overnight from California. It was a beautiful sight to behold. Although, after her class, students had trouble locating many of the fresh-from-the-garden or brought-to-the-back-door-by-the-forager ingredients used at Chez Panisse, it was already clear that the Alice Waters style of cooking would have a great impact on the future of American cooking.

In this recipe Alice introduced the use of fresh, edible flowers to the class. Chefs across the country soon began using them as a beautiful addition to salads and as an edible plate garnish. Nasturtium blossoms have a flavor similar to the more mundane watercress.

8 dozen nasturtium blossoms

6 whole shallots, peeled and minced

2 tablespoons finely minced fresh flat-leaf parsley leaves

2 teaspoons finely minced fresh savory

2 teaspoons finely minced fresh thyme leaves

Coarse salt and freshly ground white pepper to taste

¾ cup (1½ sticks) unsalted butter, at room temperature

12 tiny yellow squash with blossoms attached

12 tiny zucchini with blossoms attached

1 pound fresh tagliatelle (see Note)

1½ cups chicken stock

Separate the nasturtium blossoms from the stems, discarding the stems. Using a chef's knife, finely chop six dozen of the blossoms and reserve the remaining two dozen.

Combine the finely chopped nasturtium blossoms with the shallots, parsley, savory, and thyme. Season with salt and pepper.

Place the butter in a small bowl and, using the back of a tablespoon, press the nasturtium-blossom mixture into the butter. When well blended, cover with plastic film and refrigerate for at least 4 hours or up to 24 hours.

When ready to serve, slice the yellow squash and zucchini crosswise into thin slices and the attached flowers into thin ribbons. Set aside.

Bring a large pot of salted water to a boil. Add the pasta and cook according to the package directions.

Remove the flavored butter from the refrigerator and, while the pasta is cooking, prepare the sauce.

Heat half of the butter in a nonstick sauté pan over medium heat. Add the sliced squash and zucchini and sauté for 3 minutes. Stir in the stock and squash-blossom ribbons and simmer for 1 minute. Drain the pasta.

Add the drained pasta to the sautéed squash and toss to combine. Add the remaining flavored butter and toss.

Taste and adjust the seasoning with additional salt and pepper if necessary. Serve, sprinkled with the remaining whole nasturtium flowers.

Note: Although Alice makes her own, fresh pasta is now available at many supermarkets, specialty food stores, and Italian markets.

Serves 6

LIANG MIEN HUANG
(TWO-SIDES BROWN NOODLES)
1981

FLORENCE LIN, *Teacher, Cookbook Author*

As the leader of cooking classes at the China Institute of America, Florence Lin was quite a well-known authority on Chinese cuisine. Her cookbooks introduced many home cooks to traditional Chinese cooking. Interestingly enough, it was Chinese cooking teachers like Florence Lin and Grace Chu who helped broaden the scope of American home cooking. Even Marcella Hazan was encouraged by her experiences in Chinese cooking classes to begin teaching her native Italian cuisine. Florence's classes began an explosion of cooking schools across the country, a craze for Chinese cooking at home, and the introduction of Chinese ingredients into American restaurant cooking.

For this recipe, Florence said, "By browning a bed of noodles in a frying pan or wok, the resulting thin, cakelike patty gets a crunchy, burnt crust on both sides but is still soft on the inside. The other ingredients and the sauce are poured on top of the noodles but not mixed in when served. You can taste the distinct flavor of each ingredient with just enough sauce absorbed by the noodles."

---

1 whole boneless, skinless chicken breast

1 pound fresh egg noodles (see Note)

2½ tablespoons soy sauce

¾ cup unsalted, defatted chicken broth

1½ tablespoons plus 2 teaspoons cornstarch

Coarse salt to taste

½ pound raw shrimp, peeled, deveined, and coarsely chopped

6 dried shiitake mushrooms, rehydrated and finely shredded (see Note)

2 scallions, white parts only, finely shredded

3 cups finely shredded cabbage (or 4 cups fresh bean sprouts or a combination of both)

6 tablespoons peanut oil

Place the chicken breast in the freezer for about 45 minutes, or just until slightly frozen.

While the chicken is freezing, cook the noodles: Bring a large pot of salted water to a boil over high heat. Add the noodles and boil for about 3 minutes, or until just cooked. Drain well and rinse under cold running water. Again, drain well.

Place the noodles in a large bowl, add 1 tablespoon of the soy sauce, and toss to coat. Set aside.

To make the sauce, place the chicken broth in a small bowl. Add the remaining 1½ tablespoons of soy sauce and 1½ tablespoons of the cornstarch, whisking to combine. Set aside.

Remove the chicken from the freezer and, using a sharp knife, cut the chicken into matchsticklike pieces. Place the chicken in a small bowl, add 1 teaspoon of the remaining cornstarch and salt to taste, and toss to coat. Set aside.

Place the shrimp in a small bowl, add the remaining teaspoon of cornstarch along with salt to taste, and toss to coat. Set aside.

Preheat the oven to the warm setting or to the lowest temperature.

Place the mushrooms, cabbage, and scallions (or bean sprouts) in separate bowls. Set aside.

Preheat a large skillet or wok over medium heat until very hot but not smoking. Add 1 tablespoon of the oil and swirl to coat the bottom of the pan.

Spread the seasoned noodles over the bottom of the skillet (or wok) and cook, without stirring, for 5 minutes, or until the noodles begin to brown and even burn a little. Pour 1 tablespoon of the remaining oil down the side of the pan, allowing it to run under the noodles. Quickly flip the noodle cake over and cook, without stirring, for about 5 minutes, or until well browned and slightly burned. Slide the noodle patty onto a heatproof serving platter and place in the preheated oven to keep warm.

Add 1 tablespoon of the remaining oil to the same skillet (or wok) placed over medium-high heat. Add the reserved chicken and stir-fry for about 4 minutes, or until cooked and browned slightly. Using a slotted spoon, transfer the chicken to a plate and keep warm.

Add 1 tablespoon of the remaining oil to the same skillet (or wok) placed over medium-high heat. Add the reserved shrimp and stir-fry for about 3 minutes, or until cooked and browned slightly. Using a slotted spoon, transfer the shrimp to a plate and keep warm.

Add the remaining 2 tablespoons of oil to the same skillet (or wok) placed over medium-high heat. Add the mushrooms and cabbage (or bean sprouts) and stir-fry for 2 minutes. Add the reserved chicken and shrimp and stir-fry for about 1 minute, or just until heated through and well combined.

Whisk the reserved chicken broth mixture and pour it over the stir-fry and toss to coat. Cook for about 3 minutes, or just until a nice glaze coats all of the ingredients.

Remove the noodle patty from the oven and pour the stir-fry over it. Sprinkle the scallions over the top and serve immediately.

Note: Fresh egg noodles can be replaced with dried pasta such as spaghetti. If doing so, cook the pasta according to package directions.

Dried mushrooms can be rehydrated by soaking them in very hot water to cover by 1 inch for about 30 minutes. The soaking time will be determined by the dryness of the mushrooms.

Serves 6

AIGUILLETTES D'AGNEAU À LA BATELIERE
(THIN STRIPS OF LAMB IN THE STYLE OF THE BARGE PEOPLE)
1984

MADELEINE KAMMAN, *Teacher, Cookbook Author*

Madeleine Kamman, a French traditionalist in the kitchen, mentored many young American chefs at her cooking school in Boston. She eventually moved to California, where she led the cooking school at the Beringer Winery and continued to mentor young cooks.

Of course, in classic cooking, stock making is at the core of many great preparations. Madeleine used this class to demonstrate the making of a fine-quality classic French stock. It was her desire that home cooks master this basic that, I believe, eventually created the demand for fine-quality prepared stocks, which are now available in specialty food stores across the country.

In her note for this recipe she said, "This dish is inspired by the *Grillade des Bateliers*, a dish of beef slices prepared by the barge people who go up and down the Saône and the Rhône rivers bringing goods north and south. As quick as it is delicious."

She continued, "Professional and home cooks both should use the proportions I have given for making stock, which allows everyone to adapt the recipe to the size of the stockpot used, be it an ugly, functional, 45-quart aluminum or a pretty 5-quart, home-size copper one. One quart of water yields approximately 3 cups of good stock (see Note). Cooks who do not feel that they should be bothered weighing all of the meat have a point, for if one simply puts the browned meat at the bottom of the stockpot and adds water to reach 1 inch above the meat, one automatically obtains the correct proportions. This is probably how they were empirically calculated over the centuries." Madeleine's cooking kept us on our toes!

---

1 large saddle of lamb, about 6 pounds

6 tablespoons (¾ stick) unsalted butter

Coarse salt to taste

2 anchovy filets packed in oil, well drained

1½ cups Golden Veal Stock (recipe follows)

1 large clove garlic, peeled and finely chopped

1½ tablespoons chopped fresh flat-leaf parsley

1 to 1½ teaspoons extra-strong Dijon mustard

¼ teaspoon freshly grated lemon zest

¼ teaspoon freshly grated orange zest

Freshly ground pepper to taste

Using a boning knife, cut the lamb saddle into two sirloins and two tenderloins. Trim each piece completely free of fat and gristle. (Alternatively, have your butcher prepare the saddle.) Cut the sirloins into two pieces, 3½ inches long.

Place 2 tablespoons of the butter in a large, heavy-bottomed skillet over medium-high heat. Add the sirloin strips to the pan and sear for about 3 minutes, or until nicely browned. Turn the sirloin strips, add the tenderloins to the pan, and sear for 3 minutes, or until nicely browned. Turn and sear the remaining sides. Season each piece of meat with salt on all sides when it has browned.

Using tongs, transfer each piece of meat to a platter once it has been seared. Tent lightly with aluminum foil to keep warm.

Rinse the anchovies under cold, running water. When rinsed, place each one on a small plate and, using a fork, mash well. Set aside.

Keeping the pan on medium-high heat, add the stock and bring to a boil, stirring constantly with a wooden spoon to deglaze the pan. Continue to boil until reduced to ¾ cup. While the stock is boiling, whisk in the remaining butter.

When the stock has reduced, remove the pan from the heat

and whisk in one of the anchovies along with the garlic, parsley, mustard, and lemon and orange zests. Taste and, if more saltiness is needed, add the remaining anchovy along with freshly ground pepper to taste.

Slice the tenderloins and sirloin strips lengthwise into ⅙-inch-thin strips. Fan an equal portion of meat on each of six dinner plates. Spoon some sauce over each plate and serve immediately.

Serves 6

GOLDEN VEAL STOCK

1 pound veal (⅔ pound meat, ⅓ bone)

1 medium onion, peeled and stuck with 1 whole clove

1 piece peeled carrot, 2½ inches long by 1 inch round

⅓ cup dry white wine

1 leek, white part only, well washed

3 thick fresh parsley stems

⅓ Turkish bay leaf

¼ teaspoon dried thyme leaves

Preheat the oven to 400°F.

Trim the veal of all fat and cut it into chunks.

Place the veal, onion, and carrot in a flat roasting pan in the preheated oven and roast, turning occasionally, for about 45 minutes, or until the meat and vegetables are golden brown and a thin layer of meat juices has coagulated to a warm russet color on the surface of the pan.

Remove the pan from the oven and, using a slotted spoon, transfer the browned meat and vegetables to a stockpot. Set aside.

Place the roasting pan on the stovetop over medium heat. Add the wine and, using a wooden spoon, scrape the bottom of the pan to dislodge all of the browned bits and glaze. When the pan is well deglazed, pour the liquid into the stockpot.

Add enough water to the stockpot to cover the meat by 1 inch. Place over medium-high heat and bring to a boil. Add the leek along with the parsley, bay leaf, and thyme. Bring to a simmer, then lower the heat to barely simmering.

Place a lid on the stockpot slightly askew, so as to leave ½ inch of space for evaporation. Add lukewarm water to the pot at regular intervals to keep the water level approximately even at all times. A small, home-size batch of stock should take about three hours to be well infused with flavor, while a large, restaurant-size batch can take up to twelve hours. Very little skimming should be required, as all available surface blood and other impurities have been deeply cooked during the oven roasting.

When fully infused with flavor, remove the stock from the heat and strain through a fine sieve into a clean container.

Place the container in an ice bath (a kitchen sink filled with ice does the trick nicely) to cool quickly. If not using immediately, cover and refrigerate or freeze as soon as the liquid has cooled.

Note: The proportions given are enough to flavor 1 quart of water. If you wish to make more than 3 cups of stock, increase the proportions as needed.

POULARDE EN PAPILLON FERMIÈRE
(BUTTERFLIED ROAST CHICKEN)
1980

JULIA CHILD, *Television Personality, Cookbook Author*

There is almost nothing to be said about Julia Child that has not already been said. Julia was truly thrilled to teach a De Gustibus class in New York because, in 1980, no other classes of this type existed in the city and she loved nothing more than to talk with home cooks. She subsequently did all of our pre-Macy's classes, which were always followed by a bottle of Deutz champagne, very well chilled! At Macy's she followed tradition with her usual enthusiasm. She is greatly missed.

Back in 1980 Julia would not use the iodized salt that we were all using. Having lived in France, she had become familiar with the great sea salts and, although she preferred them, agreed to use kosher salt. At the time the use of butter was still politically correct and Julia used it freely. I suspect if she were still with us, she would still use the same amount!

For this recipe her note read, "A fine, fat roasting chicken, butterflied and roasted with fresh winter vegetables, serving 6 to 8 people. What could be better?"

One 5-pound roasting chicken or capon

¼ cup plus 2 tablespoons (¾ stick) unsalted butter, plus an optional 2 to 3 tablespoons, at room temperature

A little good-quality vegetable oil

1 cup dry white French vermouth

Coarse salt and freshly ground pepper to taste

Fragrant dried herbs such as sage, thyme, or tarragon to taste

12 to 16 pearl onions, peeled

4 or more medium carrots, peeled, trimmed, and cut into quarters (see Note)

4 or more medium turnips, peeled, trimmed, and cut into quarters (see Note)

1 large celery root, peeled and cut into pieces (see Note)

4 or more medium "boiling" potatoes, peeled and cut into quarters (see Note)

2 tablespoons chopped fresh flat-leaf parsley

Note: The vegetables should all be cut to approximately the same size.

Using a boning knife, cut the backbone out of the chicken, as well as the wishbone and the wing nubbins (at the elbows). Rinse and dry the chicken thoroughly. Chop the trimmings and the neck and reserve.

Lay the chicken on a clean work surface, flesh side down. Pound with your fist on either side of the breast to flatten it somewhat; rub generously with the ¼ cup (½ stick) of butter (use more, if you like) and place the chicken, skin side down, in a roasting pan large enough to hold it along with the vegetables to come.

Place a bit of vegetable oil in a saucepan over medium heat. Add the chicken trimmings and sauté for about 5 minutes, or until just lightly browned. Add the vermouth along with just enough water to cover the chicken. Season with a little salt and pepper and bring to a simmer. Simmer for 90 minutes, adding water as necessary to keep a steady amount of liquid in the pan. Remove from the heat and strain through a fine sieve into a clean saucepan. You should have about 1 cup of strong chicken stock. Set it aside, skimming off from time to time any fat that rises to the top.

While the sauce is cooking, prepare the chicken: Preheat the broiler. Place the buttered, seasoned chicken, flesh side up, about 8 inches from the preheated broiler and broil, basting once or twice with any fat that accumulates in the pan. This should take about 10 minutes, but watch carefully to ensure that the chicken does not burn.

Salt lightly, sprinkle the skin with about ¼ teaspoon of the dried herbs, and turn. Season the remaining side, sprinkle with herbs, and continue to broil for about 4 minutes, or until nicely browned. (This process can be done up to 24 hours in advance. If doing so, cover and refrigerate until ready to finish cooking.) When ready to roast, preheat the oven to 350°F.

Place the chicken, in the roasting pan, in the preheated oven and roast for 45 minutes, basting every 10 minutes with the accumulating pan juices.

While the chicken is roasting, prepare the vegetables: Place the onions in a small sauté pan with just enough water to come halfway up the sides. Add 1 tablespoon of the remaining butter and place over medium heat. Place a lid on the pan, slightly askew, and simmer for about 20 minutes, or until the onions are almost tender when pierced with the point of a small, sharp knife. Using a slotted spoon, transfer the onions to a plate. Pour any pan juices into the stock.

Place the carrots, turnips, and celery root in a saucepan with just enough water to come halfway up the sides. Add the remaining tablespoon of butter and place over medium heat. Place a lid on the pan, slightly askew, and simmer for about 20 minutes, or until the vegetables are almost tender when pierced with the point of a small, sharp knife. Using a slotted spoon, transfer the vegetables to the plate holding the onions. Pour any pan juices into the stock.

Place the potatoes in a medium saucepan with cold, salted water to cover over medium-high heat. Bring to a boil and boil for about 20 minutes, or until the potatoes are almost tender when pierced with the point of a small, sharp knife. Remove from the heat and drain well.

When the chicken has roasted for 45 minutes, add all of the vegetables to the roasting pan, spreading them out in a single layer. Baste the vegetables with the accumulated pan juices. Season with salt and an additional sprinkling of dried herbs. Continue roasting, basting twice, for an additional 15 minutes, or until the juices run clear yellow when the meat is pricked deeply with the sharp tines of a fork.

Remove from the oven and arrange the chicken and vegetables on a warm serving platter. Tent lightly with aluminum foil to keep warm.

Using a metal spoon, skim as much fat as possible off the juices in the roasting pan. Place the pan on the stovetop over medium-high heat, add the reserved stock, and bring to a boil. Boil, stirring frequently, for about 5 minutes, or until the sauce is syrupy.

Remove the pan from the heat and, if desired, whisk in a couple of additional tablespoons of butter. Pour the sauce over the chicken and vegetables, sprinkle with parsley, and serve.

Serves 6 to 8

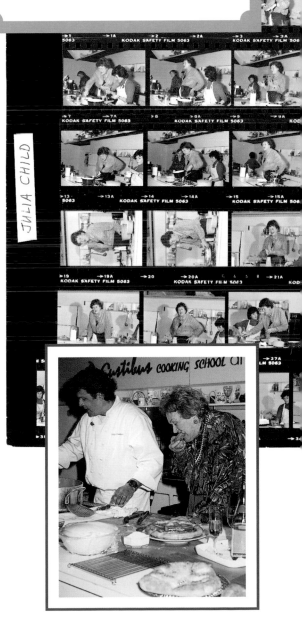

After Julia's class, we switched to **kosher salt** in the kitchen, and that was the only salt we had for quite a long period. Then came the sea salts and what a variety we had to choose from—Hawaiian Red Alae Sea Salt, Hawaiian Black Lava Salt, Black Sea Salt, Danish Smoked Salt, and many more. Every chef seemed to have a favorite, and we soon had a shelf full of options.

POULET AU VINAIGRE
(CHICKEN IN VINEGAR SAUCE)
1980

JACQUES PÉPIN, *Chef, Cookbook Author, Television Personality,*
Dean of Special Projects at The French Culinary Institute

More than being one of our most popular teachers, Jacques Pépin has been a guiding light to me at De Gustibus and a great friend. It was Jacques who first suggested that a cooking school should have assistants and that an overhead mirror would make it easier for students to observe and better understand the cooking processes. Over the years he has offered many other insights that have helped me make De Gustibus a better school. Jacques is absolutely first class at *garde manger*—he taught us how to carve lemons, tomatoes, and other fruits and vegetables for garnish as well as how to work with game, terrines, and pâtés.

Jacques grew up in Lyon with a mother who was a chef. She was a proponent of traditional French home cooking, both at home and in her restaurant. Throughout his career Jacques has been at the forefront of taking simple home cooking and reworking it for different occasions—always making sure that the results were absolutely delicious. Many other chefs now follow this same route.

1½ chickens (about 4½ pounds) (see Note)

1½ teaspoons coarse salt plus more to taste

¾ teaspoon freshly ground pepper

5 tablespoons plus 1 teaspoon unsalted butter

⅔ cup fine-quality red wine vinegar

⅓ cup water

3 cloves garlic, peeled and minced

1 tablespoon tomato paste

1 tablespoon chopped fresh flat-leaf parsley

2 teaspoons chopped fresh tarragon

Season the chicken pieces with the salt and pepper.

Divide the butter in half and set aside 2⅔ tablespoons. Place half of the remaining butter in each of two heavy skillets over medium heat. When hot, add half of the chicken to each pan, skin side down, and sear for about 4 minutes, or until golden. Turn and sear the remaining sides for about 4 minutes, or until golden. Pour off excess fat from each pan.

Divide the vinegar in half and set ⅓ cup aside. Pour half of the remaining ⅓ cup of vinegar, along with half of the water, into each skillet. Cover and simmer for 20 minutes.

Using tongs, transfer the chicken to a serving platter (see Note). Tent lightly with aluminum foil to keep warm. Do not cover tightly or the chicken may taste slightly reheated.

Remove one of the skillets from the heat and set aside. Place the garlic in the remaining skillet and sauté for 1 minute, taking care that the garlic does not begin to burn. Add the remaining ⅓ cup of vinegar and bring to a boil, scraping the bottom of the pan with a wooden spoon to deglaze.

Return the reserved skillet to medium heat and, using a spatula, scrape all of the sauce from the other skillet into it. Add the tomato paste, stirring to incorporate. This should thicken the sauce somewhat. Taste and, if necessary, add salt and pepper. This sauce should be quite peppery (see Note).

Remove the sauce from the heat and begin beating in the remaining butter a bit at a time.

Uncover the chicken and pour the sauce over the top. Sprinkle with the parsley and tarragon and serve immediately.

44

Note: You will need three chicken halves. Each half should be halved and then halved again to yield twelve pieces.

For a more elegant presentation, the chicken may be deboned after it cools slightly. The breastbone and the piece of backbone attached to the legs should pull off easily.

For a slightly different taste, you can season the sauce with 1 teaspoon of crushed green peppercorns during the final cooking.

Serves 6

Once Jacques Pépin said that he absolutely had to have a **needle-nosed pliers** to remove the bones from the salmon he was preparing. Unfortunately, we did not have one, and the team tracked down the Macy's carpenters to see if they had one. They didn't but, as luck would have it, one of the team members had tweezers in her handbag, so Jacques was able to perform his surgery. We now always have a selection of pliers on hand.

de gustibus at macy*s presents...

jacques pepin

SHRIMP ÉTOUFFÉE
1983

PAUL PRUDHOMME, *Chef/Owner, K-Paul's Louisiana Enterprises, Cookbook Author*

When Chef Paul taught his first class, we were all enchanted to be in his presence, as his graciousness was as magnanimous as his size. Before Paul Prudhomme hit the national culinary scene, "blackened" and "Cajun" were regional terms known to only a few outsiders. By the mideighties, every part of the world had been "blackened" due to the power of Chef Prudhomme's personality and skill at the stove. He went on to develop a line of seasonings that still command a strong showing in the national marketplace. This recipe showcases one of his signature seasonings.

¼ cup chopped onion

¼ cup chopped celery

¼ cup chopped green bell pepper

7 tablespoons vegetable oil

¾ cup all-purpose flour

2 tablespoons Chef Paul Prudhomme's Seafood Magic, or to taste

3 cups Basic Seafood Stock (recipe follows)

Coarse salt and freshly ground pepper to taste

1 cup (2 sticks) unsalted butter

2 pounds peeled and cleaned medium shrimp

1 cup very finely chopped scallion, green and white parts

4 cups hot cooked white rice

Combine the onion, celery, and bell pepper in a small bowl. Set aside.

Heat the oil in a large, heavy skillet, preferably cast-iron, over medium heat for about 4 minutes, or until the oil begins to smoke. Using a long-handled whisk, begin mixing in the flour, a third at a time, stirring until very smooth. Continue cooking, whisking constantly and taking care not to splatter or burn the roux, for about 25 minutes, or until the roux is dark red-brown.

Remove from the heat and immediately stir in 1 tablespoon of Seafood Magic along with the reserved vegetables. Using a wooden spoon, continue to stir for about 5 minutes, or until cooled.

Place 2 cups of the stock in a 2-quart saucepan over high heat. Whisking constantly, add the roux, a third at a time, until thoroughly dissolved. Season with salt and pepper to taste and bring to a boil. Reduce the heat to low and cook, whisking almost constantly, for about 5 minutes, or until the flour taste has disappeared. (If any of the mixture burns or scorches, do not stir it into the roux; using a metal spoon, lift it out of the pan and discard.) Remove from the heat and set aside.

Heat ½ cup of the butter in a 4-quart saucepan over medium heat. Stir in the shrimp along with the scallion and cook, whisking almost constantly, for 1 minute. Whisk in the remaining ½ cup of butter, the roux mixture, and the remaining 1 cup of stock. Cook, shaking the pan in a back-and-forth motion rather than stirring or whisking, for about 6 minutes, or until the mixture has thickened and the flavors are well blended. Stir in the remaining 1 tablespoon of Seafood Magic (or to taste) and remove from the heat. If the sauce begins to separate, add about 2 tablespoons of water (or stock) and shake the pan back and forth until it emulsifies.

Place ½ cup of rice in the center of each plate and ladle about ¾ cup of the étouffée around the rice. Serve immediately.

Serves 8

BASIC SEAFOOD STOCK

2 pounds rinsed shrimp or crawfish heads and/or shells, crab shells, or fish carcasses, heads and gills removed, or any combination of these

1 medium onion, peeled and quartered

1 large clove garlic, unpeeled and halved

1 rib celery, well washed and cut into pieces

Combine the shrimp heads and shells (or whatever shellfish or fish parts you're using) with the onion, garlic, and celery in a stockpot or large saucepan. Add enough cold water to cover the ingredients by about an inch (2 quarts will usually be sufficient).

Place the stockpot over high heat and bring to a boil. Lower the heat and simmer for about 4 hours, or until a well-flavored stock has formed, replenishing the water as needed to keep at least 1 quart of water in the pot at all times.

Remove from the heat and strain through a fine sieve into a clean container, discarding the solids.

Place the stock container in an ice bath to chill quickly. When chilled, cover and refrigerate or freeze until ready to use.

Note: Remember, if you are short on time, that using a stock simmered for 20 to 30 minutes is far better than using just water in any recipe.

Makes 1 quart

When Paul Prudhomme taught a class featuring **crayfish**, he sent boxes of the lively little creatures to my home, where I was to keep them alive over the weekend. He told me to "wrap them in damp newspaper, put them in the fridge, and visit them regularly." You can well imagine how happy I was to take my weekend "guests" to Macy's on Monday morning!

K-PAUL
LOUISIANA MAIL OR…
SUMMER

…CIAL PRICES!
…nbalaya & Etouffée
…ct to You
…ul's Louisiana
…n Smoked Meats
…n Roux Package
…Much More!!

TASTE THE CAJUN MAGIC
OF CHEF PAUL PRUDHOMME!
1-800-4KPAULS

BRIOCHE NANTERRE OR PARISIENNE
(FRENCH BRIOCHE)
1984

BERNARD CLAYTON, *Cookbook Author*

Bernie Clayton, a veteran newspaper man, was at the forefront of America's bread revolution. Long before artisanal bread bakeries began springing up across the country, Bernie was extolling the virtues of traditional European (and American) breads. Through his books, young pastry chefs began exploring traditional breadmaking, which grew to the development of small bread companies employing old techniques to make dense, fragrant loaves that had little to do with the spongy white bread for which America had become known.

By the end of the eighties, restaurants began to feature a dazzling array of house-made breads on the table, and many weekend cooks took up bread baking as a way to reduce stress. In this class Bernie focused on some of the classic breads of France. From being an almost unknown bread in the United States, brioche went on to become the bread of choice for traditional French toast—even in diners!

Approximately 5 cups all-purpose flour, plus more for flouring the work surface

2 packages dry yeast

⅓ cup nonfat powdered milk

1 tablespoon sugar

2 teaspoons coarse salt

1 cup warm (105–115°F) water

5 large eggs, at room temperature

1½ cups (3 sticks) unsalted butter, cut into chunks and softened

For the glaze

1 large egg

1 tablespoon milk

Place 2 cups of the flour in a large bowl. Stir in the yeast, powdered milk, sugar, and salt. When well blended, form a well in the center of the mixture and pour in the water. Using a large wooden spoon or pastry scraper, slowly pull the flour in from the sides to make a soft batter. One at a time, add the eggs, blending them into the batter with each addition.

While the dough remains a thick batter, begin adding and incorporating the butter, a few chunks at a time.

When all of the butter has been absorbed into the batter, beat in the remaining flour, a cup at a time, until the dough can only be worked by using your hands.

Lightly flour a clean work surface and transfer the dough to it.

Using your hands, begin kneading the dough. Break the kneading rhythm by occasionally dropping the ball of dough forcefully onto the work surface. If, after kneading for a few minutes, the dough remains sticky, add some light sprinkles of flour. Knead for 7 minutes.

Transfer the kneaded dough to a large bowl. Cover with plastic film and let rest, at room temperature, for about 1½ hours, or until the dough has doubled in bulk.

Uncover the dough and punch it down with your fingertips. Turn and again cover with plastic film. Set aside, at room temperature, for 1 hour.

Again, uncover, punch down, turn, and re-cover. Place the dough in the refrigerator and let it rest for at least 6 hours (see sidebar).

Lightly butter and flour three 8½ × 4½-inch loaf pans. (Alternatively, use nonstick pans.) Set aside. Lightly flour a clean work surface. Remove the dough from the refrigerator and divide it into two pieces.

For the *Nanterre:* for each loaf pan, cut off nine 2-ounce pieces of dough and shape them into 2½-inch balls. Place the balls in the bottom of the prepared pans in a zigzag pattern, if necessary pressing them tightly together to fit.

For the *Parisienne:* for each loaf pan, cut off eight 2-ounce pieces of dough and shape them into cylinders about 4½ inches long and 1 inch in diameter. Lay the cylinders widthwise in the bottom of each pan, making a tight fit.

You may have extra dough remaining. If so, shape it into a loaf and place it in the appropriately sized, buttered and floured loaf pan and proceed as with the other breads.

Cover the pans with waxed paper and set aside, at room temperature, for about 2½ hours, or until the dough has doubled in volume. This lengthy period is necessary because of the earlier refrigeration of the dough.

Twenty minutes before you're ready to bake, preheat the oven to 375°F.

Make the glaze by whisking the egg and milk together in a small bowl. Uncover the pans and, using a pastry brush, lightly coat the tops of the loaves with the glaze.

Place the pans on the middle shelf of the preheated oven and bake for 20 minutes. Turn the pans to allow the loaves to bake evenly for an additional 10 minutes, or until light golden brown.

Remove the pans from the oven, carefully remove the loaves from the pans, and place on wire racks to cool. To test for doneness, tap the bottom crust with your forefinger. If it sounds hollow, the bread is done. (Handle carefully, as the bread will break apart easily where the pieces of dough have been joined. They will firm up when cool.)

If the loaves are done but need more color, return to the oven, without the pans, for 5 to 8 minutes.

Makes 3 loaves

> **Brioche** is often thought of as a small breakfast bread (*brioche à tête* is the classic) when, in reality, it is an extremely versatile dough that can be used in a range of breads from hors d'oeuvres to the full-size loaves *Brioche Nanterre* and *Brioche Parisienne.*
>
> Traditionally, the dough is made the night before, punched down twice, and left in the refrigerator before being shaped into loaves the following day. Bernie modernized the recipe a bit by shortening this process to six hours.

BERNARD CLAYTON JR.

May 7, 1984

Dear Arlene:

I had a great time with you even though I lost voice which I have yet to find again. Of the three Regional French, the second class, was perhaps the I felt better that night.

Better next time, and Ihope there is one!

I just cave when those eyes look up at me under bangs.

love,

Bernie

7401

DE GUSTIBUS LEMON TART

1984

ALBERT KUMIN, *Chef, Teacher*

Albert Kumin, one of America's most distinguished pastry chefs, created many extraordinary desserts in his long career, which took him not only to great restaurants such as The Four Seasons and Windows on the World, but also to the White House. For one of his classes at De Gustibus, he created a marvelously easy-to-prepare, delicious lemon tart especially for us. He implored home cooks, unused to weighing ingredients, to be precise and exacting when making pastry. From these early classes, our audiences became more and more interested in expanding their dessert repertoire, and pastry chefs became much more in demand. Albert Kumin's influence was felt throughout the restaurant industry as pastry chefs began to have as much impact on menus as did chefs.

6 ounces (1½ cups plus 1 tablespoon) pastry flour

½ cup (1 stick) unsalted butter, cut into pieces and chilled

Pinch salt

¼ cup plus 2 tablespoons ice water

1 cup cold water

¼ cup cornstarch

½ cup plus 2 tablespoons fresh lemon juice, strained

½ cup sugar

5 large egg yolks, at room temperature

6 tablespoons unsalted butter, at room temperature

1 cup whipped cream (optional)

Place the flour in a medium mixing bowl. Using a pastry blender or a fork, cut the ½ cup of chilled butter into the flour until pea-size chunks form. Add the salt and 2 tablespoons of the ice water and, using a fork, gently toss just until the dough pulls together.

Using your hands, form the dough into a ball. Cover with plastic film and refrigerate for at least 30 minutes, or until ready to use.

When ready to prepare the tart, preheat the oven to 350°F. Lightly flour a clean work surface.

Remove the pastry from the refrigerator and unwrap. Place the pastry on the floured surface and, using a rolling pin, roll the dough out to a circle approximately 11 inches in diameter.

Fit the pastry circle into a 9-inch tart pan with a removable bottom, carefully pressing the pastry into the bottom and sides of the pan. Using a kitchen fork, randomly prick the bottom of the pastry. Fit a piece of parchment paper large enough to cover the bottom of the pan and come up the sides. Fill the bottom of the pan with pastry weights, dried beans, or peas.

Place the tart shell in the preheated oven and bake for about 15 minutes, or until set in the center and golden brown. If necessary, remove the parchment and pastry weights about 3 minutes before the pastry is baked to ensure that the pastry is an even golden brown.

While the dough is chilling and baking, prepare the filling: Measure out 3 tablespoons of the cold water and combine it with the cornstarch in a small bowl, stirring to dissolve the cornstarch. Set aside.

Place the remaining water in a heavy-bottomed saucepan. Whisk in the lemon juice and sugar and place over medium heat. Cook, whisking constantly, for about 3 minutes, or until the mixture is just about to come to a boil.

Whisk the egg yolks into the cornstarch/water mixture and, whisking constantly, add a bit of the hot lemon-juice mixture to the egg-yolk mixture to temper it. Then, whisking constantly, add the tempered egg-yolk mixture to the saucepan. Whisking constantly, bring the mixture to a full, rolling boil. Immediately remove from the heat and whisk in the butter.

Cover the top with a piece of parchment paper (to keep a film from forming) and set aside to cool slightly.

When cooled, pour the lemon filling into the baked tart shell and set aside to cool completely.

If desired, decorate the top with whipped-cream rosettes before serving.

Makes one 9-inch tart

CRÈME BRÛLÉE
1982
DIETER SCHORNER, *Pastry Chef*

Here it is—the recipe that started the landslide in crème brûlée making in restaurants all across America, and that even today leads the pack in dessert popularity surveys. Demonstrated by Dieter Schorner when he was the pastry chef at Le Cirque, this basic recipe continues its evolution as the quintessential restaurant dessert, now flavored with scents and colors once unknown and unimaginable to a French pastry chef.

¼ cup light brown sugar

2 cups heavy (whipping) cream

1 vanilla bean, split

4 large egg yolks, at room temperature

¼ cup plus 2 tablespoons extra-fine sugar

In the period since this recipe was introduced, a small, inexpensive, hand-held **torch** made especially to **caramelize** crème brûlée has been introduced into the kitchen-gadget marketplace. If you make crème brûlée frequently, you might want to invest in one, as it really does simplify the caramelization process.

Preheat the oven to 300°F.

Place the brown sugar on a baking sheet and set aside in a dry area for 24 hours, or until no longer moist.

Place the heavy cream and vanilla bean in a heavy-bottomed saucepan over medium heat. Allow to warm to about 90°F; this should take no more than 4 minutes. Remove from the heat.

Place the egg yolks in a large stainless-steel bowl and whisk to combine. Add the sugar and continue to whisk until the mixture is blended and the sugar has dissolved. Gradually add the warm cream, whisking constantly.

Using a large metal spoon, skim off any foam, then slowly pour the mixture through a fine-mesh sieve into a clean container.

Pour an equal portion of the strained mixture into each of six crème brûlée dishes. Transfer the filled dishes to a 15½ × 10½ × 1-inch jelly-roll pan. Place the pan on the lower shelf of the preheated oven, then carefully add cool water to the pan to come halfway up the sides of the filled dishes.

Bake for 30 minutes, or until the center is barely set.

Remove the pan from the oven and place the dishes on a wire rack to come to room temperature. Cover each dish with plastic film and place in the refrigerator for at least 8 hours or up to 24 hours.

Five minutes before you're ready to serve, preheat the broiler. Remove the custards from the refrigerator and unwrap.

Place the extra-fine sugar in a fine sieve and, gently tapping on the side of the sieve with your hand, lightly cover the top of each custard with the sugar.

Place the dishes under the broiler for about 15 seconds, turning the dishes once or twice, or until the sugar has caramelized and created a beautifully colored, crackling crust.

Remove from the broiler, let stand for 1 minute, and serve.

Serves 6

1986 to 1990

American Chefs Begin to Make Their Mark

During the second five-year period at De Gustibus, we were thrilled by the creativity of young American chefs and enthralled by the Americanization of a new breed of French chefs. The food was often complicated and tried the patience of even some of our most skilled home cooks when they took the recipes to their home kitchens. But everything was so exciting that complaints were few. Trained chefs and home cooks alike were challenged as American cuisine took its star turn.

Almost weekly we were introduced to new products and imaginative techniques. Once hard-to-find ethnic ingredients had become staples in both restaurants and home kitchens. Vegetable and fruit juices, rather than the traditional creams and rich stocks, became the bases for wonderfully fresh-tasting sauces. It seemed as though every chef liked to practice his or her art on a wood-fired grill. Raw and just barely cooked fish moved from the Japanese tradition to everyday acceptance. Equipment was just as likely to come from the hardware store as from the restaurant supplier. Architectural food soared upward from the plate, with beautifully designed placeware holding sculptural extravaganzas. The plates themselves were finished with Matisse-like beauty as artistry reigned in the kitchen.

"The one piece of **advice** that you gave me, Arlene, that I have never forgotten addressed my perfectionist's expectations for my first class. You said, 'Don't worry, Flo, just remember that you want your desserts to look **homemade,** not machine-made.' It has remained with me for twenty-five years, and it always works its magic by removing my self-inflicted pressure. I relax, smile, and begin teaching. That's just one of many things I have De Gustibus to be thankful for." —Flo Braker

And yet, at the same time, "mom in the kitchen"–style cooking was being felt throughout the restaurant community. Many chefs were taking their classic training and combining the skills it had given them with some of the techniques and flavors learned from their mothers and grandmothers to create a whole new style of "comfort" food. It made no difference whether the mother was Italian, American, French, or Asian.

During this period we felt the impact of two phenomena that would have far-reaching effects on the dining scene in America. First, four-star restaurants were moving with rapid speed into Las Vegas, once a culinary wasteland. By the beginning of the next century, almost every chef of import in the country would be represented on the "Vegas scene." Where innovation once occurred primarily on the two coasts as well as in Chicago, we saw creativity explode in this new venue of culinary magnificence.

Second, while culinary palaces were rising in the desert, chefs were connecting with their purveyors in a manner that had never been experienced in America. Chef and farmer, rancher, cheesemaker, wine maker, and baker began working hand-in-hand to bring organic, free-range, heirloom, and all manner of environmentally friendly products to the restaurant table. And, as we had seen time after time, what came to the high-end restaurant table would trickle down to the home kitchen.

Preceding pages (clockwise from top left): *Rick Bayless; Valentino Marcattilii; Jean-Louis Palladin; Jacques Torres; Biba Caggiano; Alfred Portale; Sarabeth Levine; Michel Richard; Roger Vergé and David Bouley; De Gustibus children's cooking class; Anne Rosenzweig; Carol Field.*
Right: *Charlie Palmer.*

1986–1990

Colman Andrews
Francesco Antonucci
Lee Bailey
Paul Bartolotta
Lidia Bastianich
Jean-Paul Battaglia
Rick Bayless
Andrew Bell
Rose Levy Beranbaum
Jean-Michel Bergougnoux
Georges Blanc
Raymond Blanc
David Bouley
Daniel Boulud
Antoine Bouterin
Flo Braker
Edward Brown
Christopher Buey
Giuliano Bugialli
David Burke
Marian Burros
Biba Caggiano
Penelope Casas
Jacques Chibois
Nicola Civetta
Patrick Clark
Gary Coyle
Rena Coyle
Marion Cunningham
Andrew D'Amico
Christian Delouvrier
Marcel Desaulniers
Jim Dodge
Sean Driscoll
Alain Ducasse
Florence Fabricant
Markus Färbinger
John Farnsworth
Dean Fearing
Susan Feniger
Carol Field
Michael Foley
Larry Forgione
Jane Freiman

George Germon
Ed Giobbi
Joyce Goldstein
Bert Greene
Vincent Guerithault
Andrea Hellrigl
Ken Hom
Michael Hutchings
Yan Jacquot
Madhur Jaffrey
Barbara Kafka
Hubert Keller
Thomas Keller
Diana Kennedy
Johanne Killeen
Albert Kumin
Gray Kunz
Jean Paul Lacombe
Viana La Place
Karen Lee
Sarabeth Levine
Edna Lewis
David Liederman
Sheila Lukins
Dennis MacNeil
Deborah Madison
Waldy Malouf
Abby Mandel
Valentino Marcattilii
Lydie Marshall
Zarela Martinez
Georges Masraff
Michael McCarty
Lorenza de'Medici
Perla Meyers
Carlo Middione
Mark Miller
Mary Sue Milliken
Anton Mosimann
Eberhard Müller
Leslie Newman
Wayne Nish
Patrick O'Connell
Bradley Ogden

Jean-Louis Palladin
Charles Palmer
Gerard Pangaud
Guy Pascal
Alex Patout
Jacques Pépin
Georges Perrier
Gennaro Picone
Debra Ponzek
Alfred Portale
Wolfgang Puck
Stephan Pyles
Jean-Jacques Rachou
Leslee Reis
Seppi Renggli
Leslie Revsin
Michel Richard
Michael Roberts
Douglas Rodriguez
Michael Romano
Anne Rosenzweig
Michel Rostang
Nicole Routhier
Albert Roux
Myra Sable
Edward Safdie
Alain Sailhac
Richard Sax
Jimmy Schmidt
Elizabeth Schneider
Julian Serrano
Joachim Splichal
Christopher Styler
Jacques Torres
Jeremiah Tower
Thomas Valenti
Jean-Georges Vongerichten
Brendan Walsh
Patricia Wells
Jasper White
Anne Willan
Christian Willer
Paula Wolfert

Rick Bayless
David Bouley
Daniel Boulud
Edward Brown

David Burke
Carol Field
Thomas Keller
Gray Kunz

Mark Miller
Charlie Palmer
Alfred Portale
Michel Richard

Anne Rosenzweig
Jacques Torres
Tom Valenti
Jean-Georges
    Vongerichten

Lidia Bastianich • Mario Batali •
Alton Brown • Michael Chiarello •
Mary Ann Esposito • Bobby Flay •
Tyler Florence • Emeril Lagasse •
Masaharu Morimoto • Sara Moulton •
Jacques Pépin • Rachael Ray •
Martha Stewart

THE WINE MAVENS

Joseph Bastianich

Cathleen Burke

Kimberly Charles

Andrea Immer

Jean-Luc Le Dû

David Lynch

Karen MacNeil

Steve Olson

Josh Wesson

25 YEARS OF

MOST POPULAR

When I'm not near the chef I
love, I love the chef I'm near;
however, if pressed, I would
have to say Emeril Lagasse,
Wolfgang Puck, Robert Del
Grande, Rachael Ray, Bobby
Flay, Mario Batali, Tyler
Florence, Jacques Pépin,
André Soltner, Alain Sailhac.

MOST
SOPHISTICATED
CHEF

JEREMIAH TOWER

ROBERT DEL GRANDE

DEAN FEARING

MARK MILLER

STEPHEN PYLES

THE SOUTHWEST
CONTINGENT

MOST IMPORTANT LESSONS LEARNED IN **THE CLASSROOM**

Prepare your mise en place

The answer to all questions is "Yes, Chef"

Keep your workplace immaculately clean

Clean as you go/Speed counts

MOST UNUSUAL SIDETRIP

DIANA KENNEDY *arrived at her class a little late. She saw the herb epazote growing in front of the FDR Drive and she made the taxi driver stop so she could collect it for the class to try.*

Superlatives

1980 to 2005

THE HEART-THROBS

SCOTT CONANT
ROBERT DEL GRANDE
ROCCO DISPIRITO
TODD ENGLISH
BOBBY FLAY
TYLER FLORENCE
THOMAS KELLER
RACHAEL RAY
MARCUS SAMUELSSON
ALAIN SAILHAC
PATRICIA WELLS

STEVE JENKINS
ROBERT KAUFELT
MAX MCCALMAN

THE RISE OF THE CHEESE MOGULS

ON THE MENU

APPETIZERS, SOUPS, AND SALADS

Cucumber and Sumac Salad
Two Hot Tamales
(Mary Sue Milliken and Susan Feniger)—1989

Manila Clams with Ancho Chilies
Mark Miller—1987

Quail Egg Canapés
Michel Richard—1988

*Uovo in Raviolo con Burro Nocciola
e Tartufi Bianchi*
(Egg in Ravioli, with Brown Butter and White Truffles)
Valentino Marcattilii and Paul Bartolotta—1989

Oyster and Endive Chowder
with Fresh American Morels
Charlie Palmer—1987

Lobster Bisque with Lemon Verbena and Ginger
Gray Kunz—1990

Squab Salad with Couscous, Croutons,
and Cumin-Coriander Vinaigrette
Alfred Portale—1987

PASTA AND GRAINS

Penne with Vodka Sauce
Biba Caggiano—1987

Pasta with Grilled Shrimp, Golden Caviar,
and Chardonnay-Cream Sauce
Michael McCarthy—1987

MEAT, GAME, AND POULTRY

Braised Lamb Shanks with White Bean Purée
Tom Valenti—1990

Duck Breasts with Green Pumpkin Seed Mole
Rick Bayless—1988

FISH AND SHELLFISH

Spiced Shrimp with Carrot Juice
Jean-Georges Vongerichten—1988

Braised Sea Bass in Tomato-Coriander Sauce
with Fried Celery Leaves and Fava Beans
David Bouley—1987

Turbot with Spring Vegetables
Alain Ducasse—1987

*Paupiettes de Sea Bass Croustillante
au Vin de Barolo*
(Crisp Paupiettes of Sea Bass in Barolo Wine Sauce)
Daniel Boulud—1988

Sautéed Shad with Chiffonade of
Collard Greens and Curry Sauce
Jean-Louis Palladin—1990

SANDWICHES

Warm Tuna and Wasabi Sandwich
with Tuna Salad and Lotus Chips
David Burke—1989

BREADS AND DESSERTS

Olive Bread
Carol Field—1987

Warm Brioche Custard with Fresh Peach Sauce
Bradley Ogden—1987

Scones
Sarabeth Levine—1990

Chocolate Almonds
Jacques Torres—1990

CUCUMBER AND SUMAC SALAD
1989
TWO HOT TAMALES (MARY SUE MILLIKEN *and* SUSAN FENIGER),
Chefs/Owners, Border Grill, Ciudad, Cookbook Authors

Two Hot Tamales was the title of their extremely successful cooking show on the Food Network, and it wasn't long before people forgot their names and called Mary Sue Milliken and Susan Feniger, two marvelous female chefs, by their television sobriquet. Their enthusiasm for easy-to-pull-together meals and their fondness for spicy and interesting ingredients made them a hit in the De Gustibus classroom. Mary Sue and Susan were two of the very few female chefs who reached stardom in the early stages of the star-chef search. Their charisma was more than evident to all of us.

In this recipe we tasted an almost unknown ingredient, the acidically refreshing sumac, in a very simple salad that they suggested serving with intensely flavored, rich main dishes. It is hard to imagine that these two marvelous but spicy cooks met in the kitchens of one of America's most revered French restaurants, Le Français, run by the esteemed chef Jean Banchet, in Wheeling, Illinois. It is also important to note that they were the first women to work in the kitchen of this august establishment.

---

2 bunches scallions

4 large Kirby (or pickling) cucumbers, well washed and dried

4 medium ripe tomatoes, well washed and dried

2 red bell peppers, well washed and dried

6 tablespoons ground sumac (see Note)

2 tablespoons extra-virgin olive oil

2 tablespoons red wine vinegar

2 pita loaves, pulled apart, toasted, and broken into bite-size pieces

Using a chef's knife, cut the scallions on the bias into thin slices. Place the scallions in a mixing bowl.

Trim the ends from the cucumbers. Using a chef's knife, cut them on the bias into ½-inch-thick slices and place them in the mixing bowl.

Core the tomatoes, cut them into small, uneven shapes, and add them to the mixing bowl.

Core, seed, and remove the white membrane from the bell peppers. Cut the peppers into small, uneven shapes and add them to the mixing bowl.

Add the sumac to the bowl and toss to combine. Pour the olive oil and then the vinegar over the vegetables and toss to coat. Cover with plastic film and refrigerate until ready to use, but for no more than six hours.

When ready to serve, add the toasted pita and toss to coat. Serve immediately.

Note: Sumac, a very astringent deep red berry, is available at Middle Eastern markets and most specialty food stores. It is sold either whole or ground and is used to add fruity acidic flavor to all types of dishes.

Serves 4 to 6

MANILA CLAMS WITH ANCHO CHILIES
1987
MARK MILLER, *Chef/Owner, Coyote Café, Cookbook Author*

Mark Miller is considered to be one of the most influential chefs in America for trying to re-create the intensity of form and color in food that he admired in primitive art. He chose the cuisine of America's Southwest in which to incorporate his philosophy and, by doing so, brought this peasant-style food to new heights. His authority was felt throughout the industry and eventually led to touches of Southwestern cuisine being introduced into almost every other style of cooking in the United States—including fast food.

When Mark Miller first came to De Gustibus, it didn't seem possible that any one person could know so much about chilies. He enlightened the class beyond anything we could have imagined about fresh chilies, dried chilies, powdered chilies, and so on. I remember we were all puzzled that a fresh poblano turned into a dried ancho.

In this recipe we saw one of the first uses of the word "pesto" to mean something other than the traditional basil-based Italian preparation. Over the years, we would see "pesto" used to define an amazing number of sauces that, often, had almost nothing to do with the original.

2 cups clam broth

2 dried New Mexico red chilies, stemmed and seeded

¼ cup extra-virgin olive oil

6 ripe plum tomatoes, roasted, peeled, cored, seeded, and chopped (see Note)

4 cloves roasted garlic (see Note)

48 baby Manila clams

Coarse salt to taste

Poblano Pesto (recipe follows)

Place the clam broth in a medium saucepan over medium heat. Add the red chilies and bring to a simmer. Remove from the heat and let stand for about 30 minutes, or until the chilies have softened. Transfer the mixture to a blender and purée until smooth. Set aside.

Place 2 tablespoons of the olive oil in a large sauté pan over medium heat. Add the tomatoes and garlic and cook, stirring frequently, for about 3 minutes, or just until the vegetables have just begun to soften. Add the clams along with the reserved chili–clam mixture. Raise the heat, cover, and cook for about 5 minutes, or until the clams open.

Remove the lid, add the remaining 2 tablespoons of olive oil, and bring to a boil. Taste and, if necessary, season with salt.

Ladle an equal portion of clams into each of four large, shallow soup bowls. Drizzle Poblano Pesto over the top and serve.

Serves 4

POBLANO PESTO

6 medium poblano chilies, roasted, peeled, stemmed, and seeded (see Note)

1 bunch cilantro, leaves only, well washed and dried

1 small clove garlic, roasted and peeled (see Note)

6 tablespoons roasted pine nuts (see Note)

4 to 6 tablespoons extra-virgin olive oil

Juice of 1 to 2 limes

1/2 teaspoon sea salt, or to taste

1 large red bell pepper, roasted, peeled, stemmed, seeded, and finely diced

Place the poblanos in a food processor fitted with the metal blade. Add the cilantro, garlic, pine nuts, and olive oil and process, using the pulse button, to make a rough paste. Add lime juice to taste along with the salt and pulse just to incorporate.

Using a rubber spatula, scrape the mixture from the processor bowl into a clean, nonreactive container. Fold in the diced bell pepper, adding just enough bell pepper to offer a nice contrast to the green sauce.

Cover and serve within a couple of hours. If made too far in advance, the sauce will lose its vibrant flavor and colors.

Note: Roasted tomatoes, chilies, and bell peppers should be well charred so that the skins can be easily removed. This can take anywhere from 10 to 30 minutes. Once roasted, they can be placed in an airtight container or in a resealable plastic bag to steam, which will facilitate the skins' removal. They can be roasted on a hot grill, over an open flame, either on the stovetop or under the broiler, or in a preheated 350°F oven. They should be turned occasionally to ensure even charring. Chilies with any degree of heat will emit noxious fumes when roasting so, for them, the preferable method is outdoors on a grill.

To roast garlic, trim off the top, rub the entire head with olive oil, wrap it firmly in aluminum foil, and bake in a preheated 350°F oven for about 1 hour, or until all of the cloves are soft. The cloves may be removed one by one, or the flesh may be pushed out of the entire head by squeezing on it.

Pine (and other) nuts may be roasted either on the stovetop or in a preheated 350°F oven. Either way, you must watch them carefully, stirring often, as their oiliness will quickly cause them to burn.

QUAIL EGG CANAPÉS

1988

MICHEL RICHARD, *Chef/Owner, Citronelle, Cookbook Author*

Michel Richard was a first-class French pastry chef who immigrated to Southern California in 1977. He is considered a pioneer in combining the essence of classic French cuisine with a California sensibility. When he opened his first restaurant, Citron, in Los Angeles, Michel's use of local, seasonal ingredients and his freedom of culinary expression centered on his old-school training opened a whole new door to California cooking.

Michel Richard is an almost larger-than-life definition of the French chef. Opinionated, passionate, well-fed, and full of enthusiasms, he is, nonetheless, very aware of the chasm between restaurant cooking and home cooking. In this recipe he introduced quail eggs in a very fancy hors d'oeuvres that could easily be replicated in the home kitchen as long as there were no budgetary constraints. He also suggested that we might try this recipe using hen eggs and larger slices of bread for a brunch dish. In the years since this recipe was introduced, quail eggs have become fairly easy to obtain and quite affordable, brioche loaves can be found in supermarket bakeries, and American caviars have made a strong impact as a replacement for the ever-more-expensive and rare Iranian and Russian caviars.

Twelve ½-inch-thick, 3-inch-round slices brioche

2 tablespoons olive oil

12 quail eggs

Freshly ground pepper to taste

2 ounces caviar, preferably osetra

When Michel Richard was preparing a recipe that required that all-American ingredient **peanut butter**, one of the students asked, "What brand?" With a great Gallic shrug and French pronunciation (Jeef) he said "Jif, what else?"

Using a canapé cutter (or any other cylindrical instrument) about the size of a quarter, cut a hole in the center of each slice of brioche. Discard the holes or reserve them for bread crumbs.

Preheat the broiler (or salamander, if you have one).

Heat the olive oil in a large ovenproof sauté pan over medium heat. Add the brioche slices in a single layer. Carefully break an egg into the center of each slice of brioche and cook for 2 minutes. Do not overcook the eggs—they should remain very soft and runny.

Place the pan under the broiler for 30 seconds.

Remove the pan from the broiler. Grind a dash of pepper over each piece of bread, then spoon a small scoop of caviar in the center of each. Serve immediately.

Serves 4 to 6

UOVO EN RAVIOLO CON BURRO NOCCIOLA
E TARTUFI BIANCHI
(EGG IN RAVIOLI, WITH BROWN BUTTER AND WHITE TRUFFLES)
1989

VALENTINO MARCATTILII *Chef/Owner, San Domenico (Imola, Italy) and*
PAUL BARTOLOTTA, *Former Chef, San Domenico (New York, Italy),*
Chef/Co-Owner, Bacchus, Ristorante Bartolotta

This recipe created by Chef Valentino Marcattilii and prepared at De Gustibus by both Chef Marcattilii and Chef Paul Bartolotta, caused a sensation when it was introduced at New York's preeminent Italian restaurant San Domenico, owned by the great restaurateur Tony May. (Tony often makes international news buying the largest truffle at the fall Italian truffle auction.) It highlights traditional ingredients in a most sophisticated way; when the sweet, runny egg yolk combines with the aromatic truffle, the flavor and aroma are blissful. Every chef in town (and from out of town) made a beeline to the restaurant to experience it. To this day, it remains on the menu at San Domenico.

½ cup finely chopped cooked spinach leaves

½ cup ricotta cheese

3½ ounces freshly grated Parmigiano-Reggiano cheese

5 large eggs, at room temperature

Freshly ground nutmeg to taste

Coarse salt and freshly ground white pepper to taste

Eight 6-inch-round pieces very thin fresh pasta dough

7 tablespoons unsalted butter

One 2-ounce white truffle

Combine the spinach and ricotta cheese with half of the Parmigiano-Reggiano cheese and one egg in a small mixing bowl. Season with nutmeg, salt, and white pepper to taste.

Place a large piece of waxed paper on a clean work surface. Place four of the pasta rounds on the paper.

Spoon an equal portion of the spinach mixture into the center of each pasta round. Using the back of a spoon, make a small indentation in the center of the spinach mixture.

Working with one at a time, carefully break open an egg and place a yolk in the indentation along with about half of the egg white.

Using a pastry brush, lightly coat the edge of each pastry round with cold water. Place one of the remaining pasta rounds over each filled round, carefully pressing down to eliminate as much air as possible, and seal the two rounds together.

Bring a large pot of salted water to a boil over high heat. When boiling, carefully add the ravioli and return to a boil. Boil for 2 minutes.

Using a slotted spoon, carefully lift the pasta from the boiling water and place on a double layer of paper towels to drain.

While the pasta is cooking, place the butter in a small skillet over high heat and heat just until the butter turns a light brown color and has a warm, nutty aroma.

Transfer one ravioli into each of four shallow soup bowls. Shave an equal portion of the white truffle over each plate, sprinkle with some of the remaining Parmigiano-Reggiano cheese, and drizzle the brown butter over all. Serve immediately.

Serves 4

OYSTER AND ENDIVE CHOWDER
WITH FRESH AMERICAN MORELS
1987

CHARLIE PALMER, *Chef/Owner, Metrazur, Dry Creek Kitchen, Kitchen 22,*
The Stirling Club, Aureole, Cookbook Author

Charlie Palmer is another larger-than-life chef, a six-foot-four all-American guy. Shy and unassuming when he first visited the De Gustibus classroom, Charlie went on to become the godfather of a huge number of American chefs, mentoring and supporting their invasion into the culinary scene. Charlie was a forerunner in the entrepreneurial chef race—he owned a dairy, then a florist, and then lots of restaurants. He had just garnered three stars at The River Cafe in Brooklyn when he taught his first class.

Charlie went on, at the ripe old age of twenty-six, to open the widely acclaimed Aureole in Manhattan. He describes his cooking as "progressive American cuisine," using American artisanal products and small-farm producers to execute his take on classic French cooking. He now has a restaurant empire and continues to be a favorite of our clients. When I think of Charlie, I always think about his tip to "season high" (to sprinkle salt over food from some height to ensure that the salt doesn't land in a clump and that the item is appropriately seasoned), as does anyone who has ever learned from him.

2 tablespoons unsalted butter

12 American morels, cleaned and halved lengthwise

2 new potatoes, peeled, cut into ¼-inch dice, and blanched

1 leek, white part only, well washed, dried, and finely diced

16 plump, meaty oysters, preferably Pacific, shucked, juices reserved

2 endives, well washed, dried, and cut on the bias into very thin pieces

6 ounces heavy cream

Coarse salt and freshly ground pepper to taste

2 tablespoons chopped fresh tarragon leaves

Place a large sauté pan over medium heat. When just warm, add the butter. When melted, add the morels, potatoes, and leek, and cook, stirring frequently, for about 5 minutes, or until the vegetables have sweated their liquid but not taken on any color.

Constantly and carefully shaking the pan back and forth, add the oysters along with their juice. Still shaking the pan, add the endives and cook for about 3 minutes, or until the oysters have tightened up slightly.

Stir in the cream and bring to a boil. Season with salt and pepper to taste.

Using a slotted spoon, transfer four oysters into each of four warm, shallow soup plates.

Return the vegetable-cream mixture to high heat and bring to a boil. Boil for about 2 minutes, or until reduced slightly.

Remove from the heat and stir in the tarragon. Taste and, if necessary, add salt and pepper. Ladle an equal portion into each soup bowl and serve immediately.

Serves 4

LOBSTER BISQUE WITH LEMON VERBENA AND GINGER
1990
GRAY KUNZ, *Chef/Owner, Café Gray, Cookbook Author*

Gray Kunz, although Swiss, is skilled in the use of Asian spices and cooking techniques, as he grew up in Singapore. He went on to train with the famous Lausanne-based chef Fredy Giradet, who made sure that he was well-versed in classic cooking, too. This training enabled Gray to combine the spices and flavors of Asia, which were little-known and infrequently used in classic European cooking, into an exciting, exploratory cuisine. Although Gray refuses to label his cooking "fusion," he has had an enormous influence on the fusion of the cuisines of Asia into contemporary American cooking.

Gray Kunz made his mark in the United States with four-star cuisine at the St. Regis Hotel's very luxe restaurant Lespinasse. His use of Asian ingredients, exotic spices and fruits, and sensational flavors brought New York food critics and foodies to their knees. In this recipe we saw how this innovative chef could turn a traditional rich, creamy bisque on its head.

1 pound lobster heads (called stiffs)

½ cup (1 stick) unsalted butter, softened

2 tablespoons olive oil

2 cloves garlic, peeled and thinly sliced

¼ cup finely diced onion

¼ cup finely diced celery root

2 tablespoons minced fresh thyme

2 tablespoons minced fresh lemon verbena, plus more to taste

2 tablespoons chopped fresh ginger root, plus more to taste

4 black peppercorns

1 whole clove

1 bay leaf

½ pound ripe tomatoes, peeled, cored, seeded, and roughly chopped

Coarse salt to taste

¾ cup white wine

¼ cup brandy, plus more to taste

Approximately 1½ cups fish stock or water

Cayenne to taste

Combine the lobster heads with 2 tablespoons of the butter in a food processor or saucepan. Either process (in the food processor) or crush with a meat mallet (in the saucepan) until the shell is smashed and the butter is incorporated into it.

Heat the olive oil in a heavy-bottomed saucepan over medium heat. Add the garlic, onion, and celery root and sauté for about 5 minutes, or until the vegetables are golden brown. Add the thyme, lemon verbena, and ginger, stirring to combine. Lower the heat and stir in the peppercorns, clove, and bay leaf.

Add the reserved lobster-butter mixture and cook, stirring vigorously, until well blended. Cook, stirring frequently, for about 10 minutes, or until all of the liquid has evaporated from the pan and the mixture begins to brown at the side of the pan.

Stir in the tomatoes. Season with a little salt to encourage the tomatoes to surrender their juices and again cook, stirring frequently, until all of the liquid has evaporated from the pan and you hear a crackling sound.

Add the wine and brandy and stir to deglaze the pan. Add just enough fish stock or water to barely cover the mixture. Bring to a simmer and simmer for 10 minutes. Using a handheld immersion blender, blend until smooth and continue cooking at a bare simmer for an additional 10 minutes. Remove from the heat and strain through a fine sieve into a clean saucepan.

Place the soup over medium heat and bring to a simmer. Simmer for about 15 minutes, or until reduced by half.

Remove from the heat. Taste and, if necessary, adjust the seasoning with cayenne and additional salt, lemon verbena, and/or ginger.

Using a handheld immersion blender, beat in the remaining 6 tablespoons of butter. Serve immediately.

Note: *Adding 2 ounces of white rice with the fish stock (or water) will bind the soup naturally.*

Serves 4

gray Kunz
Spring '92

SQUAB SALAD
WITH COUSCOUS, CROUTONS, AND CUMIN-CORIANDER VINAIGRETTE
1987

ALFRED PORTALE, *Chef/Owner, Gotham Bar and Grill, Cookbook Author*

Alfred Portale was, and remains, the king of architectural food. It was Alfred who first designed brilliantly high and towering salads that more than made a statement on the plate. While others might wow diners with spectacular desserts, Chef Portale began making his statement with the first course. But no matter how dramatic the presentation, his food is always beautifully seasoned, perfectly prepared, and contemporary in feel. Throughout the years he has remained a star on the New York dining scene with his sense of design leading contemporary food and plating in a whole new direction. Many chefs try to imitate Alfred's style, but rarely do they come near to his perfection.

Although home cooks sometimes have difficulty executing Alfred's plating, the food is always a sensation. It is amazing to me to see just how timeless Alfred's food is—his recipes from his first class are as contemporary and delicious today as they were almost twenty years ago.

---

1 cup chicken stock or water

1 tablespoon unsalted butter

¾ cup couscous

Two 1-pound squabs, cleaned, rinsed, and boned, leaving 4 breast halves and 4 leg-thigh pieces

Coarse salt and freshly ground pepper to taste

2 tablespoons peanut oil

1 small head red oak leaf lettuce, pulled apart, well washed, and dried

1 small head frisee lettuce, pulled apart, well washed, and dried

1 small head Bibb lettuce, pulled apart, well washed, and dried

Cumin-Coriander Vinaigrette (recipe follows)

1 tablespoon harissa (see Note)

2 scallions, white parts with some green, well washed, trimmed, and finely chopped

⅓ cup seedless golden raisins

8 croutons (see Note)

Place the chicken stock in a medium saucepan over medium heat. Add the butter and bring to a boil. Remove from the heat and stir in the couscous. Cover and set aside to allow the couscous to absorb the liquid.

Preheat the oven to 300°F. Season the squab pieces with salt and pepper to taste.

Heat the oil in a large sauté pan over medium-high heat. Add the squab leg pieces, skin sides down, and sear, turning frequently, until all sides are golden brown. Transfer the leg pieces to a small baking pan. Place in the preheated oven to continue cooking until an instant-read thermometer inserted into the thickest part reads 150°F for medium-well.

Place the squab breasts in the sauté pan over medium heat and sear, turning frequently, until all sides are golden brown. Cook the breasts, skin sides down, for about 7 minutes, or until an instant-read thermometer inserted into the thickest part reads 135°F. Remove from the heat and set aside to rest for 5 minutes. The breast meat should remain medium-rare.

Place the salad greens in a mixing bowl. Add just enough of the vinaigrette to moisten slightly and toss to coat.

Season the couscous with a few spoonfuls of the vinaigrette, the harissa, and salt and pepper to taste. Add the scallions and toss with a fork to fluff.

Spoon equal portions of the couscous in the center of each of four luncheon plates. Sprinkle the raisins over the couscous and arrange the lettuce around the edge of the couscous.

Cut the squab breasts, on the bias, into thin slices. Fan a breast

half out along the bottom of each plate. Cut the leg and thigh apart and nestle them into the couscous. Place two croutons on each plate and drizzle some vinaigrette over all. Serve immediately.

Serves 4

CUMIN-CORIANDER VINAIGRETTE

½ medium clove garlic, peeled and smashed

3 tablespoons chopped fresh cilantro leaves (see Note)

½ teaspoon harissa (see Note)

½ teaspoon ground cumin

¾ teaspoon coarse salt, plus more to taste

¼ teaspoon freshly ground white pepper, plus more to taste

About ¼ cup fresh lemon juice

⅔ cup peanut oil

Combine the garlic, cilantro, harissa, and cumin in a small mixing bowl. Stir in the salt and pepper. Whisk in half of the lemon juice and then the oil. Taste and, if necessary, adjust the seasoning with salt and pepper and balance the flavor with some or all of the remaining lemon juice.

Note: Harissa, an extremely hot Tunisian sauce made from chilies, garlic, spices, and olive oil, is available from Middle Eastern markets and most specialty food stores.

To most chefs, croutons are not those tiny dried-out, flavored-infused bread cubes found in boxes but a slice of baguette that has been toasted and, sometimes, seasoned with olive oil, garlic, and salt and pepper. The recipe will usually tell you whether you should season the crouton or not. Most Italian dishes will require at least a drizzle of oil.

Cilantro was once referred to as fresh coriander but is now almost always called cilantro.

PENNE WITH VODKA SAUCE
1987
BIBA CAGGIANO, *Cookbook Author, Chef/Owner, Biba*

Biba Caggiano was recommended to me by Carole Lalli, who was, at that time, the food editor at *House and Garden* magazine. Biba's recipes seemed so homey and delicious that I immediately invited her to the De Gustibus classroom. Biba turned out to be one of the most sophisticated and elegant chef/owners we had ever met. She was such a passionate teacher that she became one of our favorites.

This innovative recipe, although not a traditional Italian one, is the mother of all of those pasta with vodka sauces that are now so loved in family-style Italian restaurants across America. Vodka sauce is now found on supermarket shelves, bottled commercially. It has come so far that it is now considered a classic Italian dish.

¼ cup (½ stick) unsalted butter

¼ pound pancetta, finely diced

⅓ cup vodka

1½ cups Biba's Plain Tomato Sauce (recipe follows)

½ cup heavy cream

Coarse salt and freshly ground pepper to taste

1 pound dried penne rigate or rigatoni pasta

½ cup freshly grated Parmigiano-Reggiano cheese, or to taste

In a sauté pan large enough to accommodate the cooked pasta, heat the butter over medium heat. As soon as the butter foams, add the pancetta and sauté for about 5 minutes, or until the pancetta has taken on a light color. Add the vodka and cook, stirring frequently, for about 4 minutes, or until the vodka has evaporated. Stir in the tomato sauce and cream and bring to a simmer. Simmer for 10 minutes. Taste and, if necessary, adjust the seasoning with salt and pepper.

While the sauce is cooking, prepare the pasta. Bring a large pot of salted water to a boil over high heat. Add the pasta and cook according to the package directions for "al dente," usually about 10 minutes.

Drain the pasta and add it to the sauce, tossing to coat well. The sauce will be thick enough to coat the pasta easily.

Using tongs, place an equal portion of pasta in each of six shallow pasta bowls. Serve with the cheese sprinkled over the top.

Serves 6

BIBA'S PLAIN TOMATO SAUCE

One 28-ounce can imported Italian plum tomatoes with their juice

1 tablespoon olive oil

Coarse salt and freshly ground pepper to taste

Pass the tomatoes and their juice through a food mill or fine sieve into a clean bowl. (This is done to remove all of the seeds.)

Heat the oil in a medium saucepan over medium heat. When hot but not smoking, add the seedless tomatoes and bring to a gentle simmer. Simmer for about 15 minutes, or until thickened. Season with salt and pepper to taste and use, as is, as a simple sauce for pasta or as a base for other pasta sauces.

PASTA WITH GRILLED SHRIMP,
GOLDEN CAVIAR, AND CHARDONNAY-CREAM SAUCE
1987
MICHAEL McCARTY, *Owner, Michael's Santa Monica, Michael's NYC*

Michael McCarty's eponymous restaurant, Michael's, set the California dining scene on its ear by combining casual dining with the finest ingredients, spectacular art, glorious table settings, and fantastic floral arrangements. His cuisine was quite individual, based on the French classics with California attitude. When he opened in New York, he gave us the first glimpse of this refreshing approach to fine dining.

1½ cups all-purpose flour

6 large egg yolks

3 tablespoons unsalted butter

3 button mushrooms, cleaned and chopped

1 medium carrot, peeled, trimmed, and chopped

1 Maui onion, peeled and chopped

¼ cup chopped fresh flat-leaf parsley

18 Santa Barbara (or other large) shrimp, shells removed, and cleaned, with shells reserved

2 cups California chardonnay

Coarse salt and freshly ground pepper to taste

2 cups heavy cream

2 tablespoons olive oil

¼ cup golden caviar

2 tablespoons minced fresh chives

Place the flour in a mound on a clean work surface. Make a well in the center and pour the egg yolks into it. Using your fingertips, work the flour into the egg yolks to make a firm pasta dough. This should take about 7 minutes.

Following the manufacturer's directions, knead the dough through a pasta machine to make cappellini or angel hair pasta. Set the pasta aside.

Place 1 tablespoon of the butter in a medium saucepan over medium heat. When melted, add the mushrooms, carrot, onion, and parsley and sauté for about 4 minutes, or just until the vegetables have softened.

Stir in the shrimp shells and then the wine. Raise the heat and bring to a boil. Immediately lower the heat to a simmer. Season with salt and pepper to taste and simmer for 15 minutes.

Remove the mixture from the heat and strain through a fine sieve into a clean saucepan, discarding the solids.

Place the liquid over high heat and bring to a boil. Immediately lower the heat to a simmer and simmer for about 15 minutes, or until reduced by half.

Add the cream; again raise the heat and bring to a boil. Lower the heat and cook at a gentle simmer for about 5 minutes, or until the mixture is thick enough to coat the back of a metal spoon.

Remove the sauce from the heat and pass through a fine sieve to the top half of a double boiler. Taste and, if necessary, adjust the seasoning with salt and pepper. Place the top half over the bottom half (filled with hot water) and keep warm, uncovered.

Preheat and oil the grill (or broiler). Melt the remaining butter.

Add the olive oil to a large pot of salted water and bring to a boil over high heat.

Using a pastry brush, lightly coat the shrimp with the melted butter and season with salt and pepper to taste. Place on the preheated grill and grill for about 3 minutes, turning after 90 seconds.

While the shrimp is cooking, place the pasta in the boiling water and cook for about 3 minutes, or until al dente. Drain well and place in a large warm bowl. Immediately pour the warm sauce over the top and toss to coat.

Place equal portions of the sauced pasta into each of six shallow pasta bowls. Place three shrimp on top of each serving, place two teaspoons of caviar in the center, and sprinkle chives over all. Serve immediately.

Serves 6

BRAISED LAMB SHANKS WITH
WHITE BEAN PURÉE
1990

TOM VALENTI, *Chef/Owner, Ouest, 'Cesca, Cookbook Author*

Tom Valenti took lamb shanks from Mama's kitchen to the three-star menu. Chefs and foodies from all over made the trek to Alison on Dominick, Chef Valenti's home stove in the early nineties, to savor Tom's take on this home-style favorite. During this period, lamb shanks appeared on menus throughout the country, eventually becoming a staple on the dining scene.

For home cooks, this is a perfect recipe for entertaining, as it can be made a couple of days in advance and reheated just before serving—and it tastes even better, as the flavors have had a chance to blend during the resting period. Even if you are not serving ten people, it is a good idea to make the entire recipe as it freezes well.

10 lamb shanks

Coarse salt and freshly ground pepper to taste

½ cup olive oil

8 stalks celery, trimmed, well washed, dried, and cut crosswise into ½-inch-thick slices

5 cloves garlic, peeled and crushed

2 medium carrots, peeled, trimmed, and cut crosswise into ½-inch-thick slices

1 large onion, peeled and diced

3 cups red wine

Two 32-ounce cans Italian plum tomatoes, strained and crushed

2 cups veal stock

20 black or green peppercorns

6 anchovy filets

2 bay leaves

White Bean Purée (recipe follows)

Preheat the oven to 325°F.

Season the shanks with salt and pepper to taste. Set aside.

Heat the olive oil in a large sauté pan over medium heat. When hot, add the seasoned shanks and sear for about 10 minutes, turning frequently until all sides are nicely browned. This will have to be done in batches. When browned, transfer to a very large, heavy-bottomed casserole or roasting pan. (If you don't have a very large pan, divide the meat in half and use two pans.)

Keeping the sauté pan over medium heat, add the celery, garlic, carrots, and onion and sauté for about 1 minute, or until the vegetables are just heated through, taking care that the bits on the bottom of the pan do not burn.

Add about half of the wine to the casserole or roasting pan and bring to a boil, using a wooden spoon to scrape up the bits from the bottom of the pan. Immediately add the vegetables and the deglazing liquid to the lamb shanks. Add the remaining wine along with the tomatoes and veal stock. Stir to combine. The liquid should almost cover the shanks. If it doesn't, add enough water to do so. Stir in the peppercorns, anchovies, and bay leaves.

Place the casserole over medium heat and bring to a simmer. Cover and transfer to the preheated oven. Braise for 2½ hours.

Remove from the oven and, using tongs, carefully remove the shanks from the braising liquid, taking care that the meat does not fall off of the bone. Place the shanks on a serving platter and tent lightly with aluminum foil to keep warm.

Pass the braising liquid through a fine sieve into a clean saucepan. Taste and, if necessary, adjust the seasoning with salt and pepper. Place over medium-high heat and cook until reduced to a saucelike consistency. This should take 15 minutes at most.

Pour the sauce over the shanks and serve with White Bean Purée.

Serves 10

WHITE BEAN PURÉE

2 pounds dried Great Northern beans, well rinsed

6 cups unsalted, nonfat canned chicken broth

1 cup dry white wine

4 sprigs fresh thyme

3 cloves garlic, peeled and crushed, plus 1 clove, peeled and minced

2 bay leaves

Coarse salt and freshly ground pepper to taste

1 cup olive oil

Place the beans in cold water to cover by 2 inches. Soak for at least 8 hours, changing the water three or four times. Drain well and transfer to a large saucepan.

Add the chicken broth and wine to the beans. Then add the thyme, 3 cloves of crushed garlic, and bay leaves.

Place the saucepan over high heat and bring to a boil. Season with salt and pepper, lower the heat, and simmer for about 90 minutes, or until the beans are very tender, adding additional chicken broth or water if necessary to keep the beans very wet. Be sure to watch the beans and keep them moist during the long cooking process.

When the beans are very tender, remove them from the heat. Place them, in batches, in the bowl of a food processor fitted with the metal blade and purée, slowly adding the olive oil and the minced garlic to taste. If the purée is too thick, beat in a tablespoon or two of softened butter. Taste and, if necessary, adjust the seasoning with salt and pepper.

DUCK BREASTS WITH GREEN PUMPKIN SEED MOLE
1988
RICK BAYLESS, *Chef/Owner, Frontera Grill, Topolobampo, Cookbook Author*

Rick Bayless was ahead of the pack in his enthusiastic endorsement of Mexican cooking as a world-class cuisine. He examined the vibrant flavors and rich sauces of this ancient cuisine in a learned way that made other chefs take notice. In the years to follow, his exploration of the exuberant spices and herbs as well as the various mole sauces of the country had an increasing impact on a range of restaurant menus—from four-star to fast food—across the country.

Rick Bayless truly took Mexican food from the taco stand to the three-star menu. Erudite and passionate about his chosen field of expertise, Rick is the ultimate teacher. His classes always sell out, as he brings such a fresh view to this marvelously complex, ancient cuisine. His wife, Deann, and now his daughter, Lanie, make their restaurants, Frontera Grill and Topolobampo, and their cookbooks a family enterprise. It is hard to believe that Deann was pregnant with Lanie at their first De Gustibus class—Lanie is now a teenager!

---

1 large chayote, peeled and cut into ½-inch dice (see Note)

2 tablespoons olive oil

2 medium zucchini, well washed, trimmed, and cut into ½-inch dice

Coarse salt and freshly ground pepper to taste

Green Pumpkin Seed Mole (recipe follows)

3 tablespoons vegetable oil

4 whole boneless, skinless duck breasts

8 sprigs fresh cilantro, well washed and dried

4 radish roses (optional)

Preheat the oven to 400°F.

Place the chayote on a baking sheet. Add the olive oil and toss to coat. Place in the preheated oven and roast for 6 minutes, or until the squash has just begun to soften.

Remove from the oven and add the zucchini, along with salt and pepper to taste, and toss to combine. Return to the hot oven and continue to roast for an additional 8 minutes, or until the vegetables are tender and nicely colored.

Remove from the oven, tent lightly with aluminum foil, and set aside to keep warm. Lower the oven temperature to 250°F.

Place the mole sauce in a medium saucepan over low heat and cook, stirring frequently, until hot. Set aside and keep warm.

Heat the vegetable oil in a large, nonstick sauté pan over medium-high heat. Season the duck breasts with salt and pepper to taste. When the oil is very hot but not smoking, add the seasoned duck breasts in a single layer and cook, turning occasionally, for about 8 minutes, or until nicely browned and medium-rare, about 160°F on a meat thermometer.

If the vegetables are not still warm, return them to the low oven to reheat.

Using a chef's knife, cut each duck breast on the diagonal into thin slices.

Place one duck breast, in slightly overlapping slices, in the center of each of four dinner plates. Spoon a liberal amount of the hot mole sauce over the duck, sprinkle an equal portion of roasted vegetables on each plate, and garnish with two cilantro sprigs and, if desired, a radish rose. Serve immediately.

Serves 4

GREEN PUMPKIN SEED MOLE

¼ pound shelled pumpkin seeds (pepitas)

3 cups poultry broth, plus more as needed (see Note)

6 black peppercorns

2 whole cloves

One ¾-inch piece cinnamon stick

½ teaspoon cumin seeds

¾ pound tomatillos, husked, well washed, and dried (see Note)

3 hot green chilies (serrano or jalapeño), stemmed and seeded

5 large romaine lettuce leaves, well washed and dried

3 cloves garlic, peeled and chopped

3 large sprigs fresh cilantro, well washed and dried

½ medium onion, peeled and chopped

1½ tablespoons lard or vegetable oil

Coarse salt to taste

Heat a medium skillet over medium-low heat. Add the pumpkin seeds in a single layer. When the first seed pops, begin stirring with a wooden spoon and continue stirring for about 5 minutes, or until all of the seeds have popped and are toasted.

Transfer the toasted pumpkin seeds to a spice grinder (or a blender fitted with the mini-container and blade) and pulverize.

Transfer the seeds to a small bowl and stir in 1 cup of the broth. Set aside.

Place the peppercorns, cloves, cinnamon stick, and cumin seeds in a mortar (or a spice grinder) and, using a pestle, work until the spices are pulverized. Set aside.

Combine the tomatillos and green chilies in a small saucepan with salted water to cover. Place over medium heat and bring to a simmer. Simmer for 10 minutes, or until very tender.

Remove from the heat and drain well. Transfer to a blender or food processor fitted with the metal blade. Add the lettuce leaves, garlic, cilantro, and onion, along with the reserved pulverized spices. Process until smooth.

Heat the lard in a large saucepan over medium heat. When very hot but not smoking, stir in the reserved pumpkin seed–broth mixture and cook, stirring constantly with a wooden spoon, for about 5 minutes, or until the mixture thickens and turns quite dark in color. Add the reserved vegetable purée and continue cooking and stirring for about 4 additional minutes, or until very thick.

Stir in the remaining 2 cups of poultry broth, season with salt to taste, and bring to a simmer. Lower the heat and loosely cover. Cook for about 30 minutes, or until the flavors have blended and the sauce is very thick.

Remove from the heat and, if desired, return the sauce to a blender to process to a very smooth purée, adding additional poultry stock if necessary to thin to desired consistency. Taste and, if necessary, adjust the seasoning with salt.

If not using immediately, transfer to a nonreactive container, cover, and refrigerate until ready to use. Reheat before using.

Note: Chayote (also known as mirliton and cho-cho) is a bland, pear-shaped fruit used both raw and cooked. It is crisp and watery with a cucumber-zucchini flavor. Tomatillos are green, husk-covered, golf-ball-sized fruits used extensively in Mexican cooking. They are rather tart and are generally cooked before using in sauces and salads. They are both available at Latin American markets and some specialty food stores.

Rick Bayless uses a strong poultry broth made with either turkey or chicken. A good, strong chicken broth can be substituted.

SPICED SHRIMP WITH CARROT JUICE
1988

JEAN-GEORGES VONGERICHTEN, *Chef/Owner, Jean Georges, Vong, Mercer Kitchen,*
Spice Market, JoJo, 66, Lipstick Café, Prime Steakhouse, V Steakhouse, Cookbook Author

In 1986, Jean-Georges hit the New York restaurant scene flying. His use of Asian ingredients and exotic seasonings, combined with his classic French training, produced spectacular meals. When he introduced vegetable juices as sauces, every chef in the country made a beeline for Jean-Georges's first showcase, Restaurant Lafayette, to sample his wares and take some of his experimentation back to their own kitchens. The use of vegetable juice as the base for a light and flavorful sauce was soon found throughout the country.

For his first visit to De Gustibus, Jean-Georges brought almost his whole restaurant team, including a couple of his brothers. Although they all had chef's jackets, they thought that since they were in Macy's and in front of an audience, it would be nice to wear a tie. So, attired in their chef's coats, the entire group made their way down to the men's department, where they all bought the same very, very narrow tie. They all felt quite dressed up and, to quote them, "classy."

We all know that Jean-Georges went on to build a restaurant empire across the globe from which he still causes a stir with culinary exploration. This classic Jean-Georges recipe exemplifies his cooking—simple and sublime!

---

6 large carrots, peeled and trimmed

Juice of 1 lemon, or to taste

Pinch ground cinnamon

Pinch ground cloves

Pinch ground nutmeg

Pinch cayenne plus more to taste

½ cup (1 stick) unsalted butter, at room temperature

Coarse salt to taste

32 medium shrimp, peeled and deveined, with tails intact

Fresh chervil

Chop four of the carrots and place them in a juice extractor. Process to make approximately 2 cups of juice. Set aside.

Bring a small saucepan of salted water to a boil over high heat. Add the remaining 2 carrots and blanch for 4 minutes. Immediately drain well and refresh in an ice-water bath to stop the cooking. Using a tiny melon baller, cut the carrots into tiny balls. Pat dry and set aside.

Combine the reserved carrot juice with the lemon juice and a pinch each of cinnamon, cloves, nutmeg, and cayenne. Place over medium heat and whisk in half of the butter. Add the carrot balls and bring to a boil. Season with salt to taste, remove from the heat, and keep warm.

Heat the remaining butter in a large sauté pan. When melted, add the shrimp along with salt and cayenne to taste. Sauté for about 4 minutes, or until bright pink and just cooked through.

Spoon an equal portion of the shrimp into each of six shallow soup bowls. Ladle equal portions of the sauce and carrots over each bowl, sprinkle with some chervil, and serve immediately.

Serves 4

BRAISED SEA BASS IN TOMATO-CORIANDER SAUCE
WITH FRIED CELERY LEAVES AND FAVA BEANS
1987

DAVID BOULEY, *Chef/Owner, Bouley, Danube, Cookbook Author*

David Bouley made quite a splash in the New York restaurant scene when he departed the stove at the much-acclaimed Montrachet to open his own restaurant. He quickly garnered four stars and went on to have great influence on young cooks for years to come. David's insistence on highlighting the pure flavor of food, and his demand for the highest-quality ingredients and for preparing food his way, have changed the face of fine dining in New York. He was one of the first chefs to encourage diners to allow the chef to prepare dishes according to his wishes and to the market-fresh foods available rather than off of a set menu.

David is, to me, a chef who never fails to dazzle. His use of "tomato water" quickly made its way to the to-do lists of many chefs as well as home cooks. I like to say that David emits such an aura, the audience actually believes that he walks on tomato water!

5 ribs celery, bottoms trimmed, well washed and dried

6 tablespoons olive oil

Coarse salt and freshly ground pepper to taste

¼ cup plus 2 tablespoons Nouilly Prat dry vermouth or vin de paille

¼ cup coriander seeds

1 teaspoon tomato paste

6 very ripe medium tomatoes, peeled, cored, seeded, and finely chopped

4 shallots, peeled and finely chopped, skins reserved

1 red bell pepper, roasted, peeled, cored, seeded, membrane removed, and finely chopped

24 fava bean pods

Six 6- to 8-ounce skin-on black sea bass filets, all scales removed

2 tablespoons celery seeds

2 teaspoons honey

Juice of 1 lemon

1 teaspoon white wine vinegar

3 tablespoons unsalted butter, at room temperature

2 teaspoons chopped fresh cilantro leaves

Pull the celery leaves from the ribs and reserve them.

Chop the celery ribs and place them in a medium saucepan. Add 2 quarts of cold water and place over high heat. Bring to a simmer, lower the heat, and simmer for about 30 minutes, or until the liquid has reduced by a quarter and is infused with celery flavor. Remove from the heat and strain through a fine sieve, discarding the celery. Set aside and keep warm.

Place the olive oil in a small saucepan over medium heat. When the oil reaches 325°F on a candy thermometer, add the celery leaves and fry for 45 seconds, or until just crisped. Using a slotted spoon, lift the fried celery leaves from the oil and place on a double layer of paper towels to drain. Reserve the cooking oil.

Season the leaves with salt and pepper to taste and set them aside.

Place the vermouth in a small, nonreactive saucepan. Add the coriander seeds and tomato paste and place over medium-high heat. Bring to a simmer and simmer, stirring occasionally, for about 5 minutes, or until the liquid has reduced by half.

Add the chopped tomatoes, shallots, and bell pepper along with ¼ cup of the reserved celery stock. Bring to a simmer, lower the heat, and cook at a bare simmer for 10 minutes.

Remove from the heat and transfer to a blender or food processor fitted with the metal blade. Process for 1 minute.

Pass the mixture through a fine sieve, pressing on the solids with a rubber spatula, into the top half of a double boiler placed over simmering water. Season with salt and pepper to taste. Keep warm.

Preheat the oven to 400°F.

Bring a small saucepan of salted water to a boil over high heat.

Remove the fava beans from their pods and drop them into the boiling water. Blanch for 2 minutes.

Remove the beans from the boiling water and immediately place in an ice-water bath. Working with one bean at a time, pop the beans from their outer skins. Set aside.

Place the fish in a shallow baking pan with a cover. Add the remaining reserved celery stock, celery-leaf frying oil, and shallot skins along with the celery seeds. Season with salt to taste. Cover, place in the preheated oven, and simmer for 8 minutes, or until the fish is opaque.

While the fish is cooking, heat the honey in a small saucepan over medium heat. When bubbling, add the lemon juice and vinegar along with the reserved fava beans. Stir to combine, then add 1 tablespoon of the butter. Cook for about 5 minutes, or until the beans are nicely glazed.

Whisk the remaining 2 tablespoons of butter into the reserved sauce in the double boiler. Taste and, if necessary, adjust the seasoning with salt and pepper. Stir the cilantro into the fava beans.

Ladle equal portions of the hot sauce into the center of each of six warm dinner plates. Using a slotted spatula and working with one piece of fish at a time, place a fish filet in the center of the sauce on each plate. Spoon equal portions of the glazed beans around the fish and garnish each plate with fried celery leaves. Serve immediately.

Serves 6

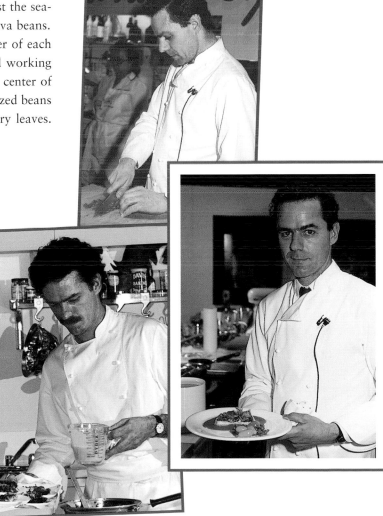

TURBOT WITH SPRING VEGETABLES
1987

ALAIN DUCASSE, *Chef/Owner, to date: 27 Restaurants, 4 Country Inns,*
Bakery, 2 Cooking Schools, Publishing House; Cookbook Author

Alain Ducasse has, I would guess, influenced more chefs throughout the world than any other chef practicing today. At the time of this class, he was the executive chef of one restaurant; today he is involved with at least twenty-three restaurants, is the author of several cookbooks, and has a hand in many other entrepreneurial businesses. Although his cuisine is quite simple and truly product driven, his innovative approach seems to capture the pulse of the dining public. To replicate his cooking one has to have the absolutely pristine ingredients that Alain demands.

The appearance of Alain Ducasse was one of the more serendipitous moments for De Gustibus. One of our out-of-town customers told me that there was an extraordinary chef working in Juans Les Pins in the south of France who, they hoped, would be moving to their hometown of Pittsburgh, Pennsylvania. The chef was going to be visiting Pittsburgh and, at the student's urging, I made contact with the chef and invited him to teach.

The chef, I was told, did not speak English but would come with his maitre d', who did. They came and taught to much applause, and the next thing I heard was that Chef Ducasse had been summoned to Monte Carlo by Prince Rainier. I'm sure that you know the rest of the story: Alain Ducasse went on to receive three Michelin stars in Monte Carlo as he began his ascent to the heights of the culinary world. He eventually became the only chef to gather nine stars from the guide. We have been lucky enough to have him come back from time to time and never cease to be awed by his genius.

Six 9-ounce pieces skinless, boneless turbot (or halibut)

6 baby artichokes, outer leaves removed, 1 inch cut from the top, well washed and dried

12 violet asparagus tips (see Note)

9 tablespoons (1 stick plus 1 tablespoon) unsalted butter

¾ cup extra-virgin olive oil, plus more to taste

Sea salt to taste

> "It was Arlene's good taste that helped me discover the **brilliant name,** De Gustibus, and inspired me to call one of my companies by this name."
> —Alain Ducasse

You will need six small (6 to 7 inches in diameter) ceramic baking dishes with lids to prepare this recipe.

Preheat the oven to 450°F.

Place one piece of turbot in each of six ceramic baking dishes. Place a trimmed artichoke into each dish, along with two asparagus tips. Place 1½ tablespoons of butter on top of each piece of fish, then add 5 tablespoons of water and 2 tablespoons of olive oil to each dish. Sprinkle with a few grains of sea salt and cover.

Place the dishes in the preheated oven and bake for 10 minutes.

Remove the dishes from the oven, uncover, and add 1 tablespoon of peas to each one. Cover and return to the oven for 5 minutes.

Remove the dishes from the oven, uncover, and add 5 slices of the zucchini skin and some cèpes to each one. Cover and return to the oven for 5 minutes.

Remove the dishes from the oven, uncover, and add 1 tablespoon of the diced tomatoes, olives, zucchini blossoms, and lima beans to each dish, along with equal portions of the basil julienne. Cover and return to the oven for 3 minutes.

6 tablespoons fresh English peas

Thirty 1-inch-long by ½-inch-wide slices zucchini skin

10 ounces fresh cèpes, stems removed, wiped clean and thinly sliced

6 tablespoons diced ripe tomatoes

6 tablespoons pitted niçoise olives

6 tablespoons thinly sliced zucchini blossoms

6 tablespoons fresh baby lima beans

12 fresh basil leaves, julienned

Freshly ground pepper to taste

Remove the dishes from the oven. Uncover and carefully remove the black skin from the turbot. There should be about 3 tablespoons of *jus* in each dish.

Taste and, if necessary, adjust the seasoning with sea salt and pepper. Drizzle a bit of extra-virgin olive oil over all and serve immediately.

Note: Violet asparagus, also known as viola, is generally available only in the spring at farmers' markets or fine produce stores. Small, tender, green stalks may be substituted.

Serves 6

PAUPIETTES DE SEA BASS
CROUSTILLANTE AU VIN DE BAROLO
(CRISP PAUPIETTES OF SEA BASS IN BAROLO WINE SAUCE)
1988

DANIEL BOULUD, *Chef/Owner, Restaurant Daniel, Café Boulud,*
db Bistro Moderne, Feast & Fêtes Catering, Cookbook Author

I first met Daniel Boulud when he was sous-chef at the Polo restaurant in New York City's Westbury Hotel. He was so self-assured and talented that I invited him to teach a class. This was the first time I had invited a sous-chef to teach a class on his own and something I never did again. A pretty good choice, eh? After Daniel accepted my invitation, he moved on to become the executive chef at the Plaza Athenée as his career began its rise.

Throughout the restaurant industry, Daniel is known as the consummate chef-restaurateur. Although he stays true to his French country roots, he has been able to incorporate the American love of entrepreneurship into expanding his enterprises. Almost any American chef you ask will say that Daniel is the "master."

This is another recipe that reverberated around the culinary world. Coating a piece of white fish with thinly sliced potatoes and then saucing it with red wine—*ooh, la la—quel horreur!* But it worked and worked beautifully. Within minutes, it seemed, every chef had done a take on Daniel's innovation. This is just a tiny measure of Daniel Boulud's influence on American dining.

---

2 large Idaho potatoes, peeled and wiped dry

¼ cup clarified butter (see Note page 94)

Coarse salt to taste

Six 6-ounce skinless, boneless sea bass filets

1 bottle Barolo

3 shallots, peeled and chopped

1 sprig fresh thyme

3 tablespoons heavy cream

Freshly ground pepper to taste

14 tablespoons (1¾ sticks) unsalted butter, at room temperature

2 leeks, white part only, well washed and thinly sliced crosswise

Pinch sugar

12 chive points (see Note)

Note: Chive points are simply the 2- to 3-inch top ends of fresh chives that are used as a garnish.

Using a mandoline, cut the potatoes lengthwise into paper-thin slices. Place the slices in a bowl, add 1½ tablespoons of the clarified butter, season with a hint of salt, and toss to coat.

Using your hands, force each piece of fish into a compact shape.

Cut six pieces of parchment paper large enough to enfold the fish. Place seasoned potato slices, slightly overlapping, in the exact shape of the fish in the center of each piece of parchment paper. Place a piece of fish on top of the potatoes and wrap the potatoes up and over to cover the fish completely. Wrap the parchment paper tightly closed to seal the packet. Refrigerate until ready to cook.

To make the sauce, combine the Barolo, shallots, and thyme in a medium, nonreactive saucepan over medium-low heat. Bring to a boil, lower the heat, and simmer for about 90 minutes, or until the wine has reduced to about 3 tablespoons. Do not allow the wine to boil quickly or it will become bitter. Begin slowly whisking in the cream, and when incorporated, season with salt and pepper. Set aside.

Heat 2 tablespoons of the butter in a sauté pan over low heat. Add the leeks and sauté for about 10 minutes, or until very soft. Season with salt and pepper to taste. Set aside and keep warm.

Return the sauce to low heat and begin whisking in the remaining 12 tablespoons of butter. Add a pinch of sugar, taste,

and, if necessary, adjust the seasoning with salt and pepper. Strain through a fine sieve into the top half of a double boiler set over simmering water to keep warm. Do not cover.

Heat the remaining clarified butter in a large, nonstick skillet over high heat. Unwrap the fish packets and discard the paper. Place the *paupiettes* into the hot butter and sear for about 4 minutes per side, or until the potatoes are crisp and golden brown and the fish is cooked through. If the fish is very thick, place it in a preheated 400°F oven and bake for about 5 minutes to complete the cooking.

Place equal portions of the sautéed leeks in the center of each of six dinner plates. Place a *paupiette* on top of the leeks on each plate and spoon equal portions of the sauce around each *paupiette*. Garnish each with two chive points and serve.

Serves 6

de gustibus at Macy*s
presents...
daniel boulud

SAUTÉED SHAD
WITH CHIFFONADE OF COLLARD GREENS AND CURRY SAUCE
1990
JEAN-LOUIS PALLADIN, *Chef, Cookbook Author*

Jean-Louis Palladin came to the De Gustibus classroom as a replacement for André Daguin, a famous French chef from Gascony. Jean-Louis, also from Gascony, was the chef at the Watergate Hotel, which had become infamous during the Nixon administration.

Jean-Louis was quite an extravagant character: expansive, generous, fun-loving, and absolutely brilliant in the kitchen. His untimely death deeply affected the entire food community.

His embrace of the world of food is seen in this recipe, where he combines traditional American ingredients in a very French way and accents them with a touch of Asian flavor.

⅓ cup ⅛-inch-dice Granny Smith apple

½ cup (1 stick) plus 2 tablespoons unsalted butter

1 tablespoon mild green curry paste (see Sidebar)

8 large collard leaves, well washed and dried, cut into ⅛-inch julienne (about 3 cups)

2 tablespoons fish stock (or clam broth, chicken stock, or water)

Coarse salt and freshly ground pepper to taste

2 tablespoons olive oil

Four 8-ounce boneless shad filets

There are various red and green **curry pastes** available in Asian markets, ranging from **mild** to extremely **hot**. They are usually sold as Thai or Vietnamese curry paste. If you can't locate a brand that is labeled "mild," use a smaller amount of a hot one.

Place 1 cup of water in a small saucepan over high heat. Bring to a boil and add the diced apple. Lower the heat and simmer for 3 minutes. Immediately remove from the heat and drain well.

When cool, combine the apple, ½ cup of the butter, and the curry paste in the bowl of a food processor fitted with the metal blade. Process to a smooth purée. Scrape the mixture from the bowl into a nonreactive container, cover, and refrigerate for at least 1 hour or up to 12 hours.

Bring a large pot of salted water to a boil over high heat. Add the collard leaves and cook for 3 minutes. Drain well and immediately plunge the leaves into an ice-water bath to stop the cooking.

When cool, using your hands, lift the leaves, in batches, from the bath and squeeze out all excess water. Set aside on a double layer of paper towels to continue draining.

Remove the apple-curry butter from the refrigerator and combine it with the stock in a small saucepan over medium heat. Bring to a simmer, whisking constantly. When hot, remove from the heat and strain through a fine sieve into a clean saucepan. Set aside.

Heat the remaining 2 tablespoons of butter in a large sauté pan over low heat. Add the drained collards, season with salt and pepper to taste, and cook, tossing constantly, for about 7 minutes, or until hot. Remove from the heat and keep warm.

Heat the olive oil in a large sauté pan over high heat. Season the shad with salt and pepper to taste and carefully place them in the hot oil. Fry, turning once, for about 6 minutes, or until crisp and golden.

Place equal portions of the collard greens in the center of each of four dinner plates. Place a shad filet on top of the greens and spoon an equal portion of the curry sauce over each serving. Serve immediately.

Serves 4

WARM TUNA AND WASABI SANDWICH
WITH TUNA SALAD AND LOTUS CHIPS
1989

DAVID BURKE, *Chef/Owner, davidburke & donatella, Cookbook Author*

David Burke is known as one of the most creative, innovative chefs working in America. His imagination is astounding and he always excites his students. David introduced the pork shank, pastrami salmon, and savory lollipops, each of which had an enormous impact on menus all over the world. David always says that his greatest influence came from fast food, which he loves to combine with the classic training that he received at The Culinary Institute of America.

David is absolutely fearless in experimenting with new foods and new techniques as well as in taking risks with old favorites. He is also a master of presentation, using old Matchbox trucks as containers, canning jars filled to the brim with vegetables or sauces, and extraordinary and unexpected artifacts to highlight his food. This sandwich is a classic example of David's taking an old standard and putting a whole new spin on it.

3 lotus roots, peeled and rinsed (see Note)

Approximately 4 quarts peanut oil (for frying)

Coarse salt

1 large egg yolk

¼ cup whole-grain mustard

1 tablespoon rice wine vinegar (see Note)

Wasabi powder to taste (see Note)

¾ cup ginger oil (see Note)

Freshly ground pepper to taste

1 small loaf homemade-style white bread

2 pounds yellowfin tuna, trimmed

2 shallots, peeled and minced

Zest of 1 lemon

1 bunch chervil, leaves only, well washed and dried

1/4 cup soy sauce or to taste

1 cup sesame seeds

Approximately ¼ cup clarified butter (see Note)

Using a chef's knife, cut the lotus root crosswise into very thin slices (thin enough to resemble potato chips).

In a deep-fat fryer with a basket, heat the peanut oil over high heat to 365°F on a candy thermometer. Drop the lotus-root slices into the hot oil and fry, turning frequently, for about 2 minutes, or until crisp and golden brown. Transfer to a double layer of paper towels to drain, and continue frying chips until all of the lotus root has been fried. Season with salt to taste and set aside.

Place the egg yolk, mustard, vinegar, and wasabi powder to taste in the bowl of a food processor fitted with the metal blade. Process to combine. With the motor running, slowly add ⅔ cup of the ginger oil, processing until a thick mayonnaise has formed. Season with salt and pepper to taste. Scrape the mayonnaise from the bowl into a clean nonreactive container. Cover and refrigerate until ready to use.

Using a serrated knife, cut the crust from all sides of the bread; then, cut the bread lengthwise into six ½-inch-thick slices, reserving the remaining bread for another use (such as fresh bread crumbs). Using a rolling pin, carefully roll each slice of bread out as thin as possible. Cut each piece in half crosswise. Set aside.

Using a serrated knife, cut six ½-inch-thick slices of tuna just large enough to fit on the bread. Place on a plate, cover with plastic film, and refrigerate until ready to use.

Cut the remaining tuna into small cubes. Place the tuna cubes in a mixing bowl and add the shallots, lemon zest, chervil, and soy sauce, along with the remaining ginger oil and salt and pepper to taste. Toss to combine, cover with plastic film, and refrigerate until ready to serve.

Spread wasabi mayonnaise to taste on each slice of bread. Remove the sliced tuna from the refrigerator and place one slice on each of six slices of the flattened bread. Top each one with a remaining piece of seasoned bread, mayonnaise side down.

Place the sesame seeds on a plate. Set aside.

Using a pastry brush, lightly coat each side of the sandwich with clarified butter. Lightly dredge each side of the sandwich in the sesame seeds.

Place a large nonstick pan over medium-high heat. When very hot but not smoking, add the sandwiches and fry, turning once, for about 5 minutes, or until both sides are golden brown.

Remove the sandwiches from the pan and cut each one into four triangles. Place one sandwich on each of six plates, mound some tuna salad on each plate, and garnish with lotus chips.

Note: Lotus root, rice wine vinegar, wasabi powder, and ginger oil are available at Asian markets and some specialty food stores.

Clarified butter is butter that has been slowly heated to separate out the water and milk solids. Since it keeps well, it is best to work with 1 pound of butter at a time. Place the butter in a medium saucepan over low heat for about 30 minutes, skimming off the white froth as it forms on the surface. Raise the heat slightly and continue skimming until the remaining liquid is clear. Do not boil or simmer. Carefully pour off the clear liquid and discard the residue at the bottom at the pan. The clear liquid is clarified butter, which has a high smoke point and clean taste and can be used to impart a butter flavor when cooking at high temperatures.

Serves 6

OLIVE BREAD

1987

CAROL FIELD, *Cookbook Author*

Carol Field's book *The Italian Baker* introduced many home cooks to the pleasures of bread baking. I remember how flexible she was in adapting her recipes to our mixer, which was smaller than she was used to, and our ovens. She was so involved with her dough that she made the greatest, most authentic, loaves of bread we had ever experienced.

¾ cup warm (115–120°F) water

3½ teaspoons active dry yeast or 1⅓ small fresh yeast cakes (24 grams)

¼ cup olive oil, plus more to coat the bowl

12 ounces Sicilian-style green olives (or 6 ounces tiny black Ligurian olives or 6 ounces small green olives), pitted, plus a few extra for garnish

3¾ cups unbleached all-purpose flour, plus ⅓ cup for kneading

1½ teaspoons coarse salt

About ⅓ cup cornmeal

This bread is difficult—if not impossible—to make by hand because the olives must be broken down enough to provide some of the liquid for the dough. The **mixer** and the **food processor** do the job nicely.

Place the warm water in the large bowl of a heavy-duty electric mixer fitted with the paddle. Stir in the yeast and let stand for 10 minutes, or until creamy.

Add the ¼ cup of olive oil and stir to mix. Add the olives, 3¾ cups of flour, and salt and mix on low speed for 2 minutes.

Remove the paddle and replace it with the dough hook. Beat on low speed for about 3 minutes, or until the olives have broken down and exuded their liquid into the dough. If necessary, add about 1½ tablespoons of warm water.

Sprinkle a clean work surface with a dusting of the remaining flour. Scrape the dough onto the surface and knead for about 2 minutes by hand, or until the dough is quite firm. It should feel soft but never smooth.

Lightly coat a mixing bowl with olive oil. Scrape up the dough and place it in the oiled bowl. Cover with plastic film and set aside to rise in a warm, draft-free spot for 1 hour, or until doubled in bulk. Flatten dough into two equal pieces, then fold each piece into thirds.

Lightly flour a clean work surface. Working with one piece at a time and using your hands, roll the dough toward you, using your thumbs to guide the dough and create tension in the rolling process. Using both hands, roll the dough into a cigar shape that is plump in the middle and tapered at both ends.

Lightly coat two baking sheets or peels with olive oil; sprinkle them lightly with cornmeal.

Place one loaf on each prepared sheet. Using a sharp knife, score the top of each loaf in a crisscross pattern. Nestle a few of the reserved olives in the top of each loaf. Cover with a clean kitchen towel and set aside to rise in a warm, draft-free spot, for 1 hour.

Preheat the oven to 400°F.

If you are using a baking stone, place the stone in the oven 30 minutes before you're ready to bake to allow it to get hot. Sprinkle cornmeal on it just before transferring the loaves to the oven.

Place the loaves in the preheated oven and bake for about 40 minutes, or until golden brown and cooked through.

Remove from the oven and place on wire racks to cool.

Makes 2 oval loaves

WARM BRIOCHE CUSTARD WITH FRESH PEACH SAUCE
1987

BRADLEY OGDEN, *Chef/Owner, Lark Creek Restaurant Group, Cookbook Author*

Bradley Ogden was one of the first hotel chefs in America to be recognized as an innovator. He imbued home-style American recipes with his classic training to create a marvelously expressive cuisine. He always said that his goal was to "keep it simple, use fresh, seasonal ingredients, and make a perfect marriage of it all."

When Bradley Ogden came to De Gustibus, he was so used to cooking in California, with beautiful produce at hand all the time, that he expected to find ripe, local peaches in New York in early June. Needless to say, this was impossible in the Northeast, so he made the recipe with ripe apricots, which we were able to find. You can make this substitution too, if ripe peaches are not at hand.

While many pastry chefs were producing desserts that grew to astounding heights and were filled with spectacular architectural elements, other chefs went back to their mothers' kitchens to recapture the desserts of their childhoods. Bradley, a proponent of great American cooking, did the latter with this recipe but took an old-fashioned bread-and-butter pudding in new directions by using brioche and a fresh peach sauce—a classic example of the combination of the classic and the home-style.

3 large eggs

1½ cups heavy cream

1 cup milk

¼ cup sugar

2 teaspoons pure vanilla extract

⅛ teaspoon ground cinnamon

Pinch freshly ground nutmeg

2 teaspoons unsalted butter, softened

Twelve ½-inch-thick slices brioche (or other egg bread), crusts trimmed

½ cup golden raisins

Fresh Peach Sauce (recipe follows)

About 2 tablespoons confectioners' sugar

Combine the eggs, cream, milk, sugar, vanilla, cinnamon, and nutmeg in a mixing bowl, whisking to blend well.

Using the butter, lightly coat the interior of a 2-quart casserole (with a lid) at least 2½ inches deep.

Place six slices of the bread into the bottom of the prepared dish. Sprinkle half of the raisins over the bread. Add another layer of six slices of bread and top with the remaining raisins.

Pour the egg mixture over the top. Cover and refrigerate for 8 hours.

Preheat the oven to 300°F. Remove the pudding from the refrigerator.

Place the casserole in a larger pan and add enough hot water to the pan to come halfway up the sides. Place in the preheated oven and bake for 30 minutes. Uncover and bake for an additional 20 minutes, or until a sharp knife inserted in the center comes out clean.

Remove from the oven and from the water bath. Place on a wire rack to cool slightly.

When ready to serve, spoon about 3 tablespoons of peach sauce onto each of six dessert plates. Cut the pudding into squares and place one square on top of the sauce in each plate.

Place the confectioners' sugar in a fine sieve and, lightly tapping on the sides of the sieve, dust each portion with sugar. Serve immediately.

Serves 6

FRESH PEACH SAUCE

1 pound ripe peaches, well washed, pitted, and chopped

2 tablespoons fresh lemon juice

1 tablespoon sugar

Combine all of the ingredients in a medium, nonreactive saucepan over medium heat. Bring to a boil, lower the heat, and simmer for 12 minutes.

Transfer the peach mixture to a food processor fitted with the metal blade and process to a smooth purée.

Pass the purée through a fine sieve into a clean container. Place in an ice-water bath to cool. The sauce should coat the back of a spoon. If not, return to medium heat and simmer until thick enough.

When cool, cover and refrigerate until ready to use.

SCONES
1990

SARABETH LEVINE, *Baker/Owner, Sarabeth's, Cookbook Author*

Sarabeth Levine was the first to bring scones to the De Gustibus classroom and to New York City diners, and now, years later, you can buy scones (although not always very good ones) almost anywhere in the country. Sarabeth took a homely little biscuit and turned it into a glamour queen with rich butter and sweet fruit additions. Her little neighborhood bakery has grown to sell wholesale baked goods throughout the United States, with her jams and preserves now also world-famous.

Sarabeth, in her namesake restaurant (which has been reincarnated), brought delicious breakfasts and brunches to the fore. Once she began, other imitative spots opened in New York and then across the country, and many of the large hotels began to feature a "power breakfast" and weekend brunch specials. Her quaint packaging of the restaurant and of her baked and prepared goods also had an enormous impact on the specialty-food business in America.

3 cups unbleached all-purpose flour, plus more for flouring the work surface

1 tablespoon sugar

1 tablespoon baking powder

¼ teaspoon salt

½ cup (1 stick) unsalted butter, chilled and cut into ¼-inch cubes

1 cup dried currants

2 large eggs

1 cup plus 1 tablespoon milk

Preheat the oven to 450°F.

Line a baking sheet with parchment paper. Set aside.

Combine the flour, sugar, baking powder, and salt in the bowl of an electric mixer. Blend on low to just mix. Add the butter and continue mixing on low for about 3 minutes, or just until the butter is incorporated into the flour. (You should see small chips of butter.) Stop the mixer and run your fingers through the mixture to break up any of the larger pieces of butter.

Add the currants and mix to just combine.

Combine 2 of the eggs with 1 cup of the milk in a small bowl. With the mixer running on low, quickly incorporate the egg mixture into the flour mixture, mixing until just blended. The dough should be sticky for tender scones.

Generously flour a clean work surface. Scrape the dough onto the floured surface. Sprinkle the top of the dough with flour and flour the rolling pin.

Roll the dough out into a ½-inch-thick circle, rolling from the center out to the edge.

Using a biscuit cutter, cut the dough into rounds and place the rounds about 1 inch apart on the prepared baking sheet.

Gently press any dough scraps together, taking care not to incorporate too much flour. Roll out and cut more scones, using all of the dough.

Using a pastry brush and the remaining 1 tablespoon of milk, lightly coat the tops of the scones.

Place in the preheated oven and bake for about 15 minutes, or until lightly browned around the edges. Remove from the oven and serve hot with clotted cream or sweet butter and jam.

Makes about 18 scones

CHOCOLATE ALMONDS
1990

JACQUES TORRES, *Pastry Chef/Owner,*
Jacques Torres Chocolate, Cookbook Author

The first time I met Jacques Torres, he was the pastry chef for Daniel Boulud and didn't speak a word of English. His friend and now partner, Kris Kruid, had to translate everything. A master baker and winner of France's most coveted culinary awards, he has, in recent years, left the pastry kitchen to devote his time to his chocolate empire. Jacques is truly Mr. Chocolate with a bit of Willy Wonka thrown in—star of television shows, author of a couple of books, owner of his own chocolate factory, and practically a national treasure. I would say that Jacques has, more than any other pastry chef, defined new paths for pastry in American restaurants today.

While still at Le Cirque, Jacques brought us a taste of things to come with this recipe for Chocolate Almonds. We always know that whatever Jacques does, it eventually comes back to chocolate.

---

2 cups granulated sugar

1 cup water

3½ cups whole unblanched almonds

1¾ cups confectioners' sugar or cocoa powder or equal portions of both

21 ounces bittersweet chocolate, tempered (see Sidebar)

> Tempered chocolate is chocolate melted to 84°F to 88°F. You can easily **temper chocolate** by placing it in a glass bowl in the microwave and heating on medium-high for 30 seconds, taking care not to overheat it. The chocolate will not be fully melted, but the residual heat will accomplish this.

Line a baking sheet with parchment paper. Set aside.

Combine the granulated sugar and water in a heavy-bottomed saucepan over medium-high heat. Bring to a boil and immediately add the almonds, stirring to coat them evenly in the sugar syrup. Continue to cook, stirring constantly, until the sugar caramelizes. You will know this has happened when the sugar is no longer sandy and has turned to a clear liquid that clings to the nuts. Watch carefully, as caramel can burn very quickly.

Using a wooden spoon, spread the nuts out onto the prepared baking sheet. Do not touch with your fingers, as the nuts are extremely hot. Set aside to cool.

When cool, break apart any nut clusters that may have formed.

Place the confectioners' sugar or cocoa powder in a small bowl. If using both, place the two in separate bowls. Set aside.

Place the cooled nuts in a large mixing bowl. Slowly add one-third of the tempered chocolate and immediately fold the nuts into the chocolate until they are thoroughly coated and the chocolate has set. Repeat this process twice to use all of the chocolate. You must work quickly, as the chocolate sets up speedily, and will cause the nuts to stick together.

Drop the chocolate-coated almonds into the confectioners' sugar and/or cocoa powder and toss to coat.

Before serving, place the nuts in a fine sieve and gently shake it to remove any excess sugar or powder.

The nuts will keep, tightly covered, at room temperature for up to 2 weeks.

Makes about 5½ cups

1991 to 1995

The Era of the Celebrity Chef

The celebrity-chef explosion began during this period with the advent of the chef as television star. Emeril Lagasse, a once quiet, unassuming New Orleans denizen, made his signature "Bam!" a household word across the country through his frenetic Food Network show, *How to Boil Water*. Although many food professionals were put off by the chef's foray into celebrity status as well as by his sometimes outrageous on-screen shenanigans, no one could deny that the growth of food-related shows and the expansion of the Food Network brought a whole new group of cooks into the kitchen. Emeril's exuberance and "macho" look, in particular, sent men to the stove. In the years to come, Emeril would be followed by many of the world's finest chefs as an ever-expanded viewing audience demanded new and engaging food personalities.

During this period, "Nuevo Latino," a totally unknown phrase a few years before, became a catchword for a new style of cooking that brought Latin ingredients into mainstream cooking. This would have a major impact on dining all across America, as family-dining establishments and fast-food chains began to introduce once-unimagined spicy flavors and tropical produce into the burger-and-fries consciousness.

We once had a married chef who brought his girlfriend along to his class. When he thought no one was looking, he would take her out into the hall and do some **smooching.** Since it was after store hours, Macy's security team, with its dogs and guns, was patrolling the halls and, of course, discovered the duo. This stopped the action, as the chef thought that his wife had put a contract out on him. It must have set the tone because through the years, we have had, from time to time, a hot **chef romance** going on behind the scenes.

In the restaurant kitchen the pastry chef was also becoming a star. It became imperative to end a starred restaurant meal with not only one spectacular dessert but a tableful. Warm chocolate desserts were of particular note, with "molten," "lava," and other heat-indicative words describing their gooey lusciousness. Plates of handmade candies and chocolate truffles, candied fruit peel, and other specialties of the house pastry chef became the restaurant's final tribute to the diner.

As they were being exposed to all of this extravagance, educated, knowledgeable consumers were also being bombarded with information on low-fat, low-cholesterol "healthy" dining. Fat-free foods took over the commercial marketplace, and chefs tried to maintain their integrity while responding to the dietary demands of their clientele. SOS (sauce on the side) became the cry of the dining public as chefs bemoaned the quest (which would turn out to be momentary) for what was thought to be healthier eating.

Preceding pages (clockwise from top left):
Mollie Katzen; Lynne Rossetto Kasper; Michael Romano; Gordon Hamersley; Vincent Guerithault; Mark Strausman; Emily Luchetti; Eric Ripert; Norman Van Aken; Emeril Lagasse and Ella Brennan; Michael Lomonaco; Marta Pulini.
Right: *Bobby Flay.*

Jody Adams

Marcia Adams

Jeffrey Alford

Colman Andrews

Francesco Antonucci

Nancy Verde Barr

Lidia Bastianich

Mario Batali

Stefano Battistini

Rick Bayless

Jean-Michel Bergougnoux

David Bouley

Philippe Boulot

Daniel Boulud

Antoine Bouterin

Charles Bowman

Wayne Brachman

Flo Braker

Georgeanne Brennan

Jane Brody

Edward Brown

Giuliano Bugialli

David Burke

Hugh Carpenter

Penelope Casas

Dominick Cerrone

Sarah Leah Chase

Judith Choate

Patrick Clark

Thomas Colicchio

Michael Cordua

Andrew D'Amico

Gary Danko

Robert Del Grande

Christian Delouvrier

Marcel Desaulniers

Traci Des Jardins

Yamuni Devi

Eric Di Domenico

Jim Dodge

Roberto Donna

Naomi Duguid

Nathalie Dupree

Toy Kim Dupree

Lisa Ekus

Lou Ekus

Todd English

Florence Fabricant

Susan Feniger

Carol Field

Bobby Flay

Jim Fobel

Susanna Foo

George Germon

Elka Gilmore

Charles Gold

Joyce Goldstein

Joni Greenspan

Vincent Guerithault

Gordon Hamersley

Chris Hollis

Josefina Howard

Eric Hubert

Madhur Jaffrey

Raji Jallepalli

Patricia Jamieson

Lynne Rossetto Kasper

Mollie Katzen

Matthew Kenney

Johanne Killeen

Abigail Kirsch

Evan Kleiman

Craig Kominiak

Deborah Krasner

Aglaia Kremezi

Gray Kunz

Emeril Lagasse

Anna Tasca Lanza

Viana La Place

Daniel Leader

Karen Lee

Dan Lenchner

Sarabeth Levine

Michael Lomonaco

Susan Loomis

Emily Luchetti

Sheila Lukins

Waldy Malouf

Noel Mantel

Lydie Marshall

Zarela Martinez

Alice Medrich

Michael Meehan

Perla Meyers

Mark Militello

Mary Sue Milliken

Rick Moonen

Pamela Morgan

George Morrone

Helen Nash

Joan Nathan

Wayne Nish

Bradley Ogden

Steven Olson

Molly O'Neill

Jean-Louis Palladin

Charles Palmer

Cindy Pawlcyn

François Payard

Caprial Pence

James Peterson

Don Pintabona

Debra Ponzek

Alfred Portale

Wolfgang Puck

Marta Pulini

Stephan Pyles

Michel Richard

Eric Ripert

Gary Robins

Douglas Rodriguez

Michael Romano

David Rosengarten

Betty Rosbottom

Anne Rosenzweig

Michel Roux

Maury Rubin

David Ruggerio

Claudio Scaduto

John Schenk

Amy Scherber

Chris Schlesinger

Patrick Clark
Traci Des Jardins
Vincent Guerithault
Gordon Hamersley

Lynne Rossetto Kasper
Mollie Katzen
Emily Luchetti
Mark Militello

Rick Moonen
Cindy Pawlcyn
Marta Pulini
Eric Ripert

Michael Romano
Norman Van Aken
Geoffrey Zakarian

Jimmy Schmidt

Sally Schneider

Michele Scicolone

Vincent Scotto

Martha Rose Shulman

Nancy Silverton

Nina Simonds

André Soltner

Marlene Sorosky

Roger Souvereyns

Joachim Splichal

Mark Strausman

Allen Susser

Alan Tardi

Jacques Torres

Claude Troisgros

Barbara Tropp

Michele Urvater

Thomas Valenti

Norman Van Aken

Jean-Georges Vongerichten

Brendan Walsh

David Waltuck

Sylvia Weinstock

Patricia Wells

Joshua Wesson

Anne Willan

Faith Heller Willinger

Paula Wolfert

Peri Wolfman

Bill Yosses

Geoffrey Zakarian

Kevin Zraly

Left: *Todd English.*

THE FRENCH CONTINGENT

JEAN PAUL BATTAGLIA
GEORGES BLANC
GERARD BOYER
EDOUARD CARLIER
FRANK CERRUTTI
MICHEL CHABRAN
JACQUES CHIBOIS
ALAIN DUCASSE
DOMINIQUE FRERARD
PIERRE HERMÉ
YVES JACQUOT
JEAN-PAUL LACOMBE
GASTON LENÔTRE
JACQUES MAXIMIM
FLORENCE MIKULA
NOEL MANTEL
PIERRE ORSI
MICHEL ROSTANG
REINE SAMMUT
ROGER VERGÉ
PATRICIA WELLS
CHRISTIAN WILLER

CHEFS WE MISS

James Beard
Simone Beck
Julia Child
Craig Claiborne
Patrick Clark
Pierre Franey
Bert Greene
Andrea Hellrigl
Raji Jallepalli

Florence Lin
Maurice Moore-Betty
Leslee Reis
Leslie Revsin
Felipe Rojas-Lombardi
Richard Sax
Barbara Tropp
Alfredo Viazzi

25 YEARS OF

CHANGES AT DE GUSTIBUS

Kitchen upgraded and remodeled four times • The addition of tables—from simple classroom style, food in lap, to tasting at tables • Nice stemware • Fine china • Bottled water • Sparkling wine, white wine, and red wine for each class • Coat check • Store discounts

TRENDS THAT HAVE COME AND STAYED—OR WENT

Anti-French • Architectural food • Artisanal foods • Bistro cuisine • Bottled water • Bruschetta • California Chardonnay • Crostini • Day-boat seafood • Extra-virgin olive oil with many pedigrees • Family-style service • Fancy china • Foraging • High heat • High-protein diets • Home-style cooking • Large plates with little food • Large portions • Las Vegas restaurants • Line-caught fish • Low-fat • Low-heat • Modern plated design • Nonstick pans • Nouvelle cuisine • Old-fashioned desserts • Organic • Panna cotta • Plancha cooking • Plated food • Raw foods • Regional cuisine • Risotto • Salsas • Signature chocolate • Silicone pans and utensils • Slow food • Small bites • Small plates with lots of food • Southwestern-style cooking • Spa cuisine • Specialty food stores • Specialty salts • Squeeze bottles • Steak houses • Sugar cages • Sushi • Take-out foods • Tapas • Tartares • The cheese course • The wine explosion • The Zagat guides • Villeroy and Boch Basketweave pattern placeware

MOST EXTRAORDINARY STORYTELLER

MADHUR JAFFREY
describing the spice man coming to her family home in India to grind the spices for the evening meal.

MOST DRAMATIC EVENT

GERARD BOYER
sabered (cut the top off) a bottle of Champagne, an ancient tradition from the Champagne region of France, leaving an indelible mark on our mylar mirror.

Superlatives
1980 to 2005

JOE BAUM, *Restaurateur (Windows on the World, Forum of the Twelve Caesars), Innovator-Consultant*

SIRIO MACCIONI, *Owner, Le Cirque*

DANNY MEYER, *Owner, Union Square Cafe, Gramercy Tavern, Blue Smoke, Tabla, Eleven Madison Park*

ANDRÉ SOLTNER, *Chef-Owner, Lutèce*

BARRY WINE, *Chef-Owner, The Quilted Giraffe*

THE MOST INFLUENTIAL RESTAURATEURS

HAPPY YOU BECAME BI-COASTAL

THOMAS KELLER'S
first class for us was when he was the chef at Raoul's in New York's Greenwich Village doing great bistro food. He went on to make his mark, internationally, at the French Laundry in Yountville, California. Then, many years later, he made a triumphant return to New York with his magnificent restaurant Per Se in the Time-Warner building.

ON THE MENU

APPETIZERS, SOUPS, AND SALADS

Seviche of Bay Scallops
Eric Ripert—1995

Shrimp and Cilantro Quesadilla
Bobby Flay—1992

Spanakopita
Mollie Katzen—1992

Chili-Orange Cold Noodles
Barbara Tropp—1993

Chilled Summer Vegetable Soup
with Spanish Vinegar and Quinoa Salad
Mark Militello—1995

*Insalata Tiepidadi Petto di Cappone
All'Aceto Balsamico Tradizionale di Modena*
(Warm Capon Breast Salad with Balsamic Vinaigrette)
Marta Pulini—1995

SAUCES AND SIDES

Ginger-Roasted Winter Vegetables
Michael Lomanoco—1991

Parsnip Purée
Vincent Guerithault—1993

PASTA AND GRAINS

Tagliarini with Tart Anchovy-and-Almond Sauce
Lynne Rossetto Kasper—1992

Polenta with Lamb Sauce
Mark Straussman—1993

MEAT, GAME, AND POULTRY

London Broil "Smoke Gets in Your House" Style
with Lime-Marinated Red Onions and Pineapple
Chris Schlesinger—1994

Marinated Pork Loin Satay with Mango Salsa
Cindy Pawlcyn—1993

Easy Roast Chicken
Gordon Hamersley—1995

FISH AND SHELLFISH

Seared Tuna with White Beans,
Arugula, and Lemon Confit
Tom Colicchio—1993

Rum and Pepper–Painted Fish
with a Mango–Scotch Bonnet Mojo
Norman Van Aken—1993

Salmon with Olive Oil–Mashed Potatoes
and Sauce Niçoise
Traci Des Jardins—1995

BREAD AND DESSERTS

Panna Cotta
Nancy Silverton—1992

Focaccia
Amy Scherber—1993

Fig and Prosciutto Pizza
Todd English—1994

Double Chocolate Biscotti
Emily Luchetti—1993

SEVICHE OF BAY SCALLOPS
1995

ERIC RIPERT, *Chef/Owner, Le Bernardin, Cookbook Author*

Eric Ripert is one of America's very few four-star chefs. Under his mentor, Gilbert Le Coze, their home, the restaurant Le Bernardin, became the preeminent seafood restaurant in New York City. With Gilbert's untimely passing in 1994, Eric Ripert has, year after year, maintained the four-star rating. Under his stewardship, the kitchen at Le Bernardin continues to garner superlatives and remains without equal on the New York restaurant scene.

Eric's wish to serve fish in its purest form has changed the way all chefs now deal with seafood. His use of classic French techniques and his respect for ingredients combined with his willingness to experiment with the cuisines of other cultures results in spectacular dishes, of which this seviche is a prime example. Unfortunately, this is a dish that can only shine when made at the last minute and when absolutely pristine scallops are available.

---

20 bay scallops, alive in their shells (see Note)

¼ cup fresh mint-leaf chiffonade (see Note)

½ cup fresh cilantro-leaf chiffonade (see Note)

1 tablespoon very finely diced tomato

1 tablespoon very finely diced jalapeño chili

Fine-quality sea salt and freshly ground pepper to taste

Extra-virgin olive oil to taste

½ lemon

½ lime

Open the scallop shells, reserving twenty half-shells (or five per person). Wash and rinse the reserved shells and pat them dry. Set aside.

Remove the main white muscle from each scallop. Rinse the scallops and pat dry. Cut the scallops into ⅛-inch dice.

Using two forks (to avoid handling the scallops with your fingers), place equal portions of the diced scallop in each of the twenty reserved half-shells. You should have enough diced scallop meat to cover the interior of each shell.

Sprinkle each shell with about five strands of the mint and then with about fifteen strands of the cilantro. Place a pinch of diced tomato and a pinch of jalapeño over each. Season with sea salt and pepper to taste, drizzle with a bit of extra-virgin olive oil, and squeeze a few drops of lemon and lime juice over each one. Serve immediately.

Note: Live bay scallops in their shells are available from fine fishmongers, some specialty food stores, or from Browne Trading Company (see Sources, page 247).

Chiffonade, a French term for thin shreds of green vegetables, can easily be made by rolling up the leaves, cigar-fashion, and cutting them crosswise into extremely thin rounds, which, when unraveled, become thin strips.

Serves 4

When De Gustibus classes began, we were still warning our students about **"fake" scallops** cut from inexpensive fish and sold as the real thing. Since then we have seen the availability of fresh scallops almost eliminate this problem. Larger sea scallops are found across the country throughout the fall and winter.

SHRIMP AND CILANTRO QUESADILLA
1992
BOBBY FLAY, *Chef/Owner, Mesa Grill, Bolo, Bar Americain, Television Personality, Cookbook Author*

Who doesn't know Bobby Flay, the boy and his grill? He's a New York boy who made his name cooking in the style of America's Southwest and went on to television fame with his technique on the grill—two styles of cooking rarely experienced in the metropolitan area. I would say that, although a group of Southwestern chefs had done much to bring their cuisine to the attention of the American dining public, Bobby Flay was solely responsible for making New York City diners take notice of this zesty fare.

I met Bobby when he was planning to take a class at De Gustibus. He queried me for about ten minutes concerning the credentials of the person teaching the class. I finally asked him, "Who are you?" and he proudly answered, "I'm Bobby Flay, the executive chef at the Miracle Grill!" He assured me that he would one day be teaching at De Gustibus and, sure enough, he has become one of our most in-demand teachers and a national television star. It has been great fun to watch his career soar.

When Bobby was fully entrenched in our program, he said that he had a friend who had a small Italian restaurant downtown called Pó. He thought his friend would give a really great class. I'll bet you've guessed—it was Mario Batali, whose career has taken a path similar to Bobby's.

In this recipe Bobby brought the homey quesadilla to gourmet standards. Though a bit ahead of the pack at the time, he was certainly one of the chefs instrumental in making the quesadilla the appetizer and snack food of choice that it has become. Even school lunches now feature them!

---

4 large shrimp, peeled and deveined, tails on

Coarse salt and freshly ground pepper to taste

3 tablespoons olive oil

Three 6-inch-round tortillas (see Note)

¼ cup Cilantro Pesto (recipe follows)

¼ cup grated Monterey Jack cheese

¼ cup grated white Cheddar cheese

½ teaspoon ancho chili powder (see Note)

2 teaspoons sour cream

Preheat the oven to 450°F.

Season the shrimp with salt and pepper to taste.

Heat 2 tablespoons of the olive oil in a small sauté pan over medium heat. Add the seasoned shrimp and sear for 1½ minutes; turn and sear the remaining side for 1½ minutes. Remove from the heat, set aside, and keep warm.

Place one tortilla on a baking sheet. Spread 1½ tablespoons of the pesto over the tortilla, then sprinkle half of the Jack and Cheddar cheeses over the pesto, leaving a little edge so that the cheese does not ooze out the sides. Season with salt and pepper to taste. Place another tortilla on top and repeat the layering using 1½ tablespoons of the pesto, the remaining portions of each cheese, and salt and pepper to taste. Top with the remaining tortilla.

Using a pastry brush and the remaining 1 tablespoon of olive oil, lightly coat the top of the last tortilla. Very lightly sprinkle ancho chili powder over the top. (The quesadilla may be prepared up to this point and stored, covered and refrigerated, for up to 6 hours before finishing. If making ahead, do not cook the shrimp until ready to serve.)

112

Place the stacked tortillas in the preheated oven and bake for 10 minutes, or until the tortilla edges are slightly crisp and the cheese has melted.

Remove from the oven and let stand for a couple of minutes so the cheese doesn't run out when the quesadilla is cut.

Cut the quesadilla into quarters. Top each quarter with a shrimp, a dollop of the remaining pesto, and a dollop of sour cream. Serve immediately.

Serves 4

CILANTRO PESTO

2 firmly packed cups fresh cilantro leaves

2 cloves garlic

2 tablespoons pumpkin seeds (pepitas; see Note)

2 tablespoons fresh lime juice

1 teaspoon coarse salt, or to taste

1 teaspoon freshly ground black pepper

5 tablespoons olive oil

Combine the cilantro, garlic, pumpkin seeds, lime juice, salt, and pepper in the bowl of a food processor fitted with the metal blade and process until just combined.

With the motor running, slowly pour in the olive oil, processing to emulsify the mixture to a smooth sauce.

If not using immediately, transfer to a nonreactive container, cover, and refrigerate until ready to use, up to two days.

Bring to room temperature before using.

Note: You may have to purchase 8-inch-round tortillas and cut them to the desired size.

Ancho chili powder and unsalted pumpkin seeds (pepitas) are available from Hispanic markets, specialty food stores, and some supermarkets.

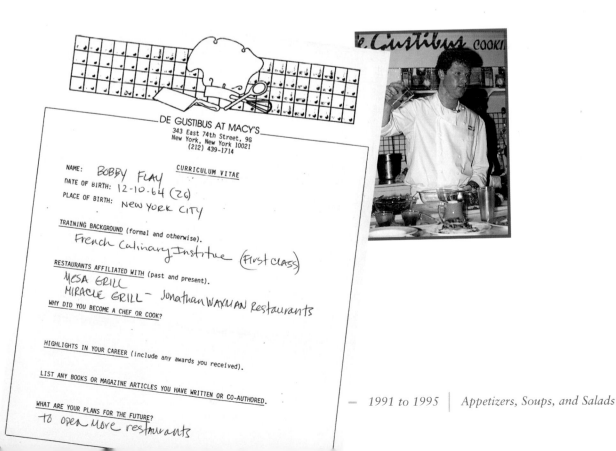

SPANAKOPITA

1992

MOLLIE KATZEN, *Cookbook Author*

Mollie Katzen has been named "one of the five women in America who have changed the way we eat" by *Health Magazine*. She came to fame through the *Moosewood Cookbook*, one of the ten best-selling cookbooks of all time. The Moosewood Café, in Ithaca, New York, was (and still is) run by a vegetarian collective. It was founded in the radical sixties when many young people embraced a nonmeat diet.

Mollie went on to build a career as an authority on vegetarian cooking. In this recipe she combined the tenets of vegetarianism with a newfound focus on health-consciousness: no eggs or butter in a traditional Greek dish that would normally be oozing both. She has done much to update traditional vegetarian recipes by putting an emphasis on clean flavors and health-promoting methods of preparation.

½ cup olive oil

2 cups minced onion (about 2 medium)

1 teaspoon minced fresh basil leaves

1 teaspoon minced fresh oregano

¼ teaspoon coarse salt, plus more to taste

2½ pounds fresh spinach, leaves only, well washed, dried, and finely chopped

5 medium cloves garlic, peeled and minced

3 tablespoons all-purpose flour

1 pound feta cheese, crumbled

1 cup small-curd cottage or pot cheese

Freshly ground black pepper to taste

1 pound frozen filo dough, thawed

Preheat the oven to 375°F.

Using a pastry brush and 1 tablespoon of the olive oil, lightly coat a 9 × 13-inch baking pan. Set aside.

Place 1 tablespoon of the remaining olive oil in a large, heavy-bottomed saucepan over medium heat. Add the onion, basil, oregano, and salt and sauté for about 5 minutes, or until the onions are very soft but have not taken on any color. Add the spinach, a handful at a time, raise the heat, and cook, stirring constantly, for about 8 minutes, or until all of the spinach has been added and is completely wilted. Stir in the garlic.

Sprinkle the flour over the top and cook, stirring constantly, for about 3 minutes, or until the flour is well incorporated. Remove from the heat.

Stirring constantly, add the feta and cottage cheeses. When well combined, season with pepper and, if necessary, additional salt to taste.

Unwrap the filo dough and remove one sheet, keeping the remaining dough covered with a barely damp kitchen towel. (You must keep the dough covered as you work or it will dry out very rapidly and be unusable.)

Place the sheet of filo dough in the prepared baking pan, allowing the edges of the dough to fit into and over the sides of the pan.

Using a pastry brush and some of the remaining olive oil, lightly coat the filo. Place another sheet of filo dough on top of the oiled sheet, then continue oiling and stacking filo until you have eight layers.

Using a spatula, spread half of the spinach-cheese mixture on top of the eight layers of oiled filo, spreading to completely cover the dough on the bottom of the pan.

Cover the filling with another stack of eight layers of filo dough, oiling and stacking each sheet. Then, using the remaining spinach-cheese mixture, cover the second layer of dough as above.

Using the remaining four sheets of filo, cover the filling as above, oiling and stacking each sheet.

Using a pastry brush, lightly coat the top sheet of dough with olive oil. Carefully tuck in the edges of the stacked dough to enfold the filling.

Place in the preheated oven and bake for about 45 minutes, or until golden brown and crisp.

Remove from the oven and allow to rest for about 10 minutes before cutting into squares. Serve warm or at room temperature.

Makes one 9 × 13-inch pie

CHILI-ORANGE COLD NOODLES
1993
BARBARA TROPP, *Restaurateur, Cookbook Author*

I first met Barbara Tropp while in Macy's Cellar (their famous kitchenware department) watching a demonstration being done by her mentor, food writer Barbara Kafka. Barbara K. said that Barbara T. was the absolute best and suggested that she teach at De Gustibus. Barbara T. agreed to teach but not until her definitive book was completed. Six years later, her first De Gustibus class was outstanding, just as Barbara K. had promised.

Through her San Francisco restaurant, China Moon, and her cookbook of the same name, food historian, Chinese-food authority, and all-around terrific woman Barbara Tropp taught many of us—trained chefs and home cooks alike—how to make authentic Chinese food. Her knowledge was astounding and her enthusiasm for her subject contagious. Her early loss to cancer left an enormous hole in the culinary scene.

This is a classic recipe which, to quote Barbara, "tastes great the next day." She also added that the oil in this recipe is "a terrific hot chili oil alive with the flavor of orange that is wonderful in cold dishes, marinades, and sauces. The 'goop' that sinks to the bottom of the oil after seasoning is terrific in noodle salads, meatloaf, hamburgers, dumplings, dipping sauces, etc." We found the sauce and "goop" so delicious that we often double the amount so there is more to savor.

1 pound fresh ¹⁄₁₆-inch-thick Chinese noodles or Italian egg noodles

¼ cup China Moon Chili-Orange Oil (recipe follows)

2 tablespoons "goop" from China Moon Chili-Orange Oil

¼ cup Superior brand black soy sauce (see Note)

¼ cup distilled white vinegar

2 tablespoons plus 2 teaspoons granulated sugar

1 teaspoon coarse salt, or to taste

2 to 3 bunches fresh cilantro, leaves and top stems, well washed and coarsely chopped

1 pound crisp bean sprouts, blanched

1 cup finely shredded carrots

¾ cup chopped roasted, unsalted peanuts, plus more for garnish

²⁄₃ cup thinly sliced white and green scallion rings, plus more for garnish

6 to 10 fresh cilantro sprigs

Fluff the noodles to separate the strands. Set a large bowl of ice water aside.

Bring a large pot of salted water to boil over high heat. Add the noodles and boil, swishing the noodles around with chopsticks, for about 2 minutes, or until al dente.

Remove from the heat, drain well, and transfer to the ice water to stop the cooking and chill.

Drain the noodles well, place them in a bowl, and set aside.

Combine the chili-orange oil with the "goop" in a small mixing bowl. Whisk in the soy sauce, vinegar, sugar, and salt. When well blended, pour the dressing over the noodles and, using your fingertips, toss to coat and separate the noodles. Let rest for 5 minutes so that the noodles can absorb the dressing a bit, then toss again.

Scatter the cilantro, bean sprouts, carrots, peanuts, and scallions over the top and toss to coat. Taste and, if necessary, add a pinch more sugar.

Heap equal portions of the tossed noodles into four or six individual bowls (or pile on a serving platter). Sprinkle with some cilantro sprigs along with some peanuts and scallion rings if desired.

Serves 4 to 6 as a main course; 8 to 10 as part of an antipasto plate

CHINA MOON CHILI-ORANGE OIL

3 large oranges, preferably organic, with smooth, unblemished skins

2 large garlic cloves, peeled and lightly smashed

½ cup dried red chili flakes (see Note)

3 tablespoons fermented black beans, unrinsed and coarsely chopped, preferably Pearl River brand in a round yellow box (see Note)

2 tablespoons minced fresh ginger

2 cups corn or peanut oil

¼ cup Japanese sesame oil, preferably Kadoya (see Note)

Wash the oranges with warm water, a light liquid soap, and an abrasive scrubber. Rinse well.

Using a sharp vegetable peeler, remove the peel only, leaving all of the white pith. With a sharp chef's knife, finely mince the peel.

Place the minced peel in a nonreactive, heavy-bottomed saucepan. Add the garlic cloves, chili flakes, black beans, and ginger. Stir in the oils.

Place the saucepan over medium-low heat. Rest a deep-fat thermometer on the rim of the pot without allowing it to touch the bottom. Bring the oil to 225°F to 250°F, stirring occasionally. Watching carefully, allow the mixture to bubble gently for 10 minutes without the temperature climbing.

Remove from the heat and let stand until very cool or up to twelve hours.

Pour the oil into a clean glass jar, scraping any of the seasonings that remain in the saucepan into the jar.

Note: Most of the products recommended by Barbara Tropp are available at Asian markets or specialty food stores. When shopping for the ingredients, Barbara said, "Shop for bright red (not purple or brown) chili flakes with a ratio of about 1 part seed to 4 to 5 parts skin. Use only Japanese sesame oil packaged in glass. Chinese oils packed in plastic are typically burnt, rancid, or otherwise second-rate. Use the brands I recommend for the best results."

China Moon Chili-Orange Oil will keep indefinitely. If refrigerated, bring to room temperature before using.

CHILLED SUMMER VEGETABLE SOUP
WITH SPANISH VINEGAR AND QUINOA SALAD
1995

MARK MILITELLO, *Chef/Owner, Mark's Las Olas, Mark's City Place, Mark's South Beach, Mark's Mizner Park*

Mark Militello was one of our first "Floribbean" chefs, representing the culinary movement that also featured the inventive cuisines of Norman Van Aken and Allen Susser, Florida cooks all. Mark's class was extremely exciting, as he combined Caribbean and Latin spices and flavors with native Floridian products and traditional cooking techniques.

In this recipe Mark used quinoa, a grain that very few in the audience had cooked. Quinoa was first introduced to De Gustibus in 1985 by the late Felipe Rojas-Lombardi of the Ballroom Restaurant. Mark also introduced Spanish vinegar, which we had not seen featured before, giving us a hint of what would occur in the next few years with the explosion of Spanish foods.

---

1 small bunch fresh thyme, well washed and dried

1 small bunch fresh flat-leaf parsley, well washed and dried

1 small bunch fresh basil, well washed and dried

½ cup extra-virgin olive oil, plus more for garnish

½ pound sweet onions such as Maui or Vidalia, peeled and diced

2 cloves garlic, peeled and minced

¾ pound very ripe tomatoes, well washed, dried, cored, and quartered

¾ pound red bell peppers, well washed, dried, cored, and seeded, membrane removed, and chopped

½ pound Idaho potatoes, peeled and chopped

½ pound eggplant, well washed, dried, and chopped

½ pound zucchini, well washed, dried, and chopped

4 cups unsalted chicken stock

Coarse salt and freshly ground pepper

2 tablespoons sherry wine vinegar, plus more to taste (see Note)

Quinoa Salad (recipe follows)

Shavings of Parmigiano-Reggiano or Tome cheese for garnish

Tie the thyme, parsley, and basil in a cheesecloth bag. Set aside.

Heat the oil in a large saucepan over medium heat. Add the onions and sauté for about 5 minutes, or until they are very soft but have not taken on any color.

Stir in the garlic, tomatoes, bell pepper, potatoes, eggplant, zucchini, and cheesecloth herb bag. Add the chicken stock and bring to a boil. Season with salt and pepper to taste, lower the heat, and cook at a bare simmer for about 30 minutes, or until all of the vegetables are very soft.

Remove from the heat. Remove and discard the herb bag.

Pass the soup through the medium plate of a food mill (or process in a blender or food processor using the metal blade). Taste and, if necessary, adjust the seasoning with salt and pepper.

Place the soup in a nonreactive container with a lid, cover, and refrigerate for at least 3 hours or up to 2 days.

When ready to serve, stir in the vinegar to taste.

Place the quinoa salad in 8 small timbale molds, pressing down to make a tight fit.

Working with one soup plate at a time, invert the mold in the center of the soup plate. Lift off the mold, leaving a neat circle of salad. Carefully ladle equal portions of the chilled soup into each bowl. Drizzle extra-virgin olive oil over the soup and place thin shavings of cheese over all. Serve immediately.

Serves 8

QUINOA SALAD

1 cup quinoa (see Note)

1 cup fresh English peas, blanched

1 cup fresh corn kernels, blanched

1 cup finely diced, peeled, and seeded English cucumber

½ cup finely diced fennel

½ cup finely diced celery

½ cup chopped fresh basil leaves

⅓ cup chopped fresh mint leaves

¼ cup fresh lemon juice, plus more to taste

2 tablespoons extra-virgin olive oil

Sea salt and freshly ground pepper to taste

Place the quinoa in a fine strainer and rinse thoroughly under cold running water.

Transfer the rinsed quinoa to a saucepan. Add 2 cups of water and place over high heat. Bring to a boil, lower the heat, and simmer for 10 minutes, or until all of the water has been absorbed and the quinoa is tender and separates easily. Remove from the heat and allow to cool.

Place the cooled quinoa in a mixing bowl. Add the peas, corn, cucumber, fennel, celery, basil, and mint, tossing to combine.

Add the lemon juice and olive oil, season with sea salt and pepper, and toss to coat.

Cover with plastic film and set aside to marinate for 1 hour.

When ready to serve, taste and, if necessary, adjust the seasoning with additional lemon juice and salt.

Note: Spanish vinegar is available from specialty food stores, and quinoa is available from health-food stores, specialty food stores, and some supermarkets.

119

INSALATA TIEPIDADI PETTO DI CAPPONE
ALL'ACETO BALSAMICO TRADIZIONALE DI MODENA
(WARM CAPON BREAST SALAD WITH BALSAMIC VINAIGRETTE)
1995

MARTA PULINI, *Former Chef, Le Madri, Cookbook Author*

Watching Marta Pulini work was like watching a terrific home cook with the skills of a formally trained chef. In this recipe Marta used two ingredients that, in the nineties, began to make their mark on menus across the country: balsamic vinegar and the bitter Italian chicory, *radicchio di Treviso*. Coming from Modena, Marta was totally at home with true *balsamico* and enchanted the class with tales of the traditional methods used to make this extraordinary condiment.

Pasta making is second nature to Marta, and it is incredible to learn from and with her. Because of her teaching, many, many De Gustibus cooks decided that only fresh pasta would do in their households. She has taught classes with Pino Luongo, the owner of many of the restaurants in which she worked—they are an incomparable duo!

---

²/₃ cup golden raisins

6 tablespoons (¾ stick) unsalted butter, at room temperature

1 large capon breast, skin on

Coarse salt and freshly ground pepper to taste

2 sprigs fresh rosemary

¼ cup *Aceto Balsamico Tradizionale de Modena* (see sidebar)

⅓ cup extra-virgin olive oil

Finely grated zest of 2 lemons

2 tablespoons pine nuts

6 small heads *radicchio di Treviso,* well washed and dried, core removed, and thinly sliced (see Note)

Preheat the oven to 400°F.

Place the raisins in a small heatproof bowl in hot water to cover. Set aside.

Using 1 tablespoon of the butter, generously coat a small baking pan. Season the capon breast with salt and pepper. Place the breast in the prepared pan.

Cut the remaining butter into small pieces and place the pieces on the seasoned breast. Place the rosemary sprigs on the breast and cover with aluminum foil. Place in the preheated oven and roast for 30 minutes.

Remove the foil and continue to roast for about 20 minutes, or until the skin is golden brown. The meat should register 170°F on an instant-read thermometer; it will continue to cook as it rests. Remove from the oven and set aside.

Place the balsamic vinegar in a small bowl. Whisk in the olive oil and season with salt to taste. Drain the plumped raisins and stir them in, along with the lemon zest and pine nuts. Set aside.

Using a chef's knife, cut the capon breast on the bias into thin slices.

Place equal portions of the radicchio on each of six luncheon plates. Place equal portions of the capon slices on top of the radicchio on each plate. Whisk the vinaigrette and spoon equal portions over each plate, taking care to get some raisins and pine nuts on each one. Serve immediately.

Note: Radicchio di Treviso is available at most specialty produce stores and some supermarkets.

Serves 6

Traditional **balsamic vinegar** is made from white Trebbiano grape juice aged to a rich, deep brownish-black color and provocative sweetness in changing barrels of various woods over a long period of years. The oldest and most expensive is syrupy in consistency and is used only as an accent. When I began the De Gustibus classes, balsamic vinegar was almost unknown in American cooking, but it has grown to be ubiquitous in menus worldwide.

120

GINGER-ROASTED WINTER VEGETABLES

1991

MICHAEL LOMONACO, *Chef, Guastavino's, Cookbook Author*

My introduction to Michael Lomonaco came when he worked for my husband, Alain Sailhac, at Le Cirque and then at the '21' Club. A lover of traditional American cooking, Michael went on to become executive chef at Windows on the World on top of the World Trade Center, a much-loved New York institution that perished in the attacks of September 11, 2001. He has remained a good friend and one of De Gustibus's most charismatic teachers.

This dish takes standard roasted vegetables to new heights, as they absorb the stock, are sweetly glazed with the butter and syrup, and are given a bit of exotic heat with the ginger. Michael has a wonderful understanding of contemporary American cooking, and it was through recipes like this one that vegetables went from being waterlogged afterthoughts to stars on the plate.

---

2 large carrots, peeled, trimmed, and cut into large dice

2 large parsnips, peeled, trimmed, and cut into large dice

2 large turnips, peeled, trimmed, and cut into large dice

½ cup unsalted, defatted chicken stock

¼ cup (½ stick) unsalted butter, melted

¼ cup pure maple syrup

2 tablespoons finely minced fresh ginger

Coarse salt and freshly ground pepper to taste

Preheat the oven to 375°F.

Combine the carrots, parsnips, and turnips in a large baking dish or casserole. Add the chicken stock, butter, syrup, and ginger. Season with salt and pepper to taste and toss to coat well.

Place in the preheated oven and roast, tossing occasionally, for about 20 minutes, or until the vegetables are tender and nicely glazed. The pan should be almost dry.

Remove from the oven. Taste and, if necessary, season with additional salt and pepper. Serve immediately.

Serves 4

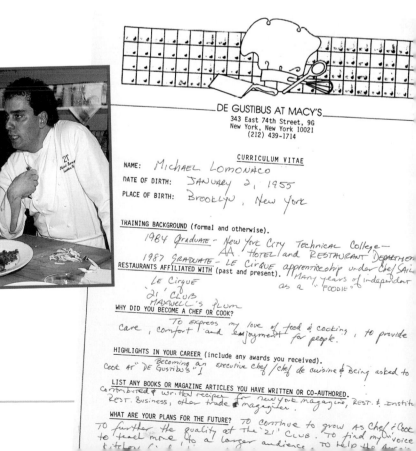

CURRICULUM VITAE

NAME: Michael Lomonaco

DATE OF BIRTH: January 2, 1955

PLACE OF BIRTH: Brooklyn, New York

TRAINING BACKGROUND (formal and otherwise).
1984 Graduate - New York City Technical College - AA. Hotel and Restaurant Department
1987 Graduate - Le Cirque apprenticeship under Chef/Sai...
Many years of independent as a "Foodie"

RESTAURANTS AFFILIATED WITH (past and present).
Le Cirque
'21' Club
Maxwell's Plum

WHY DID YOU BECOME A CHEF OR COOK?
To express my love of food & cooking, to provide care, comfort and enjoyment for people.

HIGHLIGHTS IN YOUR CAREER (include any awards you received).
Cook at "De Gustibus" ! Becoming an executive chef /chef de cuisine & Being asked to...

LIST ANY BOOKS OR MAGAZINE ARTICLES YOU HAVE WRITTEN OR CO-AUTHORED.
Contributed & written recipes for new york magazine, Rest. & Instit. Rest. Business, other trade magazines.

WHAT ARE YOUR PLANS FOR THE FUTURE? To continue to grow as Chef & Cook. To further the quality at the '21' Club. To find my own voice. to teach more to a longer audience. To help the...

PARSNIP PURÉE
1993

VINCENT GUERITHAULT, *Chef/Owner, Vincent's on Camelback, Cookbook Author*

For years, one of our very loyal clients had been recommending Vincent Guerithault to me as a teacher. I am embarrassed to say that I did not know his great reputation. On a trip to Phoenix, however, I finally met Vincent and was bowled over by the food he was serving. I quickly issued an invitation to our kitchen. He was the first classically trained French chef that I had seen use native Southwestern American ingredients to create really spectacular meals. His restaurant was the first to make Phoenix a diner's destination.

This is a wonderfully rich side dish, utilizing an underused vegetable and made without regard to calories or fat. This was the beginning of a movement to take root vegetables from the braising pan to a featured place on the plate.

---

2 pounds parsnips, peeled, trimmed, and diced

1 cup heavy cream

1 tablespoon unsalted butter, at room temperature

Coarse salt and freshly ground pepper to taste

Place the parsnips in a steamer basket over boiling water. Cover and steam for about 30 minutes, or until very tender.

While the parsnips are cooking, heat the heavy cream just until hot in a small saucepan over medium-low heat. Keep warm.

Remove the parsnips from the steamer and transfer to the bowl of a food processor fitted with the metal blade. With the motor running, slowly add the hot cream and process to a smooth purée. Add the butter and salt and pepper to taste and pulse to combine.

Scrape from the processor bowl into a serving bowl and serve immediately.

Note: This purée can be made in advance and kept hot in the top half of a double boiler over simmering water. Stir from time to time to keep the bottom from sticking.

Serves 4

TAGLIARINI
WITH TART ANCHOVY-AND-ALMOND SAUCE
1992

LYNNE ROSSETTO KASPER, *Teacher, Cookbook Author, Radio Personality*

The first time that Lynne came to De Gustibus, she was extremely nervous, as she didn't realize the skill of our staff and was concerned about their ability to assist her in getting everything done in time. As soon as she saw the depth of their knowledge, she relaxed and went shopping.

Through her best-known cookbook, *The Splendid Table,* and nationally syndicated radio show of the same name, Lynne has introduced many cooks to the glories of traditional Italian cooking. About this recipe, Lynne says, "Inspired by a traditional sauce from Modena and Ferrara's Jewish communities, this blend of tomato, lemon, anchovy, garlic, and almonds has evolved since the Middle Ages. Now it is used over pasta; centuries ago it was [used over] fish and meats. It cooks in no time and is best made just before serving. If you must work ahead, cook up to the point of adding the tomatoes. Set aside, covered, up to 3 hours."

---

10 whole salted anchovies or two 2-ounce cans anchovy filets

Enough milk to cover and soak anchovies

1 pound tagliarini or linguine, preferably homemade

¼ cup extra-virgin olive oil

1 medium onion, peeled and minced

½ cup minced fresh flat-leaf parsley

2 large cloves garlic, peeled and minced

6 canned Italian plum tomatoes, well drained and crushed

Juice of ½ lemon or to taste

1 cup blanched almonds, toasted and coarsely chopped

Freshly ground pepper to taste

If using salted anchovies, rinse them under cold running water, then open each one up like a book. Gently pull away and discard the backbone running down the center of the fish. (This does not have to be done to canned filets.)

Whichever type of anchovies are used, place them in a small, shallow bowl and add just enough milk to cover. Soak for 20 minutes; drain well and coarsely chop. Set aside.

Bring a large pot of salted water to boil over high heat. Add the pasta and cook according to the package directions, being careful to reserve some of the pasta water.

While the pasta is cooking, prepare the sauce: Heat the oil in a large skillet over medium-high heat. Add the onion and parsley and sauté for about 7 minutes, or until the onion begins to brown.

Lower the heat and stir in the reserved anchovies. Cook, stirring constantly, for 30 seconds. Add the garlic and cook, stirring frequently, for about 2 minutes, or until the garlic begins to turn pale blonde. Stir in ⅓ cup of the pasta water and cook for 2 minutes, or just long enough to melt down the anchovies without allowing the water to evaporate. If necessary, add up to 3 more tablespoons of pasta water.

Add the tomatoes and bring to a boil. Boil for 1 minute. Stir in lemon juice to taste.

Drain the pasta and immediately add it to the sauce, tossing until the pasta is well coated. Add the almonds along with pepper to taste and toss again. Transfer the pasta to a heated bowl and serve immediately. No cheese, please!

Serves 6 as a first course; 4 as a main course

In the beginning we had only anchovy filets packed in oil. With the rapid evolution of culinary standards in America, we have seen the introduction of salt-packed anchovies and, more recently, fresh **anchovies**. The latter are now de rigueur, simply grilled or roasted, on Italian and bistro menus.

POLENTA WITH LAMB SAUCE
1993
MARK STRAUSMAN, *Chef, Coco Pazzo, Cookbook Author*

Mark Strausman had a hand in the explosion of Italian home-style cooking in New York. He also introduced the richly flavored foods of the Jewish communities of Italy to the New York dining scene. What is more, he was one of the first chefs to feature family-style meals with patrons serving themselves from copious portions of "comfort" foods placed at the center of the table.

I first encountered Mark when he was a very young chef working for Pino Luongo at Sappore di Mare, a "hot-and-happening" Italian restaurant located out in the Hamptons, on the east end of New York's Long Island. I remember that he made stracotto, which gave pot roast a whole new meaning for me. The class always enjoys his cooking as much as I did that first time.

2 tablespoons olive oil

1 leg of lamb, boned, excess fat removed, meat cut into ¼-inch squares

2 cloves garlic, peeled and chopped

1 medium onion, peeled and finely chopped

3 sprigs fresh rosemary, needles only, chopped

3 sprigs fresh thyme, leaves only, chopped

2½ cups dry Italian red wine

1 cup crushed canned Italian plum tomatoes

Pinch ground cloves

Pinch ground nutmeg

Coarse salt and freshly ground pepper to taste

1 box instant polenta (to serve 8)

½ cup freshly grated Parmigiano-Reggiano cheese, plus more for garnish

¼ cup (½ stick) unsalted butter, at room temperature

Extra-virgin olive oil for garnish

Heat the 2 tablespoons of oil in a large saucepan over high heat. Add the lamb and garlic and sauté for about 5 minutes, or until the lamb just begins to color. Add the onion, rosemary, and thyme and sauté for 1 minute. Add the wine, tomatoes, cloves, nutmeg, and salt and pepper to taste and bring to a boil. Lower the heat and simmer for about 45 minutes, or until the meat is very tender.

Just before you're ready to serve, cook the polenta according to the package directions.

Beat the cheese and butter into the cooked polenta.

Scoop about three large spoonfuls of polenta into each of eight shallow soup bowls. Ladle an equal portion of lamb sauce over each. Sprinkle with additional cheese, drizzle extra-virgin olive oil over the top, and serve immediately.

Serves 8

LONDON BROIL "SMOKE GETS IN YOUR HOUSE" STYLE
WITH LIME-MARINATED RED ONIONS AND PINEAPPLE CATSUP
1994

CHRIS SCHLESINGER, *Chef, East Coast Grill, Cookbook Author*

Chris Schlesinger, along with John Willoughby, made "the thrill of the grill" a hot topic. They taught us how to barbecue everything from foie gras to sausage, accenting it all with wildly flavorful ketchups, chutneys, and marinades.

Chris did a terrific job of replicating "live fire cooking" on our electric stove. He said if he could do it there, anyone could do it anywhere. He introduced us to the stovetop grill pan, and to his triad of "lime, chilies, and salt" to make any barbecued meat sing.

2 red onions, peeled and thinly sliced

½ cup fresh lime juice

Tabasco to taste

¼ cup freshly cracked black pepper

2 tablespoons coarse salt

One beef flank steak, approximately 1½ pounds, well trimmed of fat

¼ cup all-purpose flour

Chunky Pineapple Catsup (recipe follows)

Combine the onions, lime juice, and Tabasco in a nonreactive container. Cover and refrigerate for at least 2 hours or up to 12 hours.

Combine the pepper and salt, then rub the mixture into both sides of the meat. Sprinkle the meat with the flour, using half of the flour for each side.

Place a heavy bottomed frying pan over high heat. When very hot but not smoking, place the meat in the pan (without adding any oil) and sear for 7 minutes. Turn and sear for 5 to 7 minutes more, or until an instant-read thermometer reads 135°F for rare. If you prefer your meat more well done, continue cooking until it is almost at the point you like it, noting that it will continue to cook a bit once taken from the heat.

Remove the meat from the pan and place on a serving platter. Let rest for about 5 minutes.

Using a chef's knife, cut the meat on the bias into thick slices. Serve accompanied by the marinated onions and Chunky Pineapple Catsup.

Serves 4

CHUNKY PINEAPPLE CATSUP

2 tablespoons vegetable oil

1 yellow onion, peeled and very thinly sliced

½ large, ripe pineapple, peeled, eyes removed, cored, and cut into bite-size chunks

¼ cup fresh orange juice

¼ cup white vinegar

¼ cup tightly packed light brown sugar

Pinch ground cloves

Heat the oil in a large sauté pan over medium heat until very hot but not smoking. Add the onion and sauté for 7 minutes, or until translucent.

Add the pineapple and cook, stirring constantly, for 3 minutes. Stir in the orange juice, vinegar, brown sugar, and cloves and cook, stirring constantly, for an additional 8 minutes.

Remove from the heat and serve hot. Catsup may be made in advance and stored, covered and refrigerated, for up to 2 weeks.

MARINATED PORK LOIN SATAY
WITH MANGO SALSA
1993

CINDY PAWLCYN, *Chef/Restaurateur, Mustards Grill, Cookbook Author*

Cindy Pawclyn made her first appearance at De Gustibus right off the plane returning from a visit to European kitchens. Her husband had flown her ingredients in from California, and they met up at the airport, arriving at Macy's overloaded with baggage. Her restaurant, Fog City Diner (obviously in San Francisco), was dazzling guests, so naturally she wowed the classroom with her take on comfort food, California-style.

3 cloves garlic, peeled and minced

½ bunch cilantro, well washed and chopped

3 tablespoons *ketjap manis* (or 2 tablespoons dark soy sauce or tamari plus 1 tablespoon molasses; see Note)

1 tablespoon freshly grated ginger

1 tablespoon hoisin sauce (see Note)

1 tablespoon *sambal olek* (or black bean chili paste) (see Note)

½ teaspoon freshly ground white pepper

½ cup olive oil

Two 1-pound pork tenderloins, well trimmed of all fat and sinew

Mango Salsa (recipe follows)

18 to 24 sprigs cilantro

Place the garlic and cilantro in a small bowl. Stir in the *ketjap manis*, ginger, hoisin, *sambal olek*, and white pepper. When well blended, stir in the olive oil. Set aside.

Using a chef's knife, cut the tenderloins on the bias into ¼-inch-thick slices. Place the pork in a large, shallow, nonreactive dish. Add the marinade, cover with plastic film, and place in the refrigerator for at least 2 hours or up to 12 hours.

When ready to cook the pork, remove it from the refrigerator and bring to room temperature.

Preheat and oil the grill. Place the pork slices on the preheated grill and grill, turning once, for about 3 minutes, or until nicely marked and cooked through.

Place three slices of meat on the side of each of six or eight serving plates. Spoon a line of salsa down the center and garnish with three sprigs of cilantro. Serve immediately, with rice and beans if desired.

Serves 6 to 8

MANGO SALSA

2 jalapeño chilies, grilled, stemmed, seeded, and minced

1 large ripe mango, peeled and diced

Zest and juice of 2 limes

2 tablespoons extra-virgin olive oil

Coarse salt and freshly ground pepper to taste

Combine the jalapeños and mango in a small nonreactive container. Stir in the lime juice and olive oil. Season with salt and pepper to taste.

Set aside to marinate for a few minutes before serving.

Note: Ketjap *(or kecap)* manis *is a dark, thick soy sauce sweetened with palm sugar and seasoned with garlic and star anise. Hoisin sauce is a sharp, slightly sweet, brown bean sauce made from soy mash and seasoned with sugar, vinegar, chilies, and herbs.* Sambal olek *is an Indonesian spicy chili sauce made from ground chilies, garlic, and vinegar. Ketjap manis,* hoisin sauce, *and* sambal olek *are available from Asian markets and some specialty food stores.*

EASY ROAST CHICKEN

1995

GORDON HAMERSLEY, *Chef/Owner, Hamersley's Bistro, Cookbook Author*

Long before I met Gordon, I met his wife, Fiona, who told me that her husband was a chef and that they were planning to open a restaurant in Boston. Shortly thereafter they opened Hamersley's Bistro to great critical acclaim. I then had the opportunity to meet Gordon, who is a proponent of the theory that simple food, well seasoned, is the only way to go.

Gordon has been instrumental in setting the trend of the upscale bistro across America. Although very well-schooled in the French classics, he has created a classic American bistro style that is all his own. This recipe is a classic example of his theory put to the test. No one who tries Gordon's roast chicken recipe ever returns to his or her own.

---

3 cloves garlic, peeled

3 shallots, peeled

1 bunch fresh flat-leaf parsley, leaves only, well washed and dried

3 tablespoons Dijon mustard

2 tablespoons freshly cracked black pepper

1 tablespoon dried herb mixture of your choice or dried herbes de Provence

6 tablespoons olive oil

Zest of 1 lemon

Two 3-pound roasting chickens, well rinsed and patted dry

Coarse salt and freshly ground pepper to taste

Combine the garlic, shallots, parsley, mustard, pepper, and herbs in the bowl of a food processor fitted with the metal blade. With the motor running, slowly add the olive oil and process until the mixture is slightly smooth and lime-green in color. Scrape the mixture from the processor bowl into a nonreactive container and fold in the lemon zest.

Generously coat the exterior of both chickens with the mixture. Place the chickens on a platter, cover lightly with plastic film, and refrigerate for 2 hours.

Remove the chickens from the refrigerator and let them come to room temperature. Preheat the oven to 350°F.

Season the chickens with salt and pepper to taste and place on a roasting rack in a large roasting pan.

Place the chickens in the preheated oven and roast for 1½ hours, or until the leg bone easily pulls away from the breast.

Remove the birds from the oven and transfer to a serving platter. Allow to rest for 20 minutes before carving into serving pieces.

Serves 6 to 8

SEARED TUNA
WITH WHITE BEANS, ARUGULA, AND LEMON CONFIT
1993

THOMAS COLICCHIO, *Chef/Owner, Craft, Craft Steak, Craft Bar, 'wichcraft, Cookbook Author*

Tom Colicchio first came to us when he was the chef at Mondrian, where he served deliciously tasty meals that were a terrific combination of homespun and haute. His use of market ingredients and simple, direct flavors made the restaurant an immediate hit. He is a chef of great vision and taste and never fails to share his gifts with us.

One of Tom's greatest assets is his ability to realize new concepts in restaurant dining. His restaurant Craft, in New York City, set the city afire when diners were allowed to compose their own meals, choosing from an assortment of dishes meant to be shared, offered on a very straightforward menu. He has said that he developed the menu because he found that "sharing food and passing it around the table" was an experience missing from dining in New York and one that he felt people would enjoy.

Tom feels that cooking is a craft. He loves to focus on one ingredient and take it in many different directions. Most of his menus are ingredient-driven, sparked by the seasons. In this recipe he highlights great tuna with the now well-recognized but once exotic Lemon Confit and homey white beans. This is a wonderful recipe for home cooks as both the beans and the confit can be made in advance of use.

Six 6-ounce, ¾-inch-thick tuna steaks

¼ cup crushed black peppercorns

Coarse salt to taste

White Beans (recipe follows)

Lemon Confit (recipe follows)

1 bunch arugula, tough stems removed, well washed and dried

Generously season the tuna with the crushed peppercorns and the salt to taste.

Heat a heavy-bottomed, nonstick frying pan over medium-high heat until very hot but not smoking. Add the seasoned tuna steaks and sear for about 3 minutes per side, or just until barely cooked. (You want the tuna to be rare in the center.)

Remove the tuna from the heat and set aside.

Arrange equal portions of the beans on each of six dinner plates. Place several slices of confit and a small amount of arugula on each portion.

Working with one steak at a time, cut the tuna into ½-inch-thick slices and fan them out over the top of the bean-confit mound on each plate. Spoon a bit of the confit liquid over the tuna on each plate and serve.

Serves 6

WHITE BEANS

1 pound dried white beans, well rinsed

2 strips bacon

1 medium carrot, peeled and cut into large chunks

1 medium onion, peeled and cut into large chunks

1 rib celery, well washed, trimmed, and cut into large chunks

1 leek, white part only, well washed and cut into large chunks

8 cups chicken stock

6 sprigs fresh thyme

1 bay leaf

Coarse salt and freshly ground pepper to taste

Place the beans in cold water to cover by 2 inches and set aside to soak for at least 8 hours or overnight.

Drain the beans and set aside.

Place the bacon in a large saucepan over low heat and cook, stirring occasionally, for about 5 minutes, or until slightly brown. Add the carrot, onion, celery, and leek and cook, stirring frequently, for about 3 minutes, or until the vegetables have just begun to sweat their liquid. Add the chicken stock, thyme, and bay leaf along with the beans. Raise the heat and bring to a simmer.

Lower the heat, season with salt and pepper to taste, and cook at a simmer for about 1½ hours, or until the beans are soft.

Remove from the heat. Remove and discard the carrot, onion, celery, leek, thyme, and bay leaf. If not serving immediately, transfer to a clean container, cover, and refrigerate until ready to use.

When ready to use, transfer the beans to a fine sieve and drain well, discarding most of the liquid. You want to keep just enough liquid to moisten the beans. If necessary, reheat before serving.

LEMON CONFIT

4 lemons, preferably organic, well washed

½ cup coarse salt

¼ cup sugar

5 shallots, peeled

1 head garlic, divided into cloves and peeled

2 cups olive oil

Bring a medium saucepan of water to a boil over high heat. Add the lemons and blanch for 30 seconds. Drain well and refresh under cold running water.

Using a chef's knife, cut the lemons crosswise into very thin (about ¹⁄₁₆-inch-thick) slices. Remove and discard the seeds and set the slices aside.

Combine the salt and sugar in a small bowl and set aside.

Combine the shallots and garlic and either chop together in the small bowl of a food processor fitted with the metal blade or coarsely chop by hand.

Place a single layer of lemon slices in the bottom of a small glass baking dish, sprinkle with some of the salt-sugar mixture and then with some of the shallot-garlic mixture. Continue layering until all of the ingredients have been used. Cover with plastic film and refrigerate for about 8 hours or overnight.

Remove the lemon mixture from the refrigerator, uncover, and pour the olive oil over the top. Again, cover with plastic film and refrigerate for 2 days before using. Confit will keep, covered and refrigerated, for 1 week.

RUM AND PEPPER–PAINTED FISH
WITH A MANGO–SCOTCH BONNET MOJO
1993

NORMAN VAN AKEN, *Chef/Owner, Norman's, Cookbook Author*

Norman Van Aken is the leading advocate for using Caribbean flavors and spices to high-light the natural goodness of the foods of the American South, particularly the fish of Florida's warm waters. When I first met Norman, he was a very young chef who had been working in Key West and had just written a cookbook titled *Feast Made of Sunlight*. He was planning to take a job in South Beach, but the next thing I knew he had begun to create a Van Aken empire throughout the state. In this recipe we see his style of cooking at its best—a zesty, aromatic "paint" for a smooth-tasting Gulf grouper accented with a sweet-hot Latin mojo or sauce. The flavor of the "paint" is quite intense, but when combined with the succulent fish, it mellows to perfection.

Rum and Pepper Paint (recipe follows)

Six 8-ounce skinless, boneless black grouper filets

2 tablespoons peanut oil

Mango–Scotch Bonnet Mojo (recipe follows)

Lime wedges for garnish

Preheat the oven to 400°F.

Using the Rum and Pepper Paint, generously coat one side of each piece of fish.

Place a heavy-bottomed, ovenproof frying pan over high heat. When very hot but not smoking, add the peanut oil. When the oil is hot, carefully lay the fish in the pan, painted side down, gently shaking the pan to keep the fish from sticking. When the fish is quite dark, flip (or carefully turn) it, pour off any excess oil from the pan, and transfer the pan to the preheated oven.

Bake the fish for about 9 minutes, or until just barely cooked through.

Place the mojo in a small nonreactive saucepan over medium heat and cook for a couple of minutes, or just until warm.

Ladle equal portions of the mojo into the center of each of six dinner plates. Place a piece of fish on top of the sauce in each plate. Serve immediately with lime wedges on the side.

Serves 6

RUM AND PEPPER PAINT

12 whole cloves

2½ tablespoons black peppercorns

¾ cup soy sauce

¾ cup light rum

½ cup sugar

2½ tablespoons freshly grated lemon zest

2 tablespoons fresh lemon juice

Combine the cloves and peppercorns in a small frying pan over medium-high heat and toast, stirring occasionally, for about 5 minutes, or until puffs of smoke appear. Remove from the heat and transfer to a spice grinder. Grind to a fine powder.

Combine the clove-peppercorn powder with the soy sauce, rum, sugar, lemon zest, and juice in a small, heavy saucepan over medium heat. Cook, stirring occasionally, for about 12 minutes, or until reduced by half. The mixture will begin to foam as it reduces, so watch carefully to keep it from boiling over. (It is important to take care when reducing because if the sauce reduces too much, the sugar will caramelize and taste burned, but it must reduce enough to be syrupy when cool.)

Remove from the heat and allow to cool before painting the fish.

MANGO–SCOTCH BONNET MOJO

2 very ripe juicy mangoes

1 Scotch bonnet chili, stemmed, seeded, and minced, plus more to taste

Juice of 1 lime

3 tablespoons chardonnay

Coarse salt to taste

Peel the mangoes and carefully cut the flesh away from the pits. Combine the flesh with the chili, lime juice, and wine in the bowl of a food processor fitted with the metal blade. Process to a smooth purée. Season with salt to taste; taste and, if desired, add more heat with additional chilies.

Transfer the sauce to a nonreactive container, cover, and refrigerate until ready to use or up to 24 hours. (If kept longer, the flavors will intensify but the color will fade and be drab and unappealing.)

133

Mojos, or citrus-juice based Caribbean sauces, became the pestos of the late nineties, enhancing many different cuisines. The citrus juice base can be infused with fresh herbs, garlic, spices, and salt and accented with bits of fruit. Oil may or may not be added. Traditionally, mojos are used as an accompaniment to grilled meats or fish, or as marinades, dipping sauces, or salad dressings.

SALMON WITH OLIVE OIL–MASHED POTATOES
AND SAUCE NIÇOISE
1995

TRACI DES JARDINS, *Chef/Owner, Jardinière, Mijita*

Traci Des Jardins first visited De Gustibus as sous chef to Joachim Splichal. It was apparent to all of us that she was very talented and would go far. And, then, voila! She became one of the very few female chefs to gain national recognition in the competitive San Francisco restaurant scene at Rubicon, the star-studded restaurant owned by Drew Nieporent, Robert De Niro, and Robin Williams (among others). California cuisine was her forte—great local products, simply prepared, with just a hint of classic French technique.

In this recipe Traci used the very common and healthful salmon but created a beautiful and exciting dish with French accents. Olive Oil–Mashed Potatoes were another take on the clean, fresh, California approach to dining.

Six 6-ounce skin-on salmon filets

Coarse salt and freshly ground pepper to taste

Olive Oil–Mashed Potatoes (recipe follows)

Sauce Niçoise (recipe follows)

Preheat and oil the grill.

Season the salmon with salt and pepper to taste. Place, skin side down, on the preheated grill and grill, turning once, for about 6 minutes, or until the skin is crisp and the fish is cooked to medium-rare.

Spoon equal portions of the potatoes in the center of each of six dinner plates. Place a piece of salmon on top of the potatoes on each plate and spoon some sauce around the potatoes. Serve immediately.

Serves 6

OLIVE OIL–MASHED POTATOES

6 russet potatoes, peeled and cut into chunks

½ cup extra-virgin olive oil, plus more to taste

Coarse salt and freshly ground pepper to taste

3 tablespoons chopped fresh flat-leaf parsley

Place the potatoes in a medium saucepan with enough cold, salted water to cover by 1 inch. Bring to a boil over high heat, lower the heat, and simmer for about 12 minutes, or until tender but not mushy. Remove from the heat and drain well.

Transfer the potatoes to the bowl of an electric mixer fitted with the paddle attachment. Add the olive oil, season with salt and pepper to taste, and beat at medium speed until fairly smooth. The potatoes may be prepared up to this point a few hours before serving. When ready to serve, put the potatoes in a baking dish, cover, and reheat in a preheated 400°F oven for about 10 minutes, or until hot.

Before serving, beat in a little additional olive oil to moisten. Taste and, if necessary, season with additional salt and pepper. Fold in the parsley and serve very hot.

SAUCE NIÇOISE

8 cloves garlic, peeled

1 tablespoon extra-virgin olive oil

6 Roma tomatoes, blanched, peeled, cored, seeded, and finely diced

Coarse salt to taste

12 fava beans, shucked, blanched, and peeled

4 sun-dried tomatoes, chopped

¼ cup pitted, roughly chopped niçoise olives

4 scallions, white parts only, cleaned, washed, and thinly sliced crosswise

1 bunch basil, leaves only, well washed, dried, and chopped

Balsamic vinegar to taste

Place the garlic in a small saucepan of boiling water and blanch for 30 seconds. Drain well. Again place the garlic in fresh boiling water and blanch for 30 seconds. Drain well and repeat the blanching once more using fresh boiling water. Rinse the garlic under cold running water and pat dry. Using a small, sharp knife, cut the garlic lengthwise into thin slices and set aside.

Heat the olive oil in a medium sauté pan over low heat. Add the tomatoes and just enough salt (a little less than ¼ teaspoon) to allow the tomatoes to begin releasing their juices, remembering that the sun-dried tomatoes and the olives will add saltiness.

When the tomatoes have released their liquid, stir in the sliced garlic along with the fava beans, sun-dried tomatoes, and olives. Cook for about 3 minutes, or until the flavors have blended somewhat and the mixture is hot. Keep warm until ready to serve.

Before serving, stir in the scallions and basil and add just a splash of balsamic vinegar to brighten the taste.

136

PANNA COTTA
1992

NANCY SILVERTON, *Pastry Chef, Campanile*

When I met Nancy Silverton, she was the pastry chef at the wildly popular but now defunct Maxwell's Plum in New York City. Moving to California was definitely in her plans, as was a goal of making traditional Italian breads in American ovens. Not only did she accomplish her goals, she helped revolutionize breadmaking in America with her LaBrea breads, now being baked daily in supermarket kitchens across the country.

Nancy made *panna cotta* the crème brûlée of its day. When she first introduced it to the De Gustibus classroom, absolutely no one had ever heard of this very simple, traditional Italian dessert, which translated simply means "cooked cream." Within a couple of years, it was on menus all over the country, with flavorings never imagined in rural Italy. To quote Nancy, "it tastes a bit like the custard of a crème brûlée, but since it has no egg yolks, it has a clean finish and is better for you!" *Panna cotta* must be made the day it is to be served or its texture will be too gelatinous.

---

1 tablespoon vegetable oil

1 scant tablespoon (1 envelope) granulated unflavored gelatin

3 tablespoons water

3 cups heavy cream

1 cup milk

¼ cup sugar

1 vanilla bean, split

Fresh berries, sliced stone fruit, or caramel or chocolate sauce for garnish (optional)

Using the vegetable oil and your fingertips, lightly coat the interior of each of six 6-ounce ramekins.

Place the gelatin in the water in a large stainless-steel bowl set over a pan of barely simmering water. Do not allow the bottom of the bowl to touch the simmering water. Stirring occasionally, allow the gelatin to melt completely.

Combine the cream, milk, and sugar in a large heavy-bottomed saucepan over medium heat (it must be large enough for the mixture to come to a boil without boiling over the edges). Using a small sharp knife, scrape the seeds from the vanilla bean into the cream, then add the scraped pod. Stirring occasionally, bring the mixture to a boil. Boil for exactly 1 minute.

Remove the cream mixture from the heat and, whisking constantly, slowly pour it over the melted gelatin, mixing until well blended. Strain the mixture through a fine sieve into a clean container.

Carefully pour equal portions of the cream into each of the oiled ramekins. Cover lightly with plastic film and refrigerate for 2 to 3 hours, or until set and well chilled. Do no allow to chill for more than a few hours or the texture will change.

When ready to serve, working with one ramekin at a time, place the ramekin in hot water for a few seconds and then invert it onto a serving plate.

Serve chilled, garnished with fresh berries, thinly sliced stone fruits, and a tablespoon of warm caramel or chocolate sauce if desired.

Serves 6

137

FOCACCIA
1993

AMY SCHERBER, *Owner/Baker, Amy's Bread, Cookbook Author*

The bread-baking revolution hit big-time in the nineties and Amy Scherber was at its forefront. From her shops, Amy's Bread, came marvelous loaves of rustic breads, muffins, rolls, and sweets. She became quite well-known for her much-imitated fennel-scented raisin semolina bread and her great focaccia. We were lucky enough to get the recipe for this wonderfully chewy snack bread, which can be topped with almost anything that you would use on a pizza. By the end of the nineties, through the influence of bakers like Amy Scherber, even supermarkets began to feature artisanal-style breads. And focaccia seemed to become the bagel of the twenty-first century!

2½ cups lukewarm (105–115°F) water

½ teaspoon dry yeast or 1 teaspoon fresh yeast

2 cups (or 14 ounces) Sponge Starter (recipe follows)

6 cups (2 pounds) high-gluten flour or bread flour

2 scant tablespoons coarse salt

3 tablespoons olive oil, plus more for oiling the bowl and pans

3 tablespoons milk

For topping: sliced tomatoes; fresh basil leaves; diced, sweated onions; pitted black olives

Basil Oil (recipe follows)

Combine the water and yeast in a large mixing bowl, whisking to dissolve the yeast. Let stand for 3 minutes.

Add the starter and, using your fingers, break the mixture up. Mix until slightly foamy.

Add the flour and begin mixing, lifting the wet mixture up and over the flour to incorporate. When the mixture forms a rough mass, begin to knead the dough in the bowl with your hands for about 5 minutes, or until it is smooth and somewhat elastic. Set aside to rest for 15 minutes.

Add the salt and briefly knead it into the dough. Slowly add the olive oil and milk, gently kneading into the dough. When incorporated, transfer the dough to a clean, flat work surface and knead for about 12 minutes or until very silky and elastic.

Lightly oil a large, clean bowl and transfer the dough to the bowl. Cover with plastic film and either refrigerate overnight or set in a warm, dry spot and allow to rise for about 2½ hours, or until doubled in bulk.

Using a pastry brush, lightly coat the interior of two 8-inch-square baking pans with olive oil.

Remove the risen dough from the bowl and cut it in half. Place one piece in the center of each of the prepared pans and, using your fingertips, gently press on the dough to stretch it to the edges of the pans, taking care not to tear the dough. Let the dough relax enough to stretch it fully and evenly to the edges of the pans.

Cover the dough with plastic film and set aside in a warm, dry spot to rise for 1½ hours, or until the dough looks light and airy and fills the pan.

Preheat the oven to 425°F.

Gently arrange whatever toppings you have selected in a decorative or symmetrical pattern on top of the dough in each pan, taking care not to deflate the dough.

Using a pastry brush, lightly coat the top of both the dough and the toppings with Basil Oil.

Using your fingertips, create a few dimples in the dough. Do not make too many or the dough will deflate.

Sprinkle the tops of the loaves with salt.

Place the pans in the preheated oven and bake for 3 minutes, misting with cool water three times during this brief baking period. Bake for 20 more minutes.

Reduce the oven temperature to 350°F and continue to bake for about 10 minutes, or until the bread is golden brown and crusty on the exterior but still soft and chewy on the interior.

Remove the loaves from the oven and, using a pastry brush, again lightly coat with Basil Oil.

Allow the loaves to cool in the pans for 10 minutes; then remove from the pans to prevent steaming. Serve while still warm.

Makes 2 loaves

SPONGE STARTER

1½ cups very warm (105–115°F) water

¼ teaspoon active dry yeast

3½ cups all-purpose flour

Combine the water and yeast in a medium mixing bowl. Stir in the flour, beating for about 3 minutes with a wooden spoon, or until a smooth, somewhat elastic batter has formed. (The batter will be very stiff but will get softer and more elastic after it rests.)

Cover the bowl with plastic film and set aside to rest.

You may do one of the two following things, depending upon your time frame. No matter which you choose, it is a good idea to have all of your ingredients measured and ready to go before you begin to make your focaccia.

If using the sponge later in the day, let it rest in a warm, dry spot until it has risen to the point where it begins to collapse in on itself, usually about 8 hours. It will triple in volume and small dents and folds will begin to appear in the top of the sponge as it reaches its peak and begins to deflate. You can now measure out the amount you will need for your dough and proceed with the recipe.

If you are not going to make the focaccia for a day or two, place the covered sponge in the refrigerator to rise for at least 14 hours. Remove the sponge from the refrigerator and either let it come to room temperature (which can take a couple of hours) or use it immediately, taking care that the warm water in the recipe is at 115°F. If you allow the sponge to come to room temperature, watch it carefully so that it does not collapse to more than ¾ of its size, because if it breaks down, it will not be able to do its job properly.

BASIL OIL

1 large bunch fresh basil, leaves only, well washed and dried

Coarse salt to taste

¾ cup extra-virgin olive oil

Place the basil leaves in a pot of boiling water and blanch for 30 seconds. Immediately remove from the heat, drain well, and place in an ice-water bath to stop the cooking.

Drain the cooled basil leaves and squeeze out all excess moisture.

Place the basil leaves in the bowl of a food processor fitted with the metal blade and add salt to taste (the oil should not taste salty).

With the motor running, slowly add the olive oil, processing until very smooth.

Pour the oil into a nonreactive container and immediately cover the surface with plastic film to keep it from darkening.

The oil will separate as it sits. You can either stir the oil to reincorporate the solids or use the oil that rises to the top as a drizzle and the solids as a garnish for focaccia, pasta, or whatever you like.

Over the years, as chefs became more inventive, we witnessed the creation of many different types of flavored or **infused oils**. Of all of these, basil oil seemed to be the favorite with our students. It was used for breads, pastas, roasting vegetables and fish, dipping, marinating, garnishing, and on and on. David Bouley told us to add a bit of vitamin C to keep the brilliant green color from fading. He simply added a small piece of a crushed vitamin C tablet into his and it worked.

FIG AND PROSCIUTTO PIZZA
1994

TODD ENGLISH, *Chef, The Olives Group, Entrepreneur, Cookbook Author*

When Todd English first came to De Gustibus, he was a one-restaurant guy, plying his trade in Boston. And not only was he a one-restaurant guy, he was a totally solo act. For this class Todd drove himself down from Boston with all of his food packed in the trunk and his dog in the backseat. The food came upstairs while the dog spent the day in the car, with frequent walking and watering visits from the De Gustibus team. Todd prepared a fantastic six-course meal from scratch with no assistants. Now his empire stretches all over the world—particularly his quick-food shops in airports. His Fig and Prosciutto Pizza had customers lining up for hours at his no-reservation restaurant, Olives, and it remains widely popular through its renditions in bistros and cafés worldwide. Todd truly is a chef who catches the pulse of the dining public, and he is much imitated.

1½ cups dry red wine

1 cup balsamic vinegar

⅔ cup sugar

1 cup roughly chopped dried figs

3 branches fresh rosemary, needles only

Pizza Dough (recipe follows)

Approximately 3 tablespoons extra-virgin olive oil, or to taste

6 ounces (about ½ cup) Gorgonzola cheese

4 to 5 slices prosciutto

Place the red wine in a small nonreactive saucepan over medium-high heat and cook, stirring occasionally, for about 20 minutes, or until reduced by half. Add the balsamic vinegar and continue to cook for an additional 20 minutes, or until again reduced by half.

Lower the heat and stir in the sugar. Cook for 5 minutes, then add the figs and half the rosemary. Cook for about 15 minutes, or until the figs have plumped and the liquid is thick and tacky. Remove from the heat and set aside to cool.

Preheat the oven to 450°F.

Place the dough on a clean, lightly floured work surface and, using a rolling pin, roll the dough out to the desired shape (it can be round, rectangular, or free-form). Using your fingertips, crimp the edges by folding small pinches of dough from the outside toward the center. Transfer the dough to a peel, pizza pan, or baking stone.

Drizzle the olive oil over the dough and sprinkle with the remaining rosemary. Using a spatula, carefully spread the cooled fig jam over the top in a thin, even layer. Sprinkle the jam with the Gorgonzola, then transfer the pizza to the preheated oven. Bake for 15 minutes, or until the bottom and edges are nicely browned and the cheese has melted.

Remove from the oven and place the prosciutto slices over the top. Cut into serving pieces and serve immediately.

Makes 1 pizza to serve 6

142

PIZZA DOUGH

½ cup lukewarm (105–115°F) water

½ tablespoon honey

½ tablespoon active dry yeast

2 tablespoons olive oil, plus more to oil the bowl

2 cups all-purpose flour, plus more to flour the work surface

½ teaspoon coarse salt

½ cup (1 stick) unsalted butter, at room temperature

Combine the water, honey, and yeast in a large mixing bowl. Let stand for 5 minutes.

Stir in the olive oil, then the flour and salt and begin kneading (this can be done in an electric mixer fitted with the dough hook, if desired). Knead for about 8 minutes, or until a soft, smooth dough has formed.

Lightly oil a clean, large bowl. Transfer the dough to the oiled bowl, cover with a clean kitchen towel, and set aside in a warm, dry spot to rise for 1 hour, or until doubled in bulk.

Lightly flour a clean, flat work surface. Transfer the risen dough to the floured surface. Pressing down with your hands, form the dough into a 10 × 6-inch rectangle of even thickness.

Spread the butter on half of the rectangle, smoothing it out to make an even layer. Fold the other half of the dough up and over the buttered half, forming a rectangle 5 × 6 inches. Using a rolling pin, smooth the dough out to the original 10 × 6-inch size. Again, fold in half and roll out to its original size. Repeat this process two more times.

Cover the dough with plastic film and refrigerate for 1 hour, or until ready to bake.

Makes one large pizza or six individual pizzas.

143

DOUBLE CHOCOLATE BISCOTTI
1993

EMILY LUCHETTI, *Pastry Chef, Farallon, Cookbook Author*

I have watched with admiration as Emily Luchetti has gone from pastry chef at San Francisco's famous Jeremiah Tower-owned Stars to world-renowned cookbook author, teacher, and pastry chef at Farallon, one of San Francisco's best restaurants.

I don't know if Emily was the first young American pastry chef to make biscotti, but she certainly put her mark on them. In just a few short years, biscotti, the crunchy, slightly sweet Italian biscuit often served with strong coffee or dessert wine, have been transformed from the unknown into the ubiquitous cookie packaged for mass consumption.

2$\frac{2}{3}$ cups all-purpose flour, plus more to flour the work surface

1 cup cocoa powder

2 cups sugar

1$\frac{1}{2}$ tablespoons finely ground espresso beans

1$\frac{1}{2}$ teaspoons baking soda

$\frac{1}{4}$ teaspoon salt

$\frac{1}{4}$ pound bittersweet chocolate, coarsely chopped

2 cups toasted, skinned hazelnuts

5 large eggs, at room temperature

1$\frac{1}{2}$ teaspoons pure vanilla extract

1 pound fine-quality white chocolate, tempered (see sidebar page 99)

Preheat the oven to 325°F.

Combine the flour and cocoa in the bowl of a heavy-duty electric mixer fitted with the paddle attachment; stir to blend. Add the sugar, ground espresso, baking soda, and salt.

Place the chocolate in the bowl of a food processor fitted with the metal blade. Add 1 cup of the dry-ingredient mix and process until the chocolate is very finely ground. Transfer the chocolate mixture along with the hazelnuts to the dry ingredients in the mixer bowl and stir to combine.

Place the eggs and vanilla in a small bowl; whisk to combine.

With the motor running on low, slowly add the egg mixture to the dry ingredients, mixing just until the dough comes together.

Lightly flour a clean, flat work surface and transfer the dough to it. Divide the dough into thirds and form each piece into a log shape. Place the logs on a baking sheet in the preheated oven and bake for about 30 minutes or until the outsides are firm and the tops cracked.

Remove the logs from the oven and lower the oven temperature to 300°F. Working with one log at a time, cut each log crosswise into $\frac{1}{4}$-inch-thick slices. Place the slices, cut side up, on a clean baking sheet, leaving about $\frac{1}{2}$ inch between each slice.

Place the slices back in the oven and bake for about 15 minutes, or until they are firm and dry. Remove from the oven and transfer to wire racks to cool.

Line a baking sheet with parchment or waxed paper.

While the biscotti are cooling, place the white chocolate in the top half of a double boiler set over simmering water. Heat, stirring frequently, until the chocolate has melted. Using a spatula, spread a light coating of white chocolate on the cut side of each biscotti.

Transfer the biscotti, white chocolate side down, to the parchment-lined baking sheet. Allow to rest until the chocolate has hardened. Remove the biscotti from the parchment and store, tightly covered, for up to one week.

Makes 4 dozen

1996 to 2000

The Evolution of Cooking in America

In 1998 a consumer research study on book purchasing reported that 10 percent of all adult books purchased were cookbooks. This was but one indication of how far American cooking had come in the past fifteen years. People were watching television food shows as entertainment and, in part at least, this translated to the growth of the cookbook industry, as every television personality had a book or two to promote and every chef and restaurateur produced a book to celebrate his spot.

The arrival of the famous and much-esteemed chef Alain Ducasse to the New York restaurant scene surely indicated that the American culinary stage had reached international stature. With the opening of his ultra-expensive, and what some thought to be pretentious, restaurant, Chef Ducasse told the world that Americans now understood fine dining. The fact that the restaurant took some hard knocks from the critics but righted itself and survived proved him to be right.

Many of the trends that we had observed for the past fifteen years had taken hold and had become an integral part of both American restaurants and home kitchens. Artisanal foods—those once simply known as homegrown—were to be found on supermarket shelves. Myriad unique olive oils and vinegars were widely available and were even being produced in small batches at home. The sushi revolution had taken over the country, and fresh-caught fish taken from international waters were on menus everywhere. Sophisticated diners welcomed raw fish on menus, and items like tartare or carpaccio became ubiquitous.

The food pyramid, as devised by the United States Department of Agriculture, was a topic of great discussion. In essence, it said nothing more than what we had heard many of our great chefs say for years: lots of natural grains, vegetables, and fruits with meat and fish as accents. It was interesting to note during this period that the caricature of the corpulent chef disappeared, as young, attractive cooks, who ate thoughtfully and exercised with the same passion with which they cooked, were becoming stars of stage and screen.

Perhaps the most far-reaching culinary trend that we had seen in some time made its appearance during this period. Suddenly, out of nowhere it seemed, every chef was "foaming." This was a technique devised by Ferran Adrià in Spain that quickly caught the attention of every imaginative cook. It was simply a method of placing a liquid ingredient into a pressurized canister to create a light, airy foam. In the De Gustibus classroom, the gas-charged canister was the tool of choice.

The rise in the consumption of wines was phenomenal. American wines had, in particular, made enormous strides in popularity in this country. And, unbelievably, some of these wines were beating their European counterparts in taste tests. As fine dining establishments saw their wine sales soar, family-dining chain restaurants were offering wines by the glass. The American wine industry was now a very strong international player. The wines that we served in the De Gustibus classroom were a special mix of both old- and new-world vintages, as our clients became more aware of the possibilities of pairing wine and food.

Preceding pages (clockwise from top left):
Jimmy Bradley; Claudia Fleming; Jeffrey Nathan; Karen and Ben Barker; Rocco DiSpirito; Susan Regis and Lydia Shire; Jean-Georges Vongerichten; Lidia Bastianich; Edward Brown; Arun Sampanthavivat; Melissa Kelly; Laurent Gras.
Right: *Nobu Matsuhisa.*

1996–2000

Jody Adams
Joan Adler
Hossein Aimani
Colman Andrews
Francesco Antonucci
Ben Barker
Karen Barker
Teresa Barrenechea
Paul Bartolotta
Lidia Bastianich
Mario Batali
Stefano Battistini
Marc Bauer
Rick Bayless
Andrew Bell
Rose Levy Beranbaum
Jean-Michel Bergougnoux
Philippe Bertineau
Jack Bishop
Mark Bittman
Erik Blauberg
Jim Botsacos
David Bouley
Daniel Boulud
Antoine Bouterin
Jimmy Bradley
Flo Braker
Georgeanne Brennan
Terrance Brennan
Edward Brown
Laurie Glenn Buckle
Giuliano Bugialli
Cathleen Burke
David Burke
Marian Burros
Yannick Cam
Scott Campbell
Floyd Cardoz
Jon Carloftis
Antonio Carluccio
Andrew Carmellini
Penelope Casas
Cesare Casella
Kimberly Charles

Sarah Leah Chase
James Chew
Julia Child
Judith Choate
Patrick Clark
Thomas Colicchio
Jeffrey Crawford
Ariane Daguin
Charles Dale
Gary Danko
Gerry Dawes
Dale DeGroff
Franck Deletrain
Paul Del Favero
Christian Delouvrier
Marcel Desaulniers
Traci Des Jardins
Rocco DiSpirito
Jane Doerfer
Roberto Donna
Alain Ducasse
Gillian Duffy
Wylie Dufresne
Toy Kim Dupree
Troy Dupuy
Jonathan Eismann
Todd English
Odette Fada
George Faison
Frank Falcinelli
Markus Färbinger
Bruno Feldeisen
Susan Feniger
Bobby Flay
Claudia Fleming
Susanna Foo
Larry Forgione
Diane Forley
Dominique Frérard
Gale Gand
Ina Garten
Jean-Louis Gerin
George Germon
Elka Gilmore

Michael Ginor
Alessandro Giuntoli
Rozanne Gold
Joyce Goldstein
Brian Goode
Laurent Gras
Dorie Greenspan
Joni Greenspan
Vincent Guerithault
Gordon Hamersley
Lee Hanson
Reed Hearon
Kerry Heffernan
Pierre Hermé
Amanda Hesser
Jason Hinds
Peter Hoffman
Chris Hollis
Josefina Howard
Johnny Iuzzini
Madhur Jaffrey
Steve Jenkins
Daniel Johnnes
Barbara Kafka
Stephen Kalt
John Kapon
Lynne Rossetto Kasper
Mollie Katzen
Hubert Keller
Thomas Keller
Melissa Kelly
Diana Kennedy
Matthew Kenney
Graham Kerr
Johanne Killeen
Sarah Belk King
Robert Kinkead
Abigail Kirsch
Lévana Kirschenbaum
Larry Kolar
Gray Kunz
Jean-Marie Lacroix
Emeril Lagasse
James Lahey

Lidia Bastianich
Mario Batali
Terrance Brennan
Floyd Cardoz

Rocco DiSpirito
Claudia Fleming
Laurent Gras
Melissa Kelly

Deborah Madison
Nobu Matsuhisa
Tadashi Ono
Arun Sampanthavivat

Marcus Samuelsson
Alessandro Stratta
Laurent Tourondel

Normand Laprise	Alison Nathan	Arun Sampanthavivat
Richard Leach	Jeffrey Nathan	Marcus Samuelsson
Alex Lee	Joan Nathan	Pierre Schaedelin
Jeanne Lemlin	Wayne Nish	John Scharffenberger
Dan Lenchner	Patrick Nuti	Doris Schecter
James Lenzi	Patrick O'Connell	John Schenk
Remi Leuvand	Robin Kelley O'Conner	Amy Scherber
Steve Levy	Nancy Oakes	Chris Schlesinger
Michael Lomonaco	Molly O'Neill	Sally Schneider
William Lopata	Tadashi Ono	Dieter Schorner
Emily Luchetti	Daniel Orr	Charles Scicolone
Sheila Lukins	Michael Otsuka	Michele Scicolone
Pino Luongo	David Page	Vincent Scotto
Egidiana Maccioni	Jean-Louis Palladin	Jamie Shannon
Deborah Madison	Charles Palmer	Diana Shaw
Donata Maggipinto	Jonathan Parker	Craig Shelton
Waldy Malouf	François Payard	Mimi Sheraton
Laurent Manrique	Carole Peck	Barbara Shinn
Noel Mantel	Jacques Pépin	Lydia Shire
Gil Marks	Georges Perrier	Nancy Silverton
Jeremy Marshall	Colette Peters	Nina Simonds
Lydie Marshall	James Peterson	Christopher Siversen
Zarela Martinez	Don Pintabona	Jimmy Sneed
Nobu Matsuhisa	Fred Plotkin	André Soltner
Kazuto Matsusaka	Debra Ponzek	Katy Sparks
Vicki Fan Matsusaka	Alfred Portale	Susan Spicer
Daniel Mattrocce	Nora Pouillon	Susan Spungen
Max Mc Calman	Marta Pulini	Alessandro Stratta
Robert McGrath	Anna Pump	Mark Strausman
Alice Medrich	Susan Purdy	Michel Stroot
Michael Meehan	Steven Raichlen	Allen Susser
Perla Meyers	Susan Regis	Alan Tardi
Carlo Middione	Cyril Renaud	Bill Telepan
Flora Mikula	Leslie Revsin	Jacques Torres
Bryan Miller	Michel Richard	Laurent Tourondel
Mark Militello	Eric Ripert	Claude Troisgros
Mary Sue Milliken	Gary Robins	Charlie Trotter
Michael Mina	Douglas Rodriguez	Ming Tsai
Rick Moonen	Ruth Rogers	Thomas Valenti
Pamela Morgan	Michael Romano	Norman Van Aken
Eberhard Müller	Anne Rosenzweig	Hoc Van Tran
Marc Murphy	David Ruggerio	Massimo Vidoni
Helen Nash	Alain Sailhac	John Villa
Riad Nasr	Reine Sammut	Jean-Georges Vongerichten

Brendan Walsh
David Waltuck
Alice Waters
Bill Wavrin
Susan Weaver
Eileen Weinberg

Sylvia Weinstock
Patricia Wells
Joshua Wesson
Jasper White
Anne Willan
Christian Willer

Faith Heller Willinger
Paula Wolfert
Roy Yamaguchi
Martin Yan
Eileen Yin-Fei Lo
Geoffrey Zakarian

RICHEST
DISH IN THE HISTORY OF DE GUSTIBUS

LOBSTER IN GARLIC BUTTER WITH BÉARNAISE SAUCE, *Albert Roux, Le Gavroche, London*

EQUIPMENT THAT BECAME MORE MAINSTREAM

Benriner slicer • Blow torch • Espresso machines with and without cartridges • Foamer • Food processor • Japanese knives • Mandoline • Microplane® • Paco Jet • Silicone pans • Silpat sheets • Specialty lines of cookware • Truffle slicer • Vita-Mix blender • Wasabi grater

25 YEARS OF

SEASONAL TRENDS
WE HAVE SEEN AT DE GUSTIBUS

A SEASON OF CONFIT

A SEASON OF CRÈME BRÛLÉE

A SEASON OF FISH TARTARES

A SEASON OF GNOCCHI

A SEASON OF MICROSPROUTS

A SEASON OF MOLTEN CHOCOLATE CAKE

MANY SEASONS OF PANNA COTTA

A SEASON OF PINEAPPLE UPSIDE-DOWN CAKE

A SEASON OF RISOTTO

A SEASON OF SALMON

A SEASON OF SKATE

A SEASON OF SHORT RIBS

A SEASON OF VITA-MIXING

BEST COUPLES

Jeffrey Alford and Naomi Duguid

Claudia Fleming and Gerry Hayden

Diane Forley and Michael Otsuka

Melissa Kelly and Price Kushner

Johanne Killeen and George Germon

Marco Moreira and Jo-Ann Makovitsky

Michele and Charles Scicolone

Nancy Silverton and Mark Peel

Superlatives

1980 to 2005

TRAVELED THE LONGEST DISTANCE TO THE DE GUSTIBUS KITCHEN

ELIZABETH ANDOH, *from Japan*

MOST AFFECTIONATE CHEF

GASTON LENÔTRE— *he loved to embrace all the women.*

GREAT WINES WE HAVE TASTED

For the past twenty-five years, I have worked with two fine wine companies, but for the last twenty years, I've been in partnership with the Kobrand Corporation, and it is their wines that we most remember at De Gustibus. Below are some of our favorite "go with food" wines that would probably pair well with most of the recipes we have gathered for this book:

Sparkling wine: Taittinger le Français, Le Rêve and
    Domaine Carneros
Cakebread Family Wines
Michele Redde Pouilly Fumé
All Louis Jadot Wines
All Michele Chiarlo Wines
St. Francis Old Vines Zinfandel
Sequoia Grove Chardonnay and Cabernet
Craggy Range New Zealand Wines and Mt. Redon
    Chateauneuf-de-Pape, blanc and rouge

MOST OUTRAGEOUS CHEFS

MARIO BATALI *in shorts and orange clogs (now red high-top sneakers); and* PATRICK O'CONNELL *and his whole team in their dalmation-print pants*

MOST EXTRAVAGANT TABLE SETTING

FRANCINE SCHERER *from Soho Charcuterie*

ON THE MENU

APPETIZERS, SOUPS, AND SALADS

Herring Sushi with Black Mustard
Marcus Samuelsson—1999

Cauliflower Cream
with Cauliflower Tartar Sauce
Laurent Gras—1998

Taylor Bay Scallops with Uni and Mustard Oil
Rocco DiSpirito—1998

The World's Best Quiche
Marc Bauer—1997

Frico con Patate e Cipolle
(Cheese Wafers with Potato and Onion)
Lidia Bastianich—1999

Nori-Wrapped Salmon
Jeffrey Nathan—2000

Charcoaled Beef Salad
with Pomegranate, Potato Leaves,
and a Drizzle of Robiola di Mondovi
Lydia Shire—1998

SAUCES AND SIDES

Quick Sauté of Zucchini
with Toasted Almonds and Pecorino
Jimmy Bradley—2000

Yukon Gold Potato Foam
with Black Winter Truffles
Laurent Tourondel—2000

PASTA AND GRAINS

Curried Couscous Pilaf
Melissa Kelly—1998

Pumpkin Risotto with White Truffles
Alex Lee—1998

MEAT, GAME, AND POULTRY

Jamieson Farm Baby Lamb
with Artichokes and Cippolini
Alessandro Stratta—1997

Braciolone
(Braised Pork Roll)
Mario Batali—1999

Curry Leaf–Marinated Flank Steak
with Smashed Potatoes, Haricot Verts,
and Ginger-Horseradish Raita
Floyd Cardoz—2000

Green Curry Chicken
Arun Sampanthavivat—1998

FISH AND SHELLFISH

Nobu Black Cod with Miso
Nobu Matsuhisa—1996

Grilled Rouget
with White Bean *Brandade*
and Niçoise Vinaigrette
Terrance Brennan—1999

Slow-Roasted Salmon
with Wild Mushrooms and Foie Gras Emulsion
Edward Brown—2000

Fried Oysters on Creamy Winter Succotash
with Barbecue Vinaigrette
Ben Barker—2000

BREAD AND DESSERTS

Chilled Rhubarb Soup
Claudia Fleming—1999

HERRING SUSHI WITH BLACK MUSTARD
1999
MARCUS SAMUELSSON, *Chef/Owner, Aquavit, Riingo,*
Henry at World Yacht, Cookbook Author

Marcus Samuelsson has the marvelous ability to charm an audience with a combination of total sincerity and charisma. He burst onto the New York dining scene with recipes from Sweden, his adopted homeland. I believe that his cooking led diners in New York to take Scandinavian cooking seriously for the first time. After a while, Marcus began introducing elements from Africa, his birthplace. His skill at combining elements of two extremely different cuisines using traditional ingredients and techniques created a very exciting menu.

But in this recipe, sushi is his forte! This time Marcus took the pickled herring and potatoes of the Swedish table and created a new take on Japanese tradition—truly a new style of Scandinavian cooking!

---

2 cups (about ¾ pound) warm, cooked, peeled fingerling potato chunks

1 tablespoon mustard oil (see Note)

1 teaspoon rice wine vinegar

1 teaspoon Dijon mustard

½ teaspoon wasabi (see Note)

½ teaspoon coarse salt, or to taste

2 pickled herring filets

Black Mustard (recipe follows)

Place the potatoes in a mixing bowl and, using a fork, coarsely mash them. Add the mustard oil, rice wine vinegar, Dijon mustard, wasabi, and salt to taste. Stir to blend and set aside to cool.

Using a very sharp knife, cut each herring filet lengthwise into twelve ½-inch-wide strips.

Form the potato mixture into four 9-inch-long logs, about 1 inch in diameter.

Cut each potato log into six 1½-inch pieces. Place a herring strip on top of each potato piece and serve with a dollop of Black Mustard on top.

Serves 4

BLACK MUSTARD

2 tablespoons Swedish mustard (see Note)

1 tablespoon Chinese mustard (see Note)

½ tablespoon squid ink (see Note)

½ tablespoon white miso (see Note)

½ tablespoon black bean paste (see Note)

Combine the mustards with the squid ink, miso, and black bean paste in the small bowl of a food processor fitted with the metal blade and process until well blended.

Scrape from the bowl into a nonreactive container and cover until ready to use.

Note: Mustard oil is available from East Indian and Middle Eastern markets and some specialty food stores.

Wasabi, Chinese mustard, white miso, and black bean paste are available from Asian markets and some specialty food stores.

Swedish mustard is available from Scandinavian markets.

Squid ink is available from fine fishmongers.

157

CAULIFLOWER CREAM
WITH CAULIFLOWER TARTAR SAUCE
1998
LAURENT GRAS, *Chef*

My path first crossed that of Laurent Gras at the Hôtel de Paris in Monte Carlo and then again at Alain Ducasse in Paris. Having sampled his cooking, I was thrilled when I heard that he was to be the executive chef at Peacock Alley in the Waldorf-Astoria Hotel.

In this recipe Laurent showed us how a sauce could be vegetable-based rather than stock-, butter-, or egg-based, and still be absolutely delicious. Many other chefs would follow his lead and experiment with vegetables in a whole new way.

---

1 cup cauliflower florets, well washed

¾ cup milk

Fleur de sel to taste (see Note)

Cauliflower Tartar Sauce (recipe follows)

½ cup broccoli sprouts or other fresh sprouts

Place the cauliflower in a medium saucepan with enough cold, salted water to cover. Bring to a boil over medium-high heat. Boil for about 15 minutes, or until very soft. Drain well.

Combine the cauliflower and milk in an electric mixer fitted with the paddle attachment and beat until smooth. Season with *fleur de sel* to taste.

Pass the purée through a fine sieve into a clean container. Cover with plastic film and refrigerate until chilled.

When ready to serve, place ten martini glasses in the freezer.

When the glasses are chilled, spoon equal portions of the cauliflower cream into each one. Cover the surface of each with an even layer of Cauliflower Tartar Sauce. Sprinkle a few broccoli sprouts on top and serve.

Serves 10

CAULIFLOWER TARTAR SAUCE

1 cup cauliflower florets, well washed

¼ cup mayonnaise, preferably home-made

1 hard-cooked egg, white only, finely diced

½ cup finely diced cornichons (see Note)

2 tablespoons finely chopped fresh flat-leaf parsley

4 teaspoons finely chopped fresh chives

1 tablespoon capers, well drained

¾ teaspoon sherry wine vinegar

Tabasco to taste

Fleur de sel and freshly ground pepper to taste

Place the cauliflower in a medium saucepan with enough cold, salted water to cover. Bring to a boil over medium-high heat. Boil for about 8 minutes, or until crisp-tender. Drain well and immediately place in an ice-water bath to stop the cooking. Drain well and pat dry.

Coarsely chop the cauliflower and combine with the mayonnaise in a small mixing bowl. Fold in the cooked egg white, cornichons, parsley, chives, and capers. Add the vinegar and season to taste with Tabasco, salt, and pepper.

Cover and refrigerate until ready to serve.

Note: Fleur de sel and cornichons (tiny French sour pickles) are available from most specialty-food stores and some supermarkets. Fleur de sel may be replaced by any other fine-quality sea salt.

TAYLOR BAY SCALLOPS
WITH UNI AND MUSTARD OIL
1998

ROCCO DISPIRITO, *Chef, Cookbook Author*

Mario Batali introduced me to Rocco by saying, "He's the best—you must have him at De Gustibus!" I don't think either of us knew just how far Rocco would go; his was a meteoric rise up through the New York culinary scene.

In this recipe we see raw shellfish moving from the sushi bar to haute cuisine. To make it, you will need absolutely pristine scallops with their shells as well as a sparkling fresh sea urchin. Rocco accents the sweet, sparkling fresh scallops with East Indian spice and a hint of Asia. Rocco assures us that this recipe can easily be increased to create additional servings.

½ large overripe beefsteak tomato

¼ teaspoon mirin (see Note)

Cayenne to taste

Coarse sea salt and freshly ground pepper to taste

5 small Taylor Bay scallops, cleaned, with 5 half-shells scrubbed, rinsed, and reserved for serving

1 sea urchin (uni), cleaned (see Note)

1 teaspoon mustard oil (see Note)

Pinch freshly crushed black mustard seeds (see Note)

½ ounce *ogonori* (seaweed), well rinsed and free of salt (optional; see Note)

Place the tomato in a food processor fitted with the metal blade and process to a smooth purée. Transfer to a double piece of cheesecloth lining a fine sieve that has been placed over a bowl. Using kitchen twine, tie the cheesecloth into a bag, leaving the bag in the sieve to allow the liquid to drain overnight.

When all of the liquid has drained, pass the liquid through a coffee filter into a bowl to remove any remaining solid matter.

Season the tomato liquid with mirin, cayenne, sea salt, and pepper to taste.

Place a scallop and a small piece of sea urchin in each of the cleaned scallop shells. Pour a bit of tomato water over the scallop and sea urchin and drizzle a few drops of mustard oil over the top. Garnish with crushed black mustard seeds and serve.

If you want to do a restaurant-style presentation, make a bed of crushed ice on a serving plate. Cover the ice with the seaweed, then nestle the filled shells into the seaweed. Serve immediately.

Note: Mirin, a sweet, syrupy rice wine used only for cooking, is available from Asian markets, specialty food stores, and fine supermarkets.

Cultivated Taylor Bay scallops and sea urchin are available from fine fishmongers as well as through Browne Trading Company (see Sources, page 247).

Seaweed is available from fine fishmongers and Asian fish markets, or through Browne Trading Company (see Sources, page 247).

Mustard oil and black mustard seeds are available from East Indian markets and some specialty food stores.

Serves 1

THE WORLD'S BEST QUICHE

1997

MARC BAUER, *Chef/Instructor, The French Culinary Institute*

This is probably one of our most requested recipes. Marc Bauer, chef-instructor and master roundsman (the chef able to cover all stations in a restaurant-kitchen brigade) at New York City's French Culinary Institute has, over the years, become well-known at De Gustibus for his hands-on knife-skills classes. He always follows his demonstration with a traditional French recipe. This is one of our favorites, and I can assure you, real men *do* eat quiche! In the classic fashion, when making pastry, Marc weighs his ingredients for precision.

1 tablespoon vegetable oil

3 ounces slab bacon (or smoked ham, prosciutto, smoked turkey, or other smoked meat), trimmed of rind and thinly sliced

4 large eggs

10 ounces milk

10 ounces heavy cream

Coarse salt and freshly ground white pepper to taste

Freshly grated nutmeg to taste

2 baked shells Short Pastry Crust (recipe follows)

3 ounces grated Gruyère cheese

Preheat the oven to 350°F.

Heat the oil in a small sauté pan over medium heat. Add the bacon (or desired meat) and sauté for about 5 minutes, or until lightly brown but still soft.

Using a slotted spoon, transfer the meat to a double layer of paper towels to drain.

Combine the eggs with the milk and cream in a mixing bowl. Add salt, white pepper, and nutmeg to taste. Whisk to blend well.

Spread an equal portion of the drained bacon on the bottom of each baked shell. Sprinkle equal portions of grated cheese in each shell. Pour equal portions of the egg mixture into each shell.

Place the filled shells in the preheated oven and bake for about 45 minutes, or until the custard is set in the center and the top is golden.

Remove from the oven and place on wire racks to rest for 10 minutes before cutting into wedges and serving.

Makes two 9-inch quiches

SHORT PASTRY CRUST

10 ounces (2½ cups) all-purpose flour, plus more to flour the work surface

1 teaspoon coarse salt

1 large egg yolk

3 tablespoons cold water, plus more if needed

½ pound (2 sticks) unsalted butter, cut into small pieces and chilled

Sift the flour onto a clean work space into a mound. Make an indentation in the center of the flour. Add the salt, egg yolk, water, and butter, and using your fingertips, begin working the wet ingredients into the flour.

Using a pastry scraper, slowly begin pulling the remaining flour into the mixture. When the mixture just comes together, knead it no more than twice with the heel of your palm.

Bring the pastry together into a ball, wrap with plastic film, and refrigerate for about 30 minutes, or until the dough is firm and has lost its elasticity.

When ready to use, preheat the oven to 350°F and lightly flour a clean work surface. Remove the dough from the refrigerator and unwrap.

Divide the dough in half. Working with one half at a time and using a lightly floured rolling pin, roll each piece of dough out on the lightly floured surface into a circle about 11 inches in diameter and ¼ inch thick.

Place the dough circles in each of two 9-inch tart pans, pushing down to fit the dough into the pans. Using your fingertips, pinch the dough around the edges to make an even flute.

Line each dough-filled pan with parchment paper, then cover the bottoms with pastry weights or dried beans. Place in the preheated oven and bake for about 15 minutes, or until the pastry is set and has begun to color. Remove from the heat and let cool.

FRICO CON PATATE E CIPOLLE
(CHEESE WAFERS WITH POTATO AND ONION)
1999

LIDIA BASTIANICH, *Chef/Owner, Felidia, Becco, Lidia's Kansas City, Cookbook Author, Television Personality*

Lidia embodies the whole idea of Mother Earth. She is passionate about all things Italian, especially the cuisine. But Lidia is not only a great cook; she's also a food scientist and food advocate and quite a fantastic businesswoman. Consequently, her classes could not be a bit more interesting nor her restaurants more authentic. This recipe is a perfect example of Lidia's simple approach to traditional Italian foods served at her restaurant, Felidia, in New York. Lidia even went on to open a restaurant based on *fricos*, crisp, lacy, very thin cheese wafers. She has inspired so many people, including her son, Joseph, who is now one of New York's most successful restaurateurs.

It is interesting to note that Lidia uses Montasio cheese—a traditional Italian farmhouse cheese originally made from sheep's milk but now made from cow's milk—rather than the expected Parmesan. This was at a time when American interest in artisanal and traditional European cheeses was just beginning to become more mainstream.

---

1 pound Montasio cheese, rind removed (about ¾ pound trimmed), coarsely shredded (about 3 cups)

Potato Filling (recipe follows)

2 cups baby salad greens, well washed and dressed with a bit of extra-virgin olive oil and salt and pepper (optional)

Preheat the oven to 250°F.

Place a 5-inch nonstick skillet over medium-low heat and warm until a shred of the cheese begins to sizzle about 2 seconds after it has been placed in the pan.

Scatter ⅓ cup of the cheese in an even layer over the bottom of the skillet. Spoon one-quarter of the Potato Filling over the cheese and gently press on it to flatten it out to an even layer covering the cheese. Sprinkle an additional ⅓ cup of the cheese in an even layer over the potato.

Cook the *frico*, without disturbing it or moving the pan, for about 3 minutes, or until the fat that separates from the cheese begins to bubble around the edges.

Immediately shake the skillet gently to free the *frico* from the bottom of the pan. If it sticks, let it cook for an additional minute and then try again. If it still sticks, carefully work a heatproof rubber spatula under the *frico* to free it from the pan.

Cook for an additional 2 to 3 minutes, or until the underside of the *frico* is crisp and golden brown and easily slides from the pan.

Slide the *frico* onto a small plate, then invert it back into the skillet and cook the remaining side as you did the first.

When done, slide the *frico* onto a small baking sheet and place in the preheated oven to keep warm while you make the remaining three *fricos*.

When all of the *fricos* are done, remove them from the oven and pat with a double layer of paper towels to absorb excess fat.

Place one *frico* on each of four luncheon plates. Cut the crisps in half and, if using, mound equal portions of the salad greens on top of each and serve.

Serves 4

POTATO FILLING

2 medium-large Idaho potatoes (about 1 pound), well washed

2 tablespoons extra-virgin olive oil

1 cup thinly sliced onion, well washed and drained

Coarse salt and freshly ground pepper to taste

Place the unpeeled, whole potatoes in a saucepan large enough to hold them comfortably. Cover with cold, salted water and place over high heat. Bring to a boil, lower the heat, and simmer for about 25 minutes, or until firm-tender when poked with the point of a small, sharp knife. The skin should remain unbroken. Drain well and set aside until cool enough to handle.

When the potatoes are cool enough to handle, peel and cut into ¼-inch-thick slices.

Heat the olive oil in a large skillet over medium heat. Add the onion and sauté for about 4 minutes, or until just wilted. Stir in the potatoes and cook, gently turning occasionally, for about 12 minutes, or until golden. Season with salt and pepper to taste, remove from the heat, and keep warm until ready to use.

NORI-WRAPPED SALMON
2000
JEFFREY NATHAN, *Chef/Owner, Abigael's, Cookbook Author*

Modern Kosher Cooking has, over the years, become one of our most popular classes as interest in "keeping kosher" has grown among younger cooks. Jeffrey Nathan has taken Jewish cooking to unexpected heights with his use of many nontraditional ingredients and techniques at his restaurant, Abigael's. His kosher classes are always extremely inventive—with his use of ingredients not typically associated with kosher cuisines—and his enthusiasm for this new style of cooking is infectious. This was obviously the period when sushi was being introduced into every type of cuisine. But who would have thought that it would find a place—along with ponzu sauce and other Asian ingredients—in Jewish cooking? Although this fish is cooked, the sushi principle remains.

1 pound skinless, boneless salmon filet

¼ cup canola oil

1 tablespoon minced fresh ginger

½ cup shiitake mushroom julienne

½ cup carrot julienne

½ cup snow-pea julienne

1 teaspoon toasted sesame oil (see Note)

6 sheets nori (see Note)

Soy sauce as needed

Asian Salad (recipe follows)

Abigael's Ponzu Sauce (recipe follows)

Wasabi Remoulade (recipe follows)

Using a sharp knife, cut the salmon lengthwise into six 5×1-inch pieces.

Using a paring knife, cut a lengthwise pocket into each piece of salmon, leaving ½ inch uncut at each end. Do not cut all the way through the salmon. Set aside.

Place 2 tablespoons of the canola oil in a large sauté pan over medium-high heat. Add the ginger and sauté for 1 minute. Stir in the mushrooms, carrot, and snow peas and sauté for about 2 minutes, or until just wilted. Stir in the sesame oil and remove from the heat. Scrape the mixture onto a plate and set aside to cool.

When the vegetable mixture is cool, place equal portions in the pocket of each piece of salmon.

Working with one sheet at a time, place the nori on a clean, flat surface. Using a pastry brush, lightly coat the nori with soy sauce. Place a filled piece of salmon on the bottom third of the nori, then roll the nori up and over the salmon to make a neat, tight roll.

When all of the rolls have been made, heat the remaining 2 tablespoons of canola oil in a large sauté pan over medium-high heat. Add the salmon rolls and sear, turning frequently, for about 4 minutes, or until all sides have been browned. If serving the salmon rare, proceed with the recipe. If more cooking is desired, preheat the oven to 350°F and transfer the salmon rolls to the hot oven to continue cooking to the desired degree of doneness, then proceed with the recipe.

Arrange equal portions of the Asian Salad in the center of each of six serving plates. Working with one at a time, cut each salmon roll crosswise into 1-inch pieces. Place the cut pieces of roll on top of the salad. Drizzle the ponzu sauce and remoulade over each plate and serve.

Makes 6 rolls

ASIAN SALAD

1 red bell pepper, peeled, cored, and seeded, membrane removed, and cut into fine julienne

One 2.5-ounce package enoki mushrooms (see Note)

½ pound pea shoots (see Note)

1 tablespoon toasted sesame seeds

1 to 2 tablespoons Abigael's Ponzu Sauce (recipe follows)

Combine the bell pepper, mushrooms, pea shoots, and sesame seeds in a mixing bowl, tossing to combine. (The salad may be made up to this point and covered and refrigerated until ready to serve.)

Drizzle with a bit of the ponzu sauce and toss until well dressed. Serve immediately.

ABIGAEL'S PONZU SAUCE

⅓ cup soy sauce

1 teaspoon minced fresh ginger

1 tablespoon honey

Juice of ½ orange

Juice of ½ lemon

Combine the soy sauce, ginger, and honey in a small nonreactive bowl. Whisk in the orange and lemon juices. Set aside until ready to use.

WASABI REMOULADE

1 tablespoon wasabi powder (see Note)

Rice wine vinegar as needed (see Note)

¼ cup mayonnaise, preferably homemade

1 tablespoon soy sauce, or to taste

½ teaspoon toasted sesame oil, or to taste (see Note)

Place the wasabi powder in a small nonreactive bowl. Add just enough rice wine vinegar to make a paste.

When a paste has formed, beat in the mayonnaise. Add the soy sauce and sesame oil. Taste and, if necessary, add additional soy sauce and sesame oil. Set aside until ready to serve.

If making ahead of time, cover and refrigerate until ready to use.

Note: Toasted sesame oil and rice wine vinegar are available from Asian markets, specialty food stores, and some supermarkets.

Nori and wasabi powder are available from Japanese markets and some specialty food stores.

Enoki mushrooms and pea shoots are available at fine greengrocers and some specialty food stores.

JEFF NATHAN

CHARCOALED BEEF SALAD
WITH POMEGRANATE, POTATO LEAVES,
AND A DRIZZLE OF ROBIOLA DI MONDOVI
1998

LYDIA SHIRE, *Chef/Co-Owner, Lock-Ober, Excelsior*

Lydia Shire was a leader of the Big Boston culinary movement, which resulted in many young chefs making Boston their home kitchen. She is known as the queen of offal and other meats that one doesn't usually find on restaurant menus, as well as for combining exotic ingredients. In this recipe, a long and complicated one, she hits her peak, combining the meat from a traditional prime rib of beef with pomegranate, rare and unusual salad greens, robiola cheese, and very fancy potatoes. In the class she added an oxtail dish as a topping for the potatoes but didn't offer the recipe, as even Lydia knew she had taken us over the top. As she said in the class, "At Biba [her Boston restaurant], we sometimes... only sometimes [smile], get carried away. Could this dish be simpler? Of course, but you can do the editing." You might have guessed that this is a very labor-intensive recipe, but it's well worth the effort.

For the presentation Lydia brought along some little wooden oxcarts to hold the potato sticks but, unless you have a local supplier, I suggest that you content yourself with a nice haystack of potato sticks placed directly on the plate.

This recipe requires that you purchase only half a prime rib (a whole rib consists of seven bones) that the butcher then should cut into three equal pieces. Each piece should have one bone sticking out of the end.

½ prime rib of beef (see recipe head-note), trimmed of excess fat

½ cup smashed garlic cloves

1 cup cracked black peppercorns

Coarse salt to taste

Pomegranate Marinade (recipe follows)

Straw Potatoes (recipe follows)

Salad Mix (recipe follows)

Red Wine Sauce (recipe follows)

½ cup fresh pomegranate seeds

Sea salt to taste

Robiola Fonduta (recipe follows)

Potato Leaves (recipe follows)

Generously rub both sides of each piece of meat with the crushed garlic, then generously coat with the cracked peppercorns. Place the meat on wire racks set on a baking sheet, cover loosely with plastic film, and refrigerate for 8 hours or overnight.

When ready to serve, remove the meat from the refrigerator and allow it to come to room temperature. Preheat and oil the grill.

Generously season the meat on both sides with coarse salt. Place on the preheated grill and grill, turning once, for about 10 minutes, or until very dark brown but not burned on all sides.

Using a pastry brush, generously coat the meat with the Pomegranate Marinade. Transfer the meat to the cooler outer edges of the grill, cover, and continue to grill until desired degree of doneness has been reached (135°F on an instant-read thermometer for rare). Immediately remove from the heat and set aside to rest for 15 minutes before carving. (Alternately, the meat can be seasoned then coated with the marinade and roasted in a preheated 325°F oven to the desired degree of doneness.)

Using a slicing knife, cut the rib, parallel to the bone, into thin slices. Place equal portions, slightly overlapping the pieces, in the center of each of six serving plates.

Arrange a haystack of Straw Potatoes at the edge of each plate. Place a mound of salad between the meat and potatoes. Spoon some Red Wine Sauce over the meat and then sprinkle with pomegranate seeds and sea salt. Drizzle with *Robiola Fonduta*, and then place equal portions of Potato Leaves next to each portion of salad and serve.

Serves 6

POMEGRANATE MARINADE

½ cup olive oil

10 shallots, peeled and finely diced

10 cloves garlic, peeled and chopped

1 bunch rosemary, well washed, leaves only

½ cup pomegranate molasses (see Note)

Heat the olive oil in a medium saucepan over medium heat. Add the shallots and garlic and stir to combine. Stir in the rosemary and bring to a simmer. Lower the heat and cook for about 10 minutes, or until the shallots and garlic are very soft. Add the molasses and, stirring constantly, bring to a simmer.

Remove from the heat and set aside to cool. (The marinade may be stored, covered and refrigerated, for up to one week.)

STRAW POTATOES

2 large Idaho potatoes, peeled and cut into matchsticks

Peanut oil for frying

Coarse salt to taste

Place the potato matchsticks into a bowl of ice-cold water to cover for 5 minutes. Drain well and pat dry.

Heat the oil in a deep-fat fryer with a basket over high heat to 375°F on an instant-read thermometer.

Add the potatoes, without crowding the pan, and fry for about 4 minutes, or until golden brown and crisp.

Place on a double layer of paper towels to drain. Season with coarse salt to taste and keep warm until ready to serve.

When De Gustibus was in its infancy, we never heard about **pomegranates** and most of us had no familiarity with them. It was, I believe, Paula Wolfert's writing that caused chefs to investigate their use. The tart, refreshing flavor of the fresh fruit—either its juice or its seeds—highlights many dishes just as acidic citrus would. In recent years, however, we have been introduced to pomegranate **molasses**, pomegranate **powder**, dried **seeds**, and now **Pom**, bottled pomegranate juice that is advertised as being very good for your health. Most frequently used in Middle Eastern and East Indian cooking, the pomegranate and its offspring are now used in many other styles of cooking.

SALAD MIX

6 cups upland cress, baby arugula, small mizuna leaves, purple amaranth, or other pristine baby greens

½ medium red onion, peeled and cut into slivers

¼ cup light red wine vinegar

2 tablespoons walnut oil or to taste

Coarse salt and freshly ground pepper to taste

Combine the greens and onion in a mixing bowl.

When ready to serve, whisk the vinegar and oil together. Season with salt and pepper to taste and drizzle over the greens, tossing to coat lightly.

RED WINE SAUCE

¾ cup (1½ sticks) unsalted butter

6 shallots, peeled and chopped

One 750-milliliter bottle dry red wine

¼ cup rich veal stock (see Note)

Heat 1 tablespoon of the butter in a medium saucepan over medium heat. Add the shallots and sauté for about 5 minutes, or until the shallots are golden. Add the wine and bring to a boil. Lower the heat and continue to cook at a gentle boil for about 40 minutes, or until reduced to 1 cup.

Add the veal stock, raise the heat, and again bring to a boil. Lower the heat and simmer for about 15 minutes, or until reduced to slightly under 1 cup.

Whisk in the remaining butter and keep the sauce warm until ready to serve.

ROBIOLA FONDUTA

2½ cups fine-quality white wine

½ cup heavy cream

12 ounces *Robiola di Mondovi* cheese, cut into small chunks

Place the wine in a small nonreactive saucepan over medium-high heat. Bring to a boil, then lower the heat and simmer for about 45 minutes, or until reduced to ¼ cup.

Add the heavy cream, raise the heat, and bring just to a boil. Lower the heat and simmer for about 15 minutes, or until reduced to ¼ cup.

Swirl in the cheese and stir until well blended.

Place in a warm spot or in the top half of a double boiler over hot water to keep warm until ready to serve. Do not cover.

POTATO LEAVES

3 hot baked Idaho potatoes

1 large egg white

2 tablespoons clarified butter (see Note page 94)

½ teaspoon coarse salt

Split the potatoes in half lengthwise and scoop out the flesh.

Place the flesh in a ricer and process into a bowl. Beat in the egg white, butter, and salt.

Preheat the oven to 400°F. Cover a baking sheet with parchment paper.

Place a leaf cookie cutter on the paper and spoon 1 tablespoon of the potato mixture into it, smoothing to make a neat, even layer. Continue making potato leaves, allowing about ½ inch between each one, until all of the potato mixture has been used.

Place the baking sheet in the preheated oven and bake for about 10 minutes, or until the leaves are golden brown.

Remove the leaves from the oven and, working quickly, drape each one over a rolling pin, bottle, or pan edge to form them into "fun" shapes.

Set aside to cool. Serve at room temperature.

Note: Pomegranate molasses is available at Middle Eastern markets and some specialty food stores.

Veal stock is now commercially available at fine butchers and some specialty food stores.

169

QUICK SAUTÉ OF ZUCCHINI
WITH TOASTED ALMONDS AND PECORINO
2000

JIMMY BRADLEY, Chef/Owner, The Red Cat, The Harrison, The Mermaid Inn, Pace

I first met Jimmy Bradley when he was the chef at Bryant Park Grill, a beautiful restaurant in the park behind the main branch of the New York City Public Library. I sort of lost track of him until he opened The Red Cat with his partner, Danny Abrams. They now have a number of "hip-happenin'" restaurants in New York City.

Jimmy and Danny seem to be able to "catch the vibe" and know just what young diners are looking for in a favorite spot. They have been pioneers in creating diners' favorite "neighborhood restaurants." Jimmy is a relaxed, easygoing chef who makes cooking fun and interesting. His recipes are usually fairly easy to accomplish but do require top-notch ingredients. This is one of our favorites.

2 tablespoons extra-virgin olive oil

¼ cup sliced almonds

5 cups ⅛-inch-thick zucchini matchsticks

Coarse salt and freshly ground pepper to taste

¼ pound Pecorino Romano cheese, shaved into almost paper-thin slices

Place two large sauté pans over high heat. Add a tablespoon of olive oil to each one and when hot, add half of the almonds to each pan. Sauté for about 2 minutes, or until the nuts are golden brown.

Immediately add half of the zucchini to each pan and toss to incorporate the almonds and coat the zucchini with the oil. Season with salt and pepper to taste and toss for about 30 seconds, or until the zucchini is just warmed through.

Remove from the heat and transfer to a serving plate. Layer slices of cheese over the top and serve.

Serves 4

YUKON GOLD POTATO FOAM
WITH BLACK WINTER TRUFFLES
2000

LAURENT TOURONDEL, *Chef/Owner, BLT Steak, BLT Fish, BLT Prime, Cookbook Author*

We have watched Laurent Tourondel go from working in a classically serene French restaurant, Cello, to opening an explosion of BLT (Bistro Laurent Tourondel) hot spots around town. He is such a terrific cook that it is no wonder he attracts crowds no matter what he chooses to do.

By 2000 Yukon Gold potatoes reigned supreme in the De Gustibus kitchen. If chefs were not using heirloom potatoes, Yukon Golds seemed to be their choice.

Influenced by the great Spanish chef, Ferran Adrià, many contemporary chefs began using "foams" in their presentation. In this recipe Laurent used the technique to prepare a very classic French combination of potatoes and black truffles. To complete the recipe you will need a whipped cream (or soda) charger, which can be found in most kitchen supply stores.

---

1 pound Yukon Gold potatoes, well washed

1 tablespoon coarse sea salt

2 cups heavy cream

1 cup (2 sticks) unsalted butter, at room temperature

1 tablespoon truffle oil (see Note)

½ ounce black truffle

Fleur de sel de Guèrande to taste (see Note)

Place the whole, unpeeled potatoes in a medium saucepan with cold water to cover. Add the sea salt and place over high heat. Bring to a boil, lower the heat, and simmer for about 20 minutes, or until the potatoes are tender when pierced with a knife.

Remove from the heat, drain well, and quickly peel. Immediately transfer the potatoes to a ricer and pass them through back into the saucepan.

Place the saucepan over medium heat and, using a wooden spoon or spatula, beat in the heavy cream and butter until very smooth. Beat in ½ tablespoon of the truffle oil. You should have a mixture that is the consistency of a thick soup.

Pour the potato purée into a whipped cream or soda charger fitted with the cream charger. Attach one cartridge to the canister and invert the canister so that the nozzle points downward. Vigorously shake five times.

With the nozzle pointed down, slowly dispense an equal portion of the potato "foam" into each of four small dishes. Shave equal portions of the truffle over each serving, drizzle with the remaining truffle oil, and sprinkle with *fleur de sel de Guèrande* to taste. Serve immediately.

Note: Truffle oil is available at most specialty food stores.

Fleur de sel de Guèrande is hand-raked from the salt marshes of South Brittany-Guèrande. It is 100 percent natural with no additives and is lower in sodium than regular salt. It derives its flavor from the sea and its slight ivory color from the clay present in the area where it is harvested. You can substitute any other fine sea salt.

Serves 4 to 6

CURRIED COUSCOUS PILAF
1998
MELISSA KELLY, *Chef/Owner, Primo*

Melissa Kelly first came to De Gustibus from the Old Chatham (New York) Sheepherding Company, which she had put on the map as a dining destination. Her food exemplified the simple, direct tastes that young American chefs were becoming quite famous for producing. She was a leader in what I came to call the "Gardeners," those chefs who preferred working in settings where they could grow their own produce.

This urge propelled Melissa to Maine, where she opened Primo, featuring local, seasonal foods served in a relaxed atmosphere. She is one of the chefs, along with Sam Hayward in Portland, and Mark Gaier and Clark Frasier, of Ogunquit, instrumental in putting Maine on the gastronomic radar.

Rather than the expected rice, Melissa chose Tunisian couscous as the base for this tasty, perfectly spiced pilaf that is a home cook's dream as it is made to be served at room temperature.

2 cups Tunisian couscous (see Note)

½ cup curry oil (see Note)

2 cups boiling water

¾ cup dried currants

2 jalapeño chilies, stemmed, seeded, membrane removed, and finely diced

2 small carrots, peeled, trimmed, and finely diced

1 red bell pepper, peeled, cored, seeded, membrane removed, and finely diced

1 small red onion, peeled and finely diced

2 tablespoons fresh lime juice

Green Tabasco to taste

Coarse salt and freshly ground pepper to taste

1 tablespoon fresh mint-leaf chiffonade (see Note page 111)

1 tablespoon fresh cilantro-leaf chiffonade (see Note page 111)

Place the couscous in a stainless-steel bowl. Stir in the curry oil, then pour the boiling water over all. Cover with plastic film and set aside to "bloom."

Place the currants in a small heatproof bowl with hot water to cover. Set aside for about 15 minutes to plump. Drain well.

Add the currants to the couscous along with the jalapeño, carrots, bell pepper, and onion, tossing with a fork to blend well. Add the lime juice and season with Tabasco, salt, and pepper to taste.

When ready to serve, toss in the mint and cilantro and serve at room temperature.

Note: Tunisian couscous is available from Middle Eastern and African markets. Curry oil is available from East Indian markets and some specialty food stores. You may also make your own by adding 1 tablespoon of curry powder to 1 cup of warm peanut oil and setting it aside to infuse for twenty-four hours. Strain the oil through a fine sieve lined with cheesecloth, discarding the solids. Store, covered, at room temperature, for up to one week.

Serves 6 to 8

PUMPKIN RISOTTO WITH WHITE TRUFFLES
1998

ALEX LEE, *Chef, formerly of Restaurant Daniel*

Alex Lee often took De Gustibus classes when he was working as a chef at a private club. When he attended Daniel Boulud's class, he was, naturally, very impressed with Daniel's skill and philosophy and asked if it would be possible to work in his kitchen. Daniel said, "Sure, we need someone in *garde manger* right now." Several years later Alex had moved up the ranks and was made chef de cuisine at Daniel, where he stayed for many, many years.

Alex Lee remained true to the Daniel Boulud tradition at Restaurant Daniel as he continued to bring the absolute best of the marketplace to the table. Working with classic French techniques but using contemporary (and very un-French) American ingredients as well as inspiration from other cuisines, Alex garnered as much praise as his mentor.

Where once risotto was strictly an Italian presentation of arborio rice, a bit of white wine, great chicken stock, saffron, and Parmesan cheese, by the late nineties it had been absorbed into almost every style of cuisine and transformed with every imaginable grain, vegetable, seasoning, and liquid. Many risottos were accented with confits and other rich meat preparations. Alex thrilled us with this absolutely delicious combination.

6 tablespoons (¾ stick) unsalted butter, at room temperature

¾ pound cheese pumpkin or butternut squash, peeled, seeded, and cut into ½-inch squares

Coarse salt and freshly ground white pepper to taste

7¼ cups unsalted, defatted homemade chicken stock or canned broth

½ cup finely diced onion

2 cups arborio rice

⅓ cup dry white wine

½ cup freshly grated Parmigiano-Reggiano cheese

1 tablespoon crème fraîche (see Note)

Fresh white truffle for garnish

Heat 2 tablespoons of the butter in a medium saucepan over medium heat. Add the pumpkin, season with salt and white pepper to taste, and cook, stirring frequently, for about 5 minutes, or until the pumpkin starts to soften but does not take on any color.

Add ¼ cup of the chicken stock, bring to a simmer, cover, and lower the heat. Cook for about 20 minutes, or until the pumpkin is very tender and falling apart and most of the liquid has evaporated. Remove from the heat, uncover, and, using a fork, roughly crush. Set aside.

Pour the remaining 7 cups of chicken stock into a medium saucepan and place over medium heat. Bring to a boil, lower the heat, and keep the stock at a low simmer.

Warm 3 tablespoons of the remaining butter over medium-low heat. Add the onion, season with salt and white pepper to taste, and cook, stirring frequently, for about 5 minutes, or until the onion has softened but not taken on any color.

Stir in the rice, season again with salt and white pepper, and cook, stirring frequently, for 5 additional minutes.

Pour in the wine and stir, scraping up any bits from the bottom of the pan. Raise the heat to medium and cook, stirring often, for about 5 minutes, or until all of the liquid has evaporated.

Stir in 1 cup of the hot stock and cook, stirring often, for about 10 minutes, or until the rice has absorbed most of the liquid. Continue adding stock, 1 cup at a time, stirring and cooking until you've added 6 cups of the stock. This will take about 30 minutes.

Taste and bite into the rice. If it is not yet al dente, add another ½ cup to 1 cup of stock and cook, stirring frequently, for a few more minutes.

Remove from the heat and stir in the remaining tablespoon of butter along with the reserved pumpkin, the cheese, and the crème fraîche. Taste and, if necessary, season with additional salt and white pepper.

Spoon equal portions of the risotto into each of four or six large, shallow soup bowls. Serve immediately, shaving some white truffle over each portion.

Note: Crème fraîche is available from specialty food stores and some supermarkets.

Serves 6 as an appetizer, 4 as a main course

Short-grain rices such as arborio, Carnaroli, and Vialone Nano are always used to make traditional risotto. Their fat, white kernels are coated with a soft starch that, when cooked, dissolves into a creamy sauce that marries the rice with the flavoring liquid.

JAMIESON FARM BABY LAMB
WITH ARTICHOKES AND CIPPOLINI
1997
ALESSANDRO STRATTA, *Chef, Restaurant Alex*

Alessandro Stratta is an unbelievably talented chef. He grew up in a European hotel family and was the executive chef at the Phoenician Hotel in Arizona when I first met him. It was quite a long way from his early career in Italy and France. He made his mark as the executive chef at Renoir in Las Vegas, where he garnered every accolade imaginable. So many, in fact, that he now has his own restaurant, Alex. His artistry has set the Las Vegas standard for fine dining.

Alessandro has a very Mediterranean sensibility and a love for farm-fresh ingredients. The food that he demonstrated at De Gustibus reflected all of his innate passions. With this recipe, many of us tasted high-quality Ligurian olive oil for the first time. It was a perfect match for his food.

---

2 baby lamb racks, well trimmed, trimmings reserved

2 baby lamb loins, well trimmed, trimmings reserved

1 cup extra-virgin Ligurian olive oil (see Note)

4 cloves garlic, peeled and smashed

2 sprigs fresh rosemary

Freshly ground pepper to taste

2 pounds lamb bones

4 cups defatted, unsalted chicken stock

Coarse salt to taste

8 baby artichokes, trimmed, quartered, and blanched

8 cippolini onions, peeled, blanched, and quartered

4 medium carrots (preferably farm-fresh), peeled, trimmed, and cut crosswise into ¼-inch-thick slices

½ cup 1-inch-long pieces green beans, blanched

1 teaspoon chopped fresh chives

Place the trimmed racks and loins in a glass baking dish along with ½ cup of the olive oil, 2 cloves of garlic, the rosemary, and pepper to taste. Turn the meat so that all sides receive some of the marinade. Cover with plastic film and refrigerate for 24 hours.

While the lamb is marinating, prepare the sauce.

Preheat the oven to 375°F.

Place a large heavy-bottomed, ovenproof saucepan over high heat. Add half (¼ cup) of the remaining olive oil and heat until smoking. Add the lamb bones along with the reserved meat trimmings and sauté for about 7 minutes, or until golden brown. Stir in the remaining 2 cloves of garlic and cook, stirring frequently, for about 3 minutes, or until the garlic begins to take on color.

Pour the excess fat from the pan and then, stirring constantly with a wooden spoon, add the chicken stock and deglaze the pan, taking care to scrape all of the brown bits from the bottom. Bring to a boil and, using a large metal spoon, skim off any fat that rises to the top.

Transfer to the preheated oven and cook, stirring every 20 minutes, for 2½ hours.

Remove from the oven and strain through a fine sieve into a clean container. Place the sauce in an ice-water bath to cool quickly.

When cool, cover and refrigerate until ready to use.

When ready to serve, preheat the oven to 450°F.

Heat the remaining ¼ cup of olive oil in a large ovenproof sauté pan. When smoking-hot, season the marinated racks and loins with salt and pepper to taste and place them in the pan. Sear, turning frequently, for about 10 minutes, or until all sides are well browned.

Transfer to the preheated oven and roast for 10 minutes.

Remove the sauce from the refrigerator. Transfer to a small saucepan and place over low heat to warm.

Remove the racks from the pan and transfer to a serving platter. Lightly tent with aluminum foil to keep warm. Do not turn the oven off.

Place the artichokes, onions, and carrots in the same sauté pan as the loins. Season the vegetables with salt and pepper to taste and toss to coat with the pan drippings. Continue to roast for an additional 7 minutes, or until the loins register 150°F on an instant-read thermometer when inserted into the thickest part.

Remove the pan from the oven and transfer the loins and vegetables to the serving platter that holds the racks.

Pour ¼ cup of the warm lamb *jus* into the pan, place over high heat, and cook, stirring constantly, for about 5 minutes, or until the sauce has thickened.

Cut each rack in half and cut the loins crosswise into ¼-inch-thick slices. Stir the green beans into the vegetables, then place equal portions of the vegetables on each of four dinner plates. Top each with a lamb rack and equal portions of the sliced loin. Drizzle the warm sauce around each serving and sprinkle with chopped chives. Serve immediately.

Note: Ligurian olive oil is available from some Italian markets and many specialty food stores.

Serves 4

BRACIOLONE
(BRAISED PORK ROLL)
1999

MARIO BATALI, *Chef/Co-Owner, Babbo, Lupa, Esca, Otto, Italian Wine Merchants,*
Television Personality, Cookbook Author

Not only is Mario a television star; he is a real star in the classroom. With his exuberant personality, orange high-top sneakers, and passionate interest in all things Italian, Mario Batali brings more enthusiasm to cooking than almost any other chef I know. I would say that Mario, as much as anyone else, has been responsible for bringing Italian cooking to the forefront as America's favorite cuisine.

His first De Gustibus class came when he was chef at Pó, a very tiny restaurant for such a great talent. It was a small beginning for a now very expansive restaurant group in which he is partner with Joseph Bastianich, Lidia's son, and which features many fine young chefs at the various stoves.

For this traditional recipe, Mario says, "The most difficult part of this truly spectacular dish may be finding a real butcher behind the window of the grocery store where you buy your meat. This is when it definitely pays off to have a relationship with a local butcher. He or she can make or break this dish, since a piece of pork this big is not generally laying around at the local supermarket—you do need to order it from someone special."

He adds, "The sauce in this dish is generally used to sauce the ziti, which is served first. The meat is held warm and served as a main course."

One 3-pound pork shoulder or leg, butterflied and pounded to yield one piece, ½ inch thick by 12 inches square

Coarse salt and freshly ground pepper to taste

16 thin slices (about ½ pound) prosciutto di Parma

½ cup finely chopped fresh flat-leaf parsley, leaves only, plus more for garnish

½ cup dried currants

⅓ cup freshly grated Pecorino Romano cheese, plus more for garnish

¼ cup lightly toasted pine nuts

4 large hard-boiled eggs, peeled

Freshly grated nutmeg to taste

¼ cup dried oregano

¼ cup extra-virgin olive oil

Place the pork on a large cutting board. Season with salt and pepper to taste. Place the prosciutto over the pork in an even layer.

Combine the parsley, currants, cheese, and pine nuts in a small mixing bowl. Season with salt and pepper to taste.

Spoon the parsley mixture over the prosciutto and, using a spatula, spread it out in an even layer.

Quarter the hard-boiled eggs lengthwise. Lay the quarters in three rows down the center of the meat.

Sprinkle nutmeg over the entire filling, then sprinkle 2 tablespoons of the oregano, rubbing the herb between your fingers to help it release its essential oils.

Working carefully, roll the pork up, jelly-roll-fashion. Using kitchen twine, neatly tie the roll closed. Season the outside with salt and pepper to taste.

Heat the oil in a large Dutch oven over high heat. When the oil is smoking, place the pork roll in the pan. Lower the heat and sear the roll, turning frequently, for about 15 minutes, or until well browned on all sides. Don't rush this; you want the roll to be a deep, uniform brown. Using tongs, remove the meat from the pan and set aside.

4 cloves garlic, peeled and thinly sliced

2 red onions, peeled and cut into ¼-inch dice

Three 28-ounce cans Italian plum tomatoes, crushed by hand, juices included

2 cups dry white wine

2 teaspoons red pepper flakes

Add the garlic, onions, and remaining oregano to the Dutch oven and sauté for about 10 minutes, or until golden brown.

Stir in the tomatoes, wine, and red pepper flakes and bring to a boil. Return the meat to the pan and bring to a simmer. Loosely cover and simmer, moving the meat around in the pan from time to time to prevent sticking, for 1 hour and 45 minutes. If the sauce gets too thick, add water, ¼ cup at a time.

Remove the meat from the pan and place on a serving platter. Using kitchen scissors, cut off and discard the twine. Keep warm until ready to serve.

When ready to serve, using a sharp knife, cut the *braciolone* crosswise into ¾-inch-thick slices. Place, slightly overlapping, on the serving platter. Sprinkle with grated cheese and chopped parsley and serve.

Serves 8

CURRY LEAF–MARINATED FLANK STEAK
WITH SMASHED POTATOES, HARICOTS VERTS,
AND GINGER-HORSERADISH RAITA
2000

FLOYD CARDOZ, *Chef/Partner, Tabla*

At his stove at Tabla, one of restaurateur Danny Meyer's popular New York spots, Chef Floyd Cardoz practices East Indian culinary magic. He has added a whole new dimension to classic Indian cooking. Floyd told us that he tried to cook his signature dishes in India but diners were very resistant, as they felt that his food was too experimental.

In his classes we always learn about some unknown ingredient or technique that we can incorporate into our everyday cooking. In this recipe we experienced fresh curry leaves as well as a number of traditional Indian seasonings. This recipe has several components, but the great thing is that, other than the steak, they can all be made ahead of time and served at room temperature or chilled.

8 fresh curry leaves (see sidebar)

1 dried red hot chili pepper

One 1½-inch piece fresh peeled ginger, puréed (see Note)

6 tablespoons soy sauce

1 tablespoon canola oil

1 tablespoon fresh garlic purée (see Note)

1 tablespoon finely ground cumin seed

2 teaspoons freshly ground pepper

1½-pound flank steak, trimmed of all fat

Smashed Potatoes (recipe follows)

Haricots Verts (recipe follows)

Ginger-Horseradish Raita (recipe follows)

Combine the curry leaves, dried chili, ginger, soy sauce, canola oil, garlic, cumin, and pepper in a small blender jar and process until smooth.

Place the steak in a nonreactive pan and pour the marinade over the top. Turn to coat both sides. Cover with plastic film and set aside to marinate for at least 4 hours but no more than 7 hours.

When ready to cook, oil and preheat a grill to medium-high.

Place the steak on the preheated grill and grill, turning once, for about 15 minutes, or until the desired degree of doneness (130°F on an instant-read thermometer for rare) has been reached.

Remove the steak from the grill and place on a cutting board to rest for 10 minutes.

Using a sharp knife, cut the steak, crosswise against the grain, into thin slices.

Place equal portions of the sliced steak on each of four dinner plates. Mound Smashed Potatoes on one side and Haricots Verts on the other and serve with the Ginger-Horseradish Raita on the side.

Note: Ginger and garlic can easily be puréed in a coffee grinder or a mini food processor. They can also be grated almost to a purée on a handheld rasp grater used for zesting.

Chana dal, bright-yellow Indian lentils, and red and yellow mustard seeds are available from East Indian markets.

Sugar to taste, in this instance, means just enough sugar to balance the heat for your palate.

Serves 4

Curry leaf, also called *kari parta*, is the leaf of a Southeast Asian plant. It looks like a lemon leaf but smells like curry powder when its fragrant oils are released once smashed. It is not in any way, however, related to either. Curry leaves can be purchased in some supermarkets through the wide distribution of companies such as Frieda's. It is most often available in East Indian and Asian markets.

SMASHED POTATOES

4 Yukon Gold potatoes, peeled and quartered

1 teaspoon ground turmeric

1 tablespoon canola oil

1 tablespoon *chana dal* (see Note)

1 curry leaf (see sidebar)

1 teaspoon red mustard seed (see Note)

4 cloves garlic, roasted and peeled (see Note page 65)

Coarse salt and freshly ground pepper to taste

Place the potatoes and turmeric in cold, salted water to cover over high heat. Bring to a boil, lower the heat, and simmer for about 10 minutes, or until the potatoes are partially cooked but still firm in the center. Remove from the heat and drain well.

Transfer the potatoes to a bowl and, using a potato masher or wooden spoon, smash them. Set aside.

Preheat the oven to 375°F.

Heat the oil in a medium sauté pan over medium heat. Add the *chana dal* and sauté for about 3 minutes, or until well toasted and very fragrant. Stir in the curry leaf and mustard seeds, stirring for about 2 minutes, or until the curry leaf wilts and the seeds pop.

Remove from the heat and stir in the roasted garlic.

Combine the spice mixture and salt and pepper to taste with the potatoes, tossing to combine well.

Spread the potatoes out on a baking sheet and place in the preheated oven. Bake for about 30 minutes, or until golden brown and crusty.

Remove from the oven and serve warm or at room temperature.

HARICOTS VERTS

1 tablespoon canola oil

1 teaspoon yellow mustard seeds (see Note)

2 cloves garlic, peeled and thinly sliced

One ½-inch piece fresh ginger, peeled and cut into fine julienne

¼ medium onion, peeled and thinly sliced

10 ounces fresh haricots verts (or tiny green beans), trimmed

¼ jalapeño or other hot green chili, thinly sliced

¼ cup hot, unsalted chicken stock

Coarse salt and freshly ground pepper Heat the oil in a large saucepan over medium heat. Add the mustard seeds and cook, stirring frequently, for about 2 minutes, or until well toasted.

Add the garlic and sauté for about 2 minutes, or just until the garlic has sweat its liquid but not taken on any color.

Add the ginger and onion and sauté for about 3 minutes, or until just translucent.

Add the beans along with the chili and stock, raise the heat, and bring to a hard boil. Boil rapidly for about 4 minutes, or until the beans are very tender. Remove from the heat and season with salt and pepper to taste. Keep warm until ready to serve.

GINGER-HORSERADISH RAITA

1 cup unflavored yogurt

1-inch piece fresh ginger, peeled

1 tablespoon freshly grated horseradish

Coarse salt and freshly ground pepper

Sugar to taste (see Note)

Place the yogurt in a small bowl. Using a rasp grater held over a fine mesh sieve, grate the ginger over the yogurt, allowing only the juices to fall into the yogurt. (You may have to press on the ginger to push the juice out.) Add the horseradish and season with salt, pepper, and sugar to taste. Cover and refrigerate until ready to use.

GREEN CURRY CHICKEN
1998
ARUN SAMPANTHAVIVAT, *Chef, Arun's*

By the late 1990s Thai food had almost surpassed Chinese as the favorite Asian cuisine in America. Thai food seemed to be simpler and healthier than Chinese, and its curries were much lighter than the more familiar Indian curries. Arun Sampanthavivat was one of the country's best Thai chefs, and he introduced many of the exotic ingredients that are now quite common.

I first tasted Arun's amazing cooking at his eponymous restaurant in Chicago. After this experience I tried, for three years, to get him to come to De Gustibus. When I finally got him there, he arrived with two brothers, three uncles, and a big team. What a great class—we all learned some important nuances of Thai cuisine.

2 cups coconut milk

Green Curry Paste (recipe follows)

1 pound skinless, boneless chicken breast, thinly sliced

4 baby eggplants, trimmed and quartered

2 tablespoons chopped cherry eggplant (see Note)

2 tablespoons *nam pla* or other fish sauce (see Note)

2 tablespoons palm sugar (see Note)

Coarse salt to taste

2 tablespoons sweet basil leaves (see Note)

2 cups hot, cooked rice

Place the coconut milk in a medium sauté pan over medium heat and cook for about 7 minutes, or until slightly thick.

Add the curry paste and stir vigorously to combine.

Add the chicken and cook, stirring occasionally, for about 2 minutes, or until the chicken is almost cooked through. Stir in the eggplant quarters, cherry eggplant, fish sauce, palm sugar, and salt to taste. Cook, stirring frequently, for an additional 5 minutes. Stir in the sweet basil leaves and remove from the heat.

Place a cup of rice in the center of each of two serving plates. Spoon equal portions of the chicken curry over the rice and serve immediately.

Serves 2

GREEN CURRY PASTE

5 jalapeño chilies, seeded

2 tablespoons thinly sliced shallots

2 tablespoons thinly sliced garlic

1 tablespoon finely chopped fresh lemongrass (see sidebar page 220)

1 teaspoon finely chopped galangal (see sidebar)

1 teaspoon finely chopped fresh cilantro leaves

1 teaspoon finely ground coriander seeds

¼ cup water, plus more if needed

Place the chilies, shallots, garlic, lemongrass, galangal, cilantro, and coriander in a blender. Add the water and process to a smooth paste.

Transfer the paste to a nonreactive container, cover, and refrigerate until ready to use.

Note: Cherry eggplant, nam pla, *palm sugar, sweet basil leaves, lemongrass, and galangal are available at Asian markets and some specialty food stores.*

182

NOBU BLACK COD WITH MISO
1996
NOBU MATSUHISA, *Chef/Owner/Restaurateur, Nobu Matsuhisa*

Chef Nobu Matsuhisa is known simply as Nobu throughout the world. His strict adherence to using only pristine ingredients makes each of his restaurants a top draw, whether in New York, London, or Paris. This particular recipe has resonated throughout the culinary world, with many chefs doing their own interpretations of this absolutely delicious and simple-to-execute dish.

When Nobu first came to De Gustibus, he brought his sous-chef, Morimoto, who said, "I will be back here one day!" Who could have dreamed of the Iron Chef? I have to say I wasn't at all surprised by Morimoto's rise to international fame.

A cook's note: The cod has to marinate for three days before grilling.

---

1 pound boneless, skinless black cod filet

Den Miso (recipe follows)

1 head Bibb lettuce, pulled apart into about 20 leaves, trimmed, well washed, and dried

¼ cup *kaiware* (radish sprouts; see Note)

Place the cod in a glass dish. Add all but ¼ cup of the Den Miso and turn to coat. Cover with plastic film and refrigerate, turning occasionally, for 3 days.

When ready to cook, preheat and oil a grill.

Remove the cod from the marinade and place on the preheated grill. Grill, turning once, for about 5 minutes, or until dark golden brown and well glazed.

Remove the fish from the grill and cut it into bite-size pieces. Place a piece of fish in a lettuce leaf, add a bit of Den Miso, and garnish with a few radish sprouts. Serve immediately.

Serves 4 to 6

DEN MISO

1 cup red miso paste (see Note)

¼ cup sake

¼ cup mirin

3 tablespoons sugar

Combine the miso, sake, mirin, and sugar in a small saucepan over low heat and bring to a simmer. Immediately remove from the heat and set aside to cool.

Store, covered and refrigerated, until ready to use.

Note: Radish sprouts are available from some Asian markets, health food stores, and specialty food stores.

Miso paste and mirin are available from Japanese markets and some specialty food stores.

Miso, a soybean paste, is an integral ingredient in Japanese cooking. It is sold in three varieties—wheat, rice, and barley—all malted. The type of malted grain as well as the amount of time it is allowed to age determines the flavor, color, and texture of the miso. Light-colored miso is usually quite delicate and is used for soups and broths, while the darker misos are used for intense flavor. *Dengaku* is the Japanese name for a sauce applied to grilled foods, made from red or white miso, sake, mirin, and sugar.

GRILLED ROUGET
WITH WHITE-BEAN BRANDADE AND NIÇOISE VINAIGRETTE
1999

TERRANCE BRENNAN, *Chef/Owner, Picholine, Artisanal, Artisanal Cheese Center, Cookbook Author*

When I first met Terry, he was working for my husband, Alain Sailhac, at Le Cirque in New York City. As a young chef, he would talk about how he wanted "his" restaurant(s) to look as good as the food prepared there. I remember going to his first restaurant, Picholine, and thinking how closely he had held to his dreams.

Of all of the first wave of adventuresome American chefs, Terrance Brennan has stayed closest to the traditions of the French kitchen. So much so that he has, in recent years, become an entrepreneur in the cheese business, serving as both importer and *affineur*, or guardian, of the aging of cheese. I think that this recipe clearly shows how much he respects the flavors and techniques of classic French cooking.

2 tablespoons extra-virgin olive oil

18 rouget filets (see Note)

Coarse salt and freshly ground pepper to taste

White-Bean *Brandade* (recipe follows)

Niçoise Vinaigrette (recipe follows)

Preheat the oven to 450°F. Preheat and oil a grill.

Using a pastry brush lightly coat the filets with oil. Season with salt and pepper to taste.

Place the filets, skin side down, on the hot grill and grill for 40 seconds. Immediately transfer the filets, skin side up, to a nonstick baking sheet. Place in the preheated oven and roast for 2 minutes, or until cooked through.

Place 1 tablespoon of the *brandade* in the center of each of six plates. Lay three filets on top of the *brandade* on each plate. Drizzle the vinaigrette around the plate and serve immediately.

Serves 6

WHITE-BEAN BRANDADE

¾ cup cooked white beans, well drained

2 anchovy filets packed in salt, rinsed and patted dry (see Note)

1 teaspoon minced garlic

1 tablespoon extra-virgin olive oil

Sea salt and freshly cracked black pepper to taste

Place the beans in the bowl of a food processor fitted with the metal blade. Add the anchovy filets and garlic and process to a smooth purée.

With the motor running, slowly add the olive oil. Season with sea salt and cracked pepper to taste.

Store, covered and refrigerated, until ready to use, or for up to 5 days. Bring to room temperature before serving.

NIÇOISE VINAIGRETTE

3 tablespoons red wine vinegar

½ cup finely diced peeled, seeded ripe tomato

2 tablespoons finely chopped fresh flat-leaf parsley leaves

1½ tablespoons finely chopped niçoise olives

1 tablespoon capers, well drained

1 teaspoon minced garlic

1 teaspoon finely chopped fresh thyme leaves

1 teaspoon finely chopped fresh rosemary needles

⅓ cup plus 1 tablespoon extra-virgin olive oil

Place the vinegar in a mixing bowl. Stir in the tomatoes, parsley, olives, capers, garlic, thyme, and rosemary. Whisking constantly, add the olive oil.

Set aside to allow the flavors to meld for 30 minutes before serving.

Note: Rouget, a small, sweet Mediterranean fish, can be replaced with almost any sweet-fleshed saltwater fish. For this recipe you can substitute red snapper.

Salt-packed anchovies are available from fine fishmongers and some specialty food stores.

By the beginning of the twenty-first century, **cheese service**, cheese plates, and cheese carts were very much a part of the **"haute"** restaurant scene in America. This was, in great part, due to the influence of Terrance Brennan, who had offered this traditional French service at Picholine for years. Where we once knew only the bland, processed American cheeses and a few acceptable Cheddars and packaged imported cheeses, we were now being offered prize-winning American **farmstead** cheeses and imported cheeses made from raw milks. The cheese landscape had changed drastically and the American dining public embraced it with a passion. Terrance also created a new position in America when he hired Max McCalman as cheese sommelier.

SLOW-ROASTED SALMON
WITH WILD MUSHROOMS AND FOIE GRAS EMULSION
2000
EDWARD BROWN, *Chef/Partner, The Sea Grill, Cookbook Author*

Edward Brown is a champion of environmentally friendly foods. He has his work cut out for him ensuring that only appropriately raised and caught fish make it to the restaurant table. His strong convictions have done much to make the restaurant community aware of the hazards of depleting our ocean's resources. Working at The Sea Grill in Manhattan's Rockefeller Center, Ed uses his classic French training to take fish dishes to new heights.

Ed used both emulsion and slow roasting in this recipe, which superbly illustrates these two methods, which had become familiar during this period.

One 1½-pound skinless, boneless wild salmon filet, cut into 4 equal pieces

2 tablespoons unsalted butter, at room temperature

Coarse salt and freshly ground pepper to taste

Wild Mushroom Sauté (recipe follows)

Foie Gras Emulsion (recipe follows)

Preheat the oven to 275°F.

Place the salmon pieces on a nonreactive baking sheet. Rub each piece with a bit of the butter and season with salt and pepper to taste.

Place in the preheated oven and bake for about 12 minutes, or until just barely cooked through.

Spoon equal portions of the Wild Mushroom Sauté in the center of each of four serving plates. Place a piece of salmon on top and spoon the Foie Gras Emulsion over the top. Serve immediately.

Serves 4

WILD MUSHROOM SAUTÉ

1 tablespoon olive oil

1 cup cremini mushrooms, cut into thirds

2 cups torn chanterelle mushrooms, caps only

3 shallots, peeled and minced

1 clove garlic, peeled and finely mashed

1 tablespoon unsalted butter

2 tablespoons roughly chopped fresh flat-leaf parsley leaves

2 tablespoons roughly chopped fresh tarragon leaves

2 tablespoons roughly chopped fresh chives

Coarse salt and freshly ground pepper to taste

Heat the oil in a large sauté pan until smoking.

Add the cremini mushrooms and sauté for 5 minutes. Add the chanterelles and sauté for an additional 2 minutes. Stir in the shallots, garlic, and butter and sauté for an additional 45 seconds.

Remove from the heat and stir in the parsley, tarragon, and chives. Season with salt and pepper to taste and keep warm until ready to serve.

FOIE GRAS EMULSION

¾ cup (1½ sticks) unsalted butter, softened

4 ounces foie gras

1 tablespoon Armagnac

1 teaspoon fresh lemon juice

Coarse salt and freshly ground pepper to taste

3 tablespoons heavy cream

Combine the butter, foie gras, Armagnac, lemon juice, and salt and pepper to taste in the bowl of a food processor fitted with the metal blade. Process to a smooth purée.

Scrape the mixture from the bowl into a clean container. Cover and refrigerate for about 1 hour, or until well chilled.

When ready to serve, place the cream in a small saucepan over medium heat. Remove the foie gras mixture from the refrigerator and, using a handheld blender, beat it into the cream, mixing until frothy.

Taste and, if necessary, season with salt and pepper to taste. Keep warm until ready to serve.

187

FRIED OYSTERS
ON CREAMY WINTER SUCCOTASH
WITH BARBECUE VINAIGRETTE
2000

BEN BARKER, *Chef/Owner, Magnolia Grill, Cookbook Author*

Ben Barker has put new Southern cooking on the culinary map. When Ben and his wife, Karen, made their visit to De Gustibus from their restaurant, Magnolia Grill, in Durham, North Carolina, it was as though we were transported to the Old South. Their knowledge of classic techniques and regional ingredients, combined with their respect for traditional manners and grace, made for some truly spectacular combinations. It was Southern hospitality at its best.

About this recipe, Ben Barker says, "Ahhh, fried oysters . . . we do them so many different ways, it's difficult to choose one dish. This one commingles some of the aspects we like best: crunchy, briny, salty, creamy, tangy, a little bit spicy. Plus, it's an opportunity to sneak some hominy by an unsuspecting victim who's loudly proclaimed his disdain for that lowly grain. Have everything ready before you fry the oysters; the key to success is hot and GBD (golden brown and delicious)."

1 cup coarsely ground cornmeal

½ cup all-purpose flour

½ teaspoon coarse salt

¼ teaspoon freshly ground black pepper

¼ teaspoon cayenne

1½ pints shucked oysters, reserving ¼ cup liquor for the vinaigrette

Approximately 6 cups peanut oil

Creamy Winter Succotash (recipe follows)

Barbecue Vinaigrette (recipe follows)

¼ cup chopped scallions, white and green parts

Preheat the oven to 200°F.

Combine the cornmeal, flour, salt, black pepper, and cayenne in a shallow bowl.

Place four to six large, shallow soup bowls in the oven to warm.

Working with a few at a time, place the oysters in the cornmeal mixture and toss to coat well. Lift the oysters from the dredging mixture, shaking off the excess.

Heat the oil in a deep-fat fryer over high heat until it reaches 350°F on an instant-read thermometer.

Add the oysters, a few at a time, and fry for about 2 minutes, or until golden brown and crisp. Using a slotted spoon, transfer the oysters to a double layer of paper towels to drain. Place the oysters on a baking pan in the preheated oven to keep warm while you continue to fry the remaining oysters.

Remove the serving bowls from the oven. Spoon equal portions of the succotash into each bowl. Pile equal portions of the fried oysters on top of the succotash and spoon some of the warm vinaigrette around the edge of each portion. Sprinkle with scallions and serve immediately.

Serves 4 to 6

CREAMY WINTER SUCCOTASH

2 tablespoons peanut oil

3 ounces country ham, cut into small dice

½ cup diced onion

¼ cup diced fennel bulb

¼ cup diced carrot

¼ cup diced red bell pepper

1 tablespoon minced garlic

Pinch red pepper flakes

1 bay leaf

2 cups fresh or thawed frozen baby lima beans

Chicken stock as needed

1 cup white hominy, rinsed and drained

¾ cup heavy cream

Coarse salt and freshly ground pepper to taste

1 cup coarsely chopped arugula leaves

1 tablespoon chopped fresh flat-leaf parsley leaves

1 teaspoon fresh thyme leaves

Cider vinegar to taste

Heat the oil in a large saucepan over medium heat. Add the ham and cook, stirring frequently, for about 4 minutes, or until lightly browned. Using a slotted spoon, transfer the ham to a plate.

Keeping the saucepan on medium heat, add the onion, fennel, carrot, and bell pepper. Cook, stirring frequently, for about 5 minutes, or until the vegetables have softened.

Stir in the garlic, red pepper flakes, and bay leaf and cook for 1 minute. Add the lima beans along with just enough chicken stock to barely cover. Bring to a simmer and cook for about 12 minutes, or until the beans are tender.

While the beans are cooking, combine the hominy with the cream in a small saucepan over medium heat. Bring to a boil, lower the heat, and simmer, stirring occasionally, for about 7 minutes, or until the cream has reduced slightly and thickened.

Scrape the hominy mixture into the bean mixture. Taste and, if necessary, add salt and pepper to taste. The succotash may be made up to this point and stored, covered and refrigerated, until ready to use, or for up to 3 days.

When ready to serve, return the succotash to a medium saucepan over low heat and warm through. Stir in the reserved ham along with the arugula, parsley, thyme, and cider vinegar to taste. The succotash should be served immediately after adding the greens so that they retain some of their brightness.

BARBECUE VINAIGRETTE

¼ cup strained oyster liquor

¼ cup cider vinegar

2 tablespoons honey

1 tablespoon tamarind concentrate (see Note)

Pinch red pepper flakes

2 tablespoons roasted garlic purée (see Note)

2 tablespoons tomato paste

1/4 cup peanut oil

Tabasco to taste

Coarse salt and freshly ground pepper to taste

Combine the oyster liquor, cider vinegar, honey, tamarind concentrate, and red pepper flakes in a small nonreactive saucepan over medium heat. Bring to a boil, lower the heat, and simmer for 5 minutes. Transfer to a blender.

Add the garlic and tomato paste to the warm mixture in the blender and process to combine.

With the motor running, slowly pour in the peanut oil, processing until completely emulsified. Season with Tabasco and salt and pepper to taste and keep just barely warm until ready to use. The vinaigrette may be made up to this point and stored, covered and refrigerated, until ready to use. If so, it must be gently reheated and re-emulsified in a blender before serving.

Note: Tamarind concentrate is available in Asian markets and most specialty food stores.

Roasted garlic (see Note page 65) is so soft that it is almost a purée. You need do nothing more than mash it up with a fork.

CHILLED RHUBARB SOUP
1999
CLAUDIA FLEMING, *Pastry Chef, Cookbook Author*

Claudia Fleming turned the Manhattan dessert scene on its head with new takes on old favorites. Working at Gramercy Tavern, Claudia introduced diners to many long-forgotten fruits, techniques, and recipes. In this recipe, which was part of a larger recipe that included a rhubarb napoleon and rose-flavored *panna cotta,* Claudia created one of her terrific desserts, a cold fruit soup.

Fruit soups came to the fore in the nineties, when health-conscious eating took hold. They were embraced by pastry chefs for their endless possibilities and by diners for their low calories. Claudia seemed to be able to work miracles with them, as this recipe shows. The tart rhubarb, an old-fashioned American fruit (which is technically a vegetable) makes a very refreshing finish to a rich meal. You could, if desired, add some diced, caramelized rhubarb for garnish.

6½ cups (about 2 pounds, untrimmed) fresh rhubarb, peeled, trimmed, and cut crosswise into ½-inch pieces

1-inch piece fresh ginger, peeled and cut crosswise into 12 pieces

1½ cups simple syrup (recipe follows)

4 sprigs fresh mint (optional)

Combine the rhubarb, ginger, and syrup in a medium saucepan over medium heat. Bring to a boil, lower the heat, and simmer, stirring occasionally with a wooden spoon to break up the rhubarb, for about 15 minutes, or until the rhubarb has disintegrated.

Remove from the heat and pass through a medium sieve into a clean container, discarding the solids. Cover and refrigerate for at least an hour or until well chilled.

Serve chilled and garnish with a sprig of mint, if desired.

Serves 4

SIMPLE SYRUP

2 cups sugar

1½ cups water

Combine the sugar and water in a small saucepan over medium heat. Bring to a boil, lower the heat, and simmer, stirring occasionally, for about 3 minutes, or until the sugar has dissolved.

Remove from the heat and set aside to cool.

When cool, place in a container, cover, and refrigerate until ready to use, or for up to 3 months.

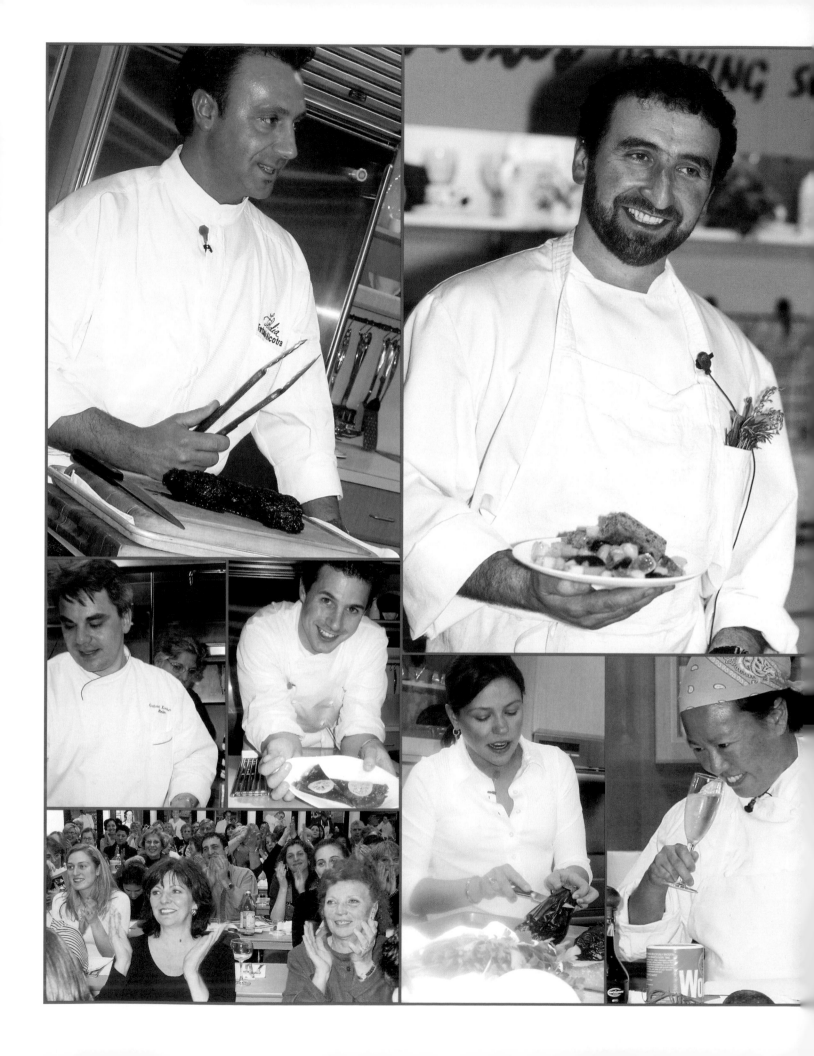

2001 to 2005

Simplicity Reigns

As far back as the early eighties, food writers were promoting the foods of Spain, but it wasn't until the late nineties when an extraordinarily gifted and imaginative chef, Ferran Adrià, made the world sit up and take notice. Experimenting in his laboratory-kitchen, El Bulli's Taller in Barcelona, and then presenting his creations at his restaurant El Bulli in northern Spain, Chef Adrià brought foams, unheard-of combinations, untried ingredients, and experimental techniques into his repertoire. His influence was felt deeply in restaurants the world over.

While American cooks were once thrilled when genuine Italian prosciutto was permitted entry into the American marketplace, at the turn of the new century, they began to make their own with great skill. House-cured *salumi* made a frequent appearance on menus as Italian and traditional American chefs delved into their heritage to create both dried and fresh meats and sausages. Along with this return to traditional ways came an interest in the revival of organ meats and innards in main-course preparations.

The television chef/personality was now firmly entrenched in the American culinary scene. While television shows were originally built around a particular chef, the new wave brought personalities with an interest in food as stars of their own programs. What was even more amazing was that chefs were becoming the featured performers in sitcoms and reality shows. It had become commonplace for the De Gustibus classroom to be filled to overflowing when a television "star" was teaching.

For New Yorkers the tragic events of September 11 reverberated in the restaurant industry with the loss of more than 200 employees and guests at the world-famous restaurant Windows on the World, which topped the World Trade Center. The financial consequences of the disaster were felt throughout the country as many thousands of employees in the restaurant industries lost their jobs due to the decrease in tourism and business travel.

One of the most deeply felt chasms to occur in the food industry was an alienation from all things French. The French government opposed America's intention to go to war with Iraq and, in protest, many restaurants took all French wines off of their lists, French fries were (momentarily) renamed, and long-established fine French dining spots found themselves faced with little or no business. Although this pique did not last for many months, it was strong enough to be instrumental in the demise of many of the nation's finest French restaurants. But then, many people said, perhaps it was simply time for America to reflect the maturity of its own cuisine.

Preceding pages (clockwise from top left):
Fortunato Nicotra; Cesare Casella; Suzanne Goin; Wylie Dufresne; L–R: Charlie Palmer, David Burke, Rick Moonen, Waldy Malouf; Sylvia Weinstock; Scott Conant; Marc Vetri; Anita Lo; Rachael Ray; De Gustibus audience; Gabriel Kreuther; Johnny Iuzzini.
Right: *Alain Ducasse and student*

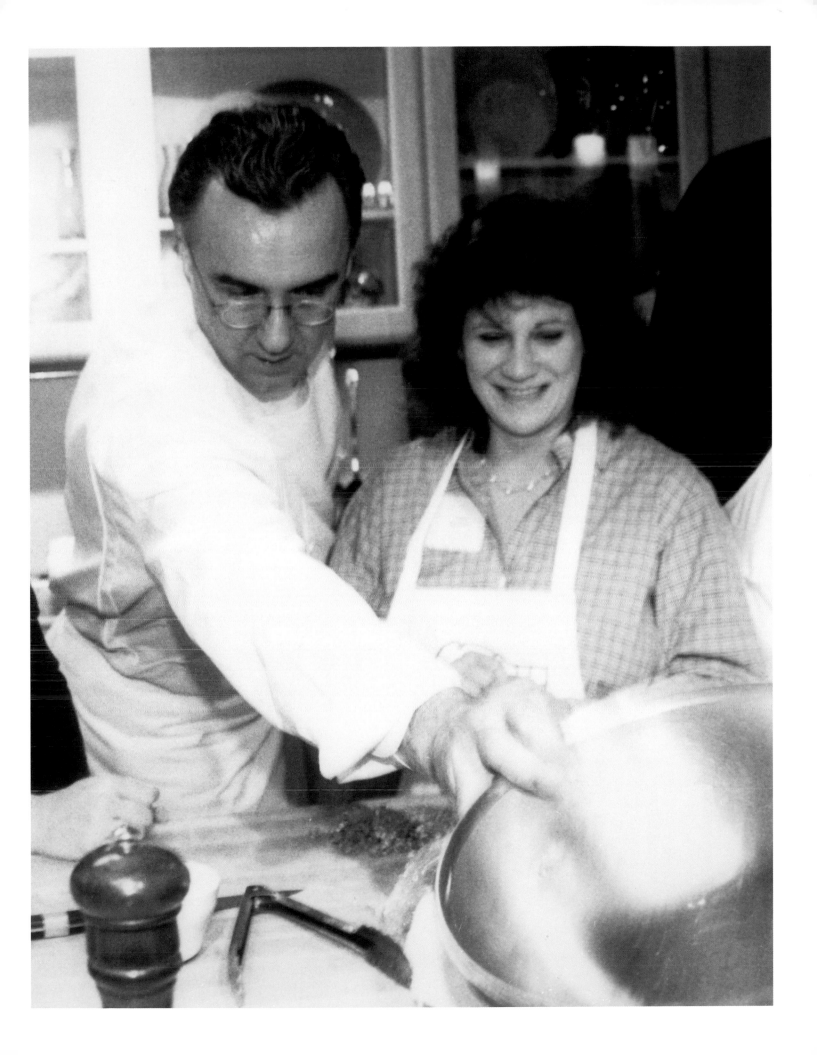

Jody Adams
Hossein Aimani
Jeffrey Alford
Pam Anderson
José Ramón Andrés
Michael Anthony
Francesco Antonucci
John Ash
Kirk Avondoglio
Dan Barber
Joseph Bastianich
Lidia Bastianich
Mario Batali
Stefano Battistini
Marc Bauer
Rick Bayless
Rose Levy Beranbaum
Jean-Michel Bergougnoux
Peter Berley
Michelle Bernstein
Bruno Bertin
Philippe Bertineau
Scott Bieber
Mark Bittman
Erik Blauberg
Jim Botsacos

James Boyce
Jimmy Bradley
Gregory Brainin
Flo Braker
Margaret Braun
Terrance Brennan
Bruce Bromberg
Eric Bromberg
Alton Brown
Jean-François Bruel
Scott Bryan
Giuliano Bugialli
Cathleen Burke
David Burke
Marian Burros
Jock Busser
Dolores and Jack Cakebread
Kenny Callaghan
Pippa Calland
Marco Canora
Floyd Cardoz
Andrew Carmellini
David Carmichael
Lincoln Carson
Cesare Casella
Rebecca Charles
Michael Chiarello
Judith Choate
Thomas Colicchio
Scott Conant
Cat Cora
Roger Dagorn
Ariane Daguin
Andrew D'Amico
Gary Danko
Gerry Dawes
Josh DeChellis
Christian Delouvrier
Traci Des Jardins
Andrew DiCataldo
Luc Dimnet
Tony DiSalvo
Rocco DiSpirito
Roberto Donna

Wylie Dufresne
Naomi Duguid
Toy Kim Dupree
Troy Dupuy
Jonathan Eismann
Didier Elena
Todd English
Workye Ephrem
Mary Ann Esposito
Odette Fada
George Faison
Mark Fiorentino
Susie Fishbein
Bobby Flay
Claudia Fleming
Diane Forley
Joseph Fortunato
George Francisco
Laura Frankel
Mark Franz
Clark Frasier
Mark Gaier
Cornelius Gallagher
Alex Garcia
Ina Garten
Rick Gencarelli
George Germon
Michael Ginor
Alessandro Giuntoli
Suzanne Goin
Rozanne Gold
Laurent Gras
Michael Green
Dorie Greenspan
Kurt Gutenbrunner
Gordon Hamersley
Gabrielle Hamilton
Lee Hanson
Craig Harzewski
Gerry Hayden
Sam Hayward
Kerry Heffernan
Thomas Henkelmann
Mark Hennessey

"De Gustibus intimidated me because their reputation was so fine. I am just a cook—why would they call me? Once I met the staff, Arlene and Amaral's staff, well, the **party** started and it has never ended. Cooking at De Gustibus is fun and easy and the **classes rock!** We have great times, great food, and huge laughs."
—Rachael Ray

David Bouley
Daniel Boulud
Anthony Bourdain

Michael Anthony
Dan Barber
Cesare Casella
Scott Conant

Wylie Dufresne
Cornelius Gallagher
Suzanne Goin
Johnny Iuzzini

Gabriel Kreuther
Anita Lo
Fortunato Nicotra
François Payard

Roger Vergé
Stanley Wong

Amanda Hesser
David Hirsch
Martha Holmberg
Andrea Immer
Johnny Iuzzini
Madhur Jaffrey
Sara Jenkins
Ramiro Jimenez
Lynne Rossetto Kasper
Mollie Katzen
Rob Kaufelt
Melissa Kelly
Matthew Kenney
Johanne Killeen
Robert Kinkead
Abigail Kirsch
Peter Klein
Craig Koketsu
David Kolotkin
Gabriel Kreuther
Price Kushner
Rick Laakkonen
Mark Ladner
Victor LaPlaca
John Larchet
Richard Leach

Anita Lo
Mario Lohninger
Michael Lomonaco
Emily Luchetti
Pino Luongo
David Lynch
Egidiana Maccioni
Sirio Maccioni
Mauro Mafrici
Jo-Ann Makovitsky
Waldy Malouf
Tony Mantuano
Silvano Marchetto
Jeremy Marshall
Lydie Marshall
Damiano Martin
Zarela Martinez
Olivier Masmondet
Shane McBride
Max Mc Calman
Leslie McEachern
George McKirdy
Alice Medrich
Jehangir Mehta
Perla Meyers
Mark Militello

Eberhard Müller
Neil Murphy
Riad Nasr
Alison Nathan
Jeffrey Nathan
Joan Nathan
Fortunato Nicotra
Ari Nieminen
Michel Nischan
Wayne Nish
Patrick Nuti
Patrick O'Connell
Steven Olson
Tadashi Ono
Ken Oringer
Daniel Orr
Michael Otsuka
David Page
Charles Palmer
Courtney Parker
Jonathan Parker
David Pasternak
Cindy Pawlcyn
François Payard
Scott Peacock
Jacques Pépin
Guillermo Pernot
Joy Pierson
Don Pintabona
Debra Ponzek
Alfred Portale
Marta Pulini
Deborah Racicot
Rachael Ray
Peter Reinhart
Cyril Renaud
Judy Rodgers
Douglas Rodriguez
Michael Romano
Ilene Rosen
David Rosengarten
Rosario Safina
Alain Sailhac
Paul Sale

> "Arlene, it was wonderful working with you. I can only say that New York City should be honoring you as one of their **treasures**. Your operation is first-rate and the epitome of professional thoroughness. Please pass my regards and thanks along to everyone. It was such a **great evening**—and no one seemed to want to leave—I thought we were going to pull out the sleeping bags for an overnighter." —Chef Richard Sandoval, Maya Restaurant

David Lebovitz
Jean Luc Le Dû
Alex Lee
Yvan Lemoine
Sarabeth Levine
Paul Liebrandt
Scott Linquist

Michael Mina
Wade Moises
Rick Moonen
Harold Moore
Marco Moreira
Masaharu Morimoto
Sara Moulton

Marcus Samuelsson
Aaron Sanchez
Damian Sansonetti
Richard Sandoval
Paulette Satur
Leslie Sbrocco
Pierre Schaedelin
Doris Schecter
Amy Scherber
Michael Schlow
Jasper Schneider
Sally Schneider
Charles Scicolone
Michele Scicolone
Vincent Scotto
Guenter Seeger
Barbara Shinn
Nancy Silverton
Christopher Siversen
André Soltner
Ana Sortun

Katy Sparks
Susan Spicer
Ivy Stark
Nick Stellino
Zanne Stewart
Alessandro Stratta
Mark Strausman
Brian Streeter
Michael Sullivan
Mark Tarbell
Geri Tashjian
Maximo Tejada
Bill Telepan
Jacques Torres
Laurent Tourondel
Cedric Tovar
Jeremiah Tower
Fabio Trabocchi
Scott Uehlein
Alex Urena
Thomas Valenti

Norman Van Aken
Roger Vergé
Marc Vetri
John Villa
Didier Virot
Brooke Vosika
Jonathan Waxman
Susan Weaver
Eileen Weinberg
Joanne Weir
Patricia Wells
Jody Williams
Paula Wolfert
Stanley Wong
Martin Yan
Sherry Yard
Patricia Yeo
Bill Yosses
Daniel Young
Geoffrey Zakarian
Galen Zamarra

Clogs in colors

Head coverings, from toques to baseball caps

Pants, from classic checks to food-fantasy prints

Jackets, from classic to the dentist's coat
in a rainbow of colors

Jody Adams wearing the first
offbeat chef's hat

ARROSER DE BEURRE
(BASTING WITH BUTTER)
CHIFFONADE
CONFIT
COULIS
CUTTING INTO
BRUNOISE
EMULSIONS
FOAMING
MONTÉ AU BEURRE
SOUS VIDE

25 YEARS OF

TECHNIQUES AND
PREPARATIONS THAT
HAVE BLOSSOMED

MOST
UNUSUAL
INGREDIENT

DRIED-AGED TUNA
to be used in salads, David Pasternak,
Esca, New York City

A NEW WORLD OF INGREDIENTS

THAT HAVE BEEN INTRODUCED OVER THE PAST TWENTY-FIVE YEARS

Aged balsamic vinegar • Arugula • Baby vegetables • Blood oranges • Bottarga • Buffalo meat • Buffalo mozzarella • Chayote •
Chipotle • Corn nuts • Couscous • Crème fraîche • Daikon • Dried cherries • Dried chilies • Dried cranberries • Dulce de leche
• Edamame • Edible flowers • Epazote • Farro • Fennel pollen • Foie gras • Free-range poultry • Fresh chilies • Fresh herbs •
Fresh pasta • Fresh wasabi • Garam masala • Gold leaf • Grains • Grapeseed oil • Honeys • Huitlacoche • Infused Oils •
Jícama • Kaffir lime leaves • Lemongrass • Lola Rosa lettuce • Meyer lemons • Microgreens • Microsprouts • Mizuna • Mojamo
• Mustard oil • Olives • Ostrich • Panko • Passion fruit • Polenta • Pomegranate • Pomegranate molasses • Preserved lemons •
Quince • Quinoa • Peruvian potatoes • Radicchio • Ramps • Ratte potatoes • Raw-milk cheese • Razor clams • Salts • Smashed
potatoes • Sriracha • Sumac • Tamarind • Tofu and other soy products • Tomatillos • Truffles and truffle products • Verjus •
Walnut oil • White balsamic vinegar • White soy sauce • Wild game • Yukon gold potatoes • Yuzu

ONLY CHEF TO RECEIVE A STANDING OVATION

JEAN BANCHET,
*of Le Français in
Wheeling, Illinois*

MOST ATHLETIC CHEFS

ALEX LEE—
marathon bike riding
ALFRED PORTALE—
tennis and skiing
MICHAEL ROMANO—
bike riding
BILL TELEPAN—
street basketball

Superlatives
1980 to 2005

MOST COMPLICATED EVENT

Getting a visa for
RAYMOND BLANC

DE GUSTIBUS AT MACY'S
1056 Fifth Avenue New York NY 10028
(212) 534-2178

September 9, 1986

EASTERN ADJUDICATIONS CENTER
52 South Main Street
St. Albans, Vermont 05478

RE: VISA APPLICATION FOR RAYMOND BLANC - HI STATUS
FORM I129B - RECEIPT #FAC-86-237-0116

Dear Sirs:

In response to the notice from your office, dated September 3, 1986, enclosed please find the original copy of I129B together with my affidavit supporting the application of Chef Blanc's visa and any other supporting documentation you had requested. I understand that your office has retained all the other information we have previously submitted.

As I indicated, Chef Blanc is scheduled to appear on behalf of De Gustibus on **September 22, 1986.** It is therefore of the utmost importance for Mr. Blanc's papers to be processed without delay.

I would like to respectfully request that Chef Blanc's visa application be given priority status in being processed. IF CHEF RAYMOND BLANC'S VISA HAS BEEN APPROVED BY YOUR OFFICE, I WOULD APPRECIATE YOUR CABLING THE AMERICAN CONSULATE IN LONDON TO VERIFY THAT MR. BLANC'S VISA HAS BEEN APPROVED.

If there is anything additionally to be done on our part to expedite this matter, please give me a call at (212) 534-2178.

We sincerely appreciate your efforts in this matter and would like to thank you for giving this matter your immediate attention.

Very truly yours,

Arlene Feltman
President

Enclosure

EASTERN ADJUDGD
52 South Main
St. Albans, Ve

RE: VISA APP
FORM I12

Dear Sirs:

This letter
Raymond Bla

I understan
cooking cl

I am curre
York. Le Cirque
The New York Times. In a...
at Deja-Vu Restaurant in Philadelphia from...
time, I received a citation from the City of Philade...
recreating a model of the town in sugar. In 1982, I was the
pastry chef in a Parisian restaurant, who reproduced the Palace
of Versailles when President Reagan visited France.

In 1984, I had the privilege of being a consulting pastry chef to
Raymond Blanc. It is my opinion that Chef Blanc is one of the
premier chefs in England and deserves the international reputation
he has earned. I believe that the American people should have
the opportunity to see and meet him in person.

Sincerely,

AFFIDAVIT

I, ARLENE FELTMAN, being duly sworn, hereby depose and sta...

1. I am the founder and President of "DeGustibus at M...
since 1978 has organized and sponsored cooking demons...
internationally famous chefs and leading cooking personalitie...
the world.

2. The purpose of the cooking demonstrations presented by...
at Macy's is to introduce Macy's customers to the finest chefs...
the world. In this way, Macy is able to teach its cu...
techniques and enjoyment of fine cooking and thereby to prom...
of Macy's cookbooks, cooking utensils, cookware, appliances, an...
products As well, these cooking demonstrations promote the o...
of Macy's as a department store offering the highest caliber se...
products to its customers.

3. In my capacity as President of DeGustibus at Mac...
organized approximately 56 such cooking demonstrations per...
1978. In connection with these demonstrations, I have conducte...
research into the elements of fine cooking. To ensure that Macy...
demonstrations are of the very highest caliber, I have also rese...
visited the finest restaurants throughout the world and have vi...
worked with many chefs having international reputations for thei...
excellence.

4. In connection with its September 1986 series of "Grea...
DeGustibus at Macy's wishes to present three cooking demonst...
Chef Raymond Blanc, Executive Chef and Owner of the award-wi...
Manoir Aux Quat' Saisons", a restaurant and hotel located in Grea...
Oxfordshire, England.

5. As part of my research, to ensure the caliber of Macy's...
demonstrations, I must be thoroughly familiar with all current...
and the prestigious guides which rate the finest internationa...
restaurants.

6. In this regard, Chef Blanc enjoys an international reputa...
the excellence of his restaurants and his cooking technic...
demonstrated by the articles attached hereto as Exhibits A and...
appeared in the New York Times on April 1, 1984 and May 15...
respectively. I hereby certify that I have personally seen...
copies of the articles, and that the enclosed Exhibits A and B a...
true and correct copies of those articles. As is stated...
articles, as a result of Chef Blanc's direction and cooking skil...
restaurant has received international acclaim.

7. Further, the Michelin Guide is the most reknown guide...
finest restaurants throughout the world and evaluates and rate...
eating establishments for the quality of their cuisine.

U.S. DEPARTME
IMMIGRATION A
SERV
P.O. BOX 1270
ALBANS

VED $ 35.0...

CIARY:
ND

I29B

08/27/86
09:57

NE FELTMAN
FIFTH AVE
YORK

ON THE MENU

APPETIZERS, SOUPS, AND SALADS

Cotton Candy Foie Gras
José Ramón Andrés—2004

Mark's Sake-Pickled Salmon
with Wasabi Crème Fraîche and Herb Salad
Mark Franz—2001

Seared Spanish Shrimp with Cauliflower Purée,
Pickled Ramps, and Blood Orange
Cornelius Gallagher—2003

Braised Baby Octopus
with Celery and Sun-Dried Tomato Ratatouille
Francesco Antonucci—2003

Ribollita
Marco Canora—2002

Polenta with Sautéed Porcini Mushrooms
Scott Conant—2003

Peasant Flour Soup
with Florida Frogs' Legs and Onion Sprouts
Gabriel Kreuther—2003

Fava Bean and Pecorino Salad
Sara Jenkins—2004

SAUCES AND SIDES

Green Beans with Prosciutto
and Celery Leaf Salsa Verde
Judy Rodgers—2002

Sweet Onion Crepe with White Truffle Fondue
Mark Vetri—2002

Green Curry Vegetables
Stanley Wong—2004

PASTA AND GRAINS

Macaroni and Cheese
with Virginia Country Ham and White Truffle
Patrick O'Connell—2001

Pasta alla Moda Rinascimentale
(Pasta in the Style of the Renaissance)
Cesare Casella—2002

MEAT, GAME, AND POULTRY

Boneless Barbecued Spareribs
with Kohlrabi, Peanuts, and Basil
Anita Lo—2003

Pork Belly with Soybean *Coulis* and Turnips
Wylie Dufresne—2003

Braised Hanger Steak
with Olive Oil–Mashed Sweet Potatoes
Fortunato Nicotra—2003

FISH AND SHELLFISH

Black Bass in Tangerine Sauce
with Farro and Black Rice
Suzanne Goin—2002

Arctic Char and Organic Beet Stew
with Soybeans and Pine Nuts
Dan Barber and Michael Anthony—2001

Fluke with Sea Beans and Radish
David Pasternak—2001

BREAD AND DESSERTS

Chocolate Tart
François Payard—2000

Chocolate Crepes Suzette
with Meyer Lemon Confit
Johnny Iuzzini—2003

Chocolate Cream with Coconut Baileys Soup
and Chocolate-Flavored Puffed-Rice Cereal
Jehangir Mehta—2004

COTTON CANDY FOIE GRAS
2004
JOSÉ RAMÓN ANDRÉS, *Chef/Owner, Jaleo, Café Atlantico,*
Minibar, Zaytinya, Oyamelk, Cookbook Author

In the United States, perhaps the greatest disciple of the renowned Spanish chef, Ferran Adrià, is José Ramón Andrés, a brilliant young chef working in Washington, D.C. In the spring of 2004, José Ramón taught us to make what might be the most unusual dish ever presented in the De Gustibus classroom: cotton candy foie gras. But it was so interesting and tasty, a number of the attendees immediately purchased cotton candy machines and have since reported that this dish has been the hit of every dinner party they have given. You will need a cotton candy machine (available at most toy stores) and six bamboo skewers to complete the recipe.

With this dish, Chef Andrés says that he "took a very humble food, cotton candy, something more often seen at amusement parks and carnivals, and sought to elevate it, transforming cotton candy into something elegant and refined." We are placing bets that this kind of cooking will be expanded upon for the next few years.

---

1 cup sugar

1 vanilla bean

4 ounces duck foie gras

Coarse salt to taste

1 cup corn nuts, crushed (see Note)

Place the sugar in a small bowl. Split the vanilla bean in half lengthwise and scrape the beans into the sugar. Add the pod, tossing to nestle it down into the sugar. Cover and set aside for 24 hours.

Chill the foie gras for a couple of hours, or until very cold.

When quite cold, cut the liver into six 1-inch cubes and lightly season with salt.

Heat a cotton candy machine.

Working with one at a time, place a piece of foie gras on each of six bamboo skewers. Roll the foie gras in the corn nuts just to cover lightly.

Remove the vanilla bean from the reserved vanilla sugar. (Do not discard as it can still be used to flavor sugar.)

As soon as the cotton candy machine is hot, add the reserved vanilla sugar to it. When cotton candy begins to form, dip the foie gras skewers into it and twirl to cover the foie gras with cotton candy.

Serve immediately.

Note: Do not crush the corn nuts too much. Their texture should be almost granular, not powdery.

Serves 6

MARK'S SAKE-PICKLED SALMON
WITH WASABI CRÈME FRAÎCHE AND HERB SALAD
2001
MARK FRANZ, *Chef/Owner, Farallon, Cookbook Author*

Mark Franz, chef at San Francisco's Farallon restaurant, came to the De Gustibus class-room along with his pastry chef, Emily Luchetti, and his sous-chef, George Francisco. They said that they had to prepare this dish as it was a favorite in the restaurant. We served it with champagne and it was delicious. It became a favorite of the entire class and remains in everyone's repertoire to this day.

It is an interesting recipe in that it features the commonplace and much-loved healthful salmon pickled in the unexpected Japanese grain alcohol, sake. This results in an almost sweet pickle which is highlighted by the rich and spicy crème fraîche and pungent herb salad. It is a good example of the type of dish we were seeing during this period.

About this recipe, Mark said, "This dish can be made as little as 2 hours in advance, but the fish really benefits from marinating for at least 4 hours, or up to 10 hours. The wasabi cream can be made 2 days in advance, but the herb salad should really be tossed just before serving."

---

4 whole star anise

2 tablespoons minced fresh ginger

1 tablespoon pickling spices

1 tablespoon Sichuan peppercorns (see Note)

1 cup rice wine vinegar

½ cup sake

¼ cup sugar

1½ tablespoons coarse salt

½ cup thinly sliced pearl onions

One 12-ounce piece skinless, bone-less salmon filet, cut into ½-inch cubes

Wasabi Crème Fraîche (recipe follows)

Herb Salad (recipe follows)

Place the star anise, ginger, pickling spices, and Sichuan pepper-corns in a square piece of cheesecloth. Using kitchen twine, tie the cheesecloth into a bag enclosing the spices. Set aside.

Place the vinegar, sake, sugar, and salt in a medium, nonreactive saucepan over medium heat. Add the spice sachet and bring to a boil.

Add the onions and again return to a boil. Lower the heat and simmer for 5 minutes. Remove from the heat and remove and discard the sachet.

Place the salmon cubes in a nonreactive bowl. Pour the pickling liquid with the onions over the salmon. If it does not quite cover the fish, either transfer it to a smaller container or add a little water. Do not add too much water, however, as it will dilute the flavor. Cover with plastic film and refrigerate for at least 2 hours, or up to 10 hours. Stir gently once or twice to ensure that all of the fish is evenly pickled.

When ready to serve, using a slotted spoon, remove the salmon from the pickling liquid and transfer to a clean kitchen towel to drain.

Place equal portions of the salmon in the center of each of four shallow soup bowls. Place a dollop of Wasabi Crème Fraîche in the center and top with a small mound of Herb Salad. Serve immediately.

Note: Sichuan peppercorns are aromatic, slightly "biting" berries from the prickly ash tree. They are usually heated to release their earthy, citrus flavor. Unrelated to black peppercorns, Sichuan peppercorns are used both whole and ground. They can be purchased from Adriana's Caravan (see page 247) but if need be a combination of equal amounts of black pepper and star anise can be substituted.

Wasabi powder is available from Japanese markets and some specialty food stores.

Serves 4

WASABI CRÈME FRAÎCHE

½ cup crème fraîche or sour cream

1 tablespoon wasabi powder (see Note)

¼ teaspoon coarse salt

Combine the crème fraîche, wasabi, and salt in a small, nonreactive container with a lid.

When well blended, cover and refrigerate until ready to use, or for up to 2 days.

HERB SALAD

1 bunch fresh chives, well washed, dried, and cut crosswise into 1-inch pieces

½ bunch fresh flat-leaf parsley, leaves only, well washed and dried

½ bunch fresh tarragon, leaves only, well washed and dried

½ bunch fresh chervil, stemmed, well washed, and dried

Toss the chives, parsley, tarragon, and chervil together in a small bowl. Cover with plastic film and refrigerate until ready to serve.

205

SEARED SPANISH SHRIMP
WITH CAULIFLOWER PURÉE, PICKLED RAMPS, AND BLOOD ORANGE
2003
CORNELIUS GALLAGHER, *Chef, Oceana*

Cornelius Gallagher is another of New York's chefs who devotes much of his repertoire to exotic seafood at Oceana, one of our finest fish restaurants. Whereas in many parts of the country, only frozen white fish filets were once available, a wide variety of fresh seafood is now being shipped all across the country due, in part, to the labors of American chefs like Cornelius. I'm sure he won't mind if you substitute your favorite shrimp for his Spanish specimens.

This recipe calls for many of the ingredients that were on the "must-have" list of chefs of this period: Spanish olive oil, exotic seafood, blood oranges, ramps, and fennel, most of which were totally unknown when I began De Gustibus. Ramps, or wild leeks, are particularly interesting. A wild vegetable commonly found along the East Coast of the United States in the springtime, they have long been popular with home cooks but until a few years ago were never seen on a restaurant menu. As chefs began using regional, seasonal ingredients, these old-fashioned aromatics became very popular on spring menus. Interestingly enough, ramps are still not cultivated.

2 tablespoons fine-quality Spanish olive oil

12 medium Carabinero (Spanish) shrimp, peeled and deveined, tails intact

Coarse salt to taste

2 tablespoons finely diced shallots

2 tablespoons fresh thyme leaves

Cauliflower Purée (recipe follows)

Pickled Ramps (recipe follows)

2 blood oranges, cut into suprêmes (see Note)

Fresh fennel greens for garnish (see sidebar)

Heat the olive oil in a large sauté pan over high heat until light plumes of smoke begin to rise from the pan. Reduce the heat to low.

Generously season the shrimp with salt and add them to the hot pan. Sear the shrimp for 2 minutes, stirring occasionally.

Add the shallots and thyme and cook for an additional 30 seconds, basting constantly.

Spoon equal portions of the Cauliflower Purée in the center of each of four plates. Top with three shrimp, Pickled Ramps, blood orange suprêmes, and fennel greens. Serve immediately.

Serves 4

Ramps are also known as wild leeks or **wild onions**. Although raw ramps have a very strong flavor, it is mellowed during cooking and ends up tasting very much like intense garlic. Ramps are available from March through June either from the wild in the eastern United States or from specialty produce stores.

CAULIFLOWER PURÉE

½ head fresh cauliflower, well washed

4 cups milk

Coarse salt and freshly ground white pepper to taste

Trim the cauliflower and break into florets. Cut the florets into pieces of roughly the same size to ensure that they can cook evenly.

Place the cauliflower in a medium saucepan along with the milk and salt to taste. Place over medium-high heat and bring to a boil. Immediately lower the heat and simmer for about 12 minutes, or until the cauliflower is very tender when pierced with the point of a small, sharp knife.

Remove from the heat and drain well, reserving ½ cup of the liquid.

Transfer the cauliflower to a blender and process, adding the least amount of the reserved liquid possible to make a smooth purée. Add pepper to taste and, if necessary, additional salt.

Either use immediately, transfer to the top half of a double boiler placed over simmering water, or place in a covered container and refrigerate until ready to use. If refrigerating, reheat before serving by transferring to the top half of a double boiler placed over simmering water.

PICKLED RAMPS

2 teaspoons olive oil

1 teaspoon curry powder

½ cup liquid from bottled cornichons (see Note)

8 ramps, white parts only, well washed and blanched (see sidebar)

Place the oil and curry powder in a small saucepan over medium heat. Cook, stirring frequently, for about 2 minutes, or until very fragrant.

Pour in the cornichon liquid and cook just until heated. Add the ramps and remove from the heat.

Set aside to cool until ready to use or transfer to a nonreactive container, cover, and refrigerate until needed. The ramps will keep, refrigerated, for about 3 months.

Note: Citrus suprêmes are simply individual segments of citrus fruit from which all of the membrane has been removed to make neat little sections.

Cornichons, tart little French gherkins, are available from most specialty food stores and some supermarkets.

Fennel is a vegetable that we began to see in all of its guises during this period. We had fresh fennel bulbs, fennel greens (the dill-like, feathery tops of the bulbs), baby fennel, fennel microgreens, and even fennel pollen. Fresh fennel is crisp and aromatic when used raw, but its aniselike flavor becomes quite elusive and sweet when cooked.

BRAISED BABY OCTOPUS
WITH CELERY AND SUN-DRIED TOMATO RATATOUILLE
2003

FRANCESCO ANTONUCCI, *Chef/Owner, Remi Restaurant, Cookbook Author*

Francesco Antonucci is a fun-loving Italian chef steeped in the traditions of Venice. Once, when stopping by to watch a Michael Romano "Italian" class, he was (I quote) "blown away" by the freedom of American chefs to interpret classic dishes in their own style. He said that, being Italian, he had to follow the traditional ways exactly. Since he was such a traditionalist, we found ourselves in one of his hands-on classes eating grilled octopus and drinking very strong grappa at eleven in the morning. We all agreed because he assured us it was the traditional way!

Octopus had become a favorite ingredient for many chefs during this period. Although it had traditionally been used in very basic Mediterranean home cooking, octopus is now found on three- and four-star menus all across America. It is interesting to note that, although Francesco thinks of himself as a traditional Italian chef, he has adopted the classic French ratatouille for this dish. The borders between cuisines are now wide open!

Preparations for this recipe must be started the day before serving. But I don't advise completing them while drinking grappa!

2 pounds fresh whole baby octopus, cleaned

1½ cups dry red wine

1½ cups red wine vinegar

2 heads radicchio (or trevisiano) well washed and cut in half lengthwise

1¼ cups extra-virgin olive oil

Juice of 2 lemons

6 sprigs fresh flat-leaf parsley

Coarse salt and pepper to taste

2 ribs celery, trimmed, peeled, and finely diced

3 ounces sun-dried tomatoes, cut into small dice

4 lemon wedges for garnish

Combine the octopus with 1 cup each of the wine and vinegar in a large nonreactive saucepan over medium heat. Bring to a boil, lower the heat, and simmer for 40 minutes, or until tender.

Remove from the heat and drain well, discarding the liquid. Set aside to cool.

While the octopus is cooking, combine the radicchio with the remaining ½ cup of wine and ½ cup of vinegar in a medium nonreactive saucepan over medium heat. Bring to a boil, lower the heat, and simmer for 30 minutes.

Remove from the heat and drain well, discarding the liquid. Tranfer to a bowl and set aside to cool.

When the octopus is cool, using a very sharp knife, cut them in half and place in a bowl.

Combine 1 cup of the olive oil with the lemon juice, parsley, and salt and pepper to taste in a small bowl, whisking constantly until well blended.

Pour three-fourths of the olive-oil mixture over the cooled, cut octopus, tossing to coat well. Cover with plastic film and refrigerate, turning occasionally, for at least 8 hours or overnight.

Pour the remaining olive-oil mixture over the radicchio, tossing to coat well. Cover with plastic film and refrigerate for at least 8 hours or overnight.

Combine the celery and sun-dried tomatoes with 2 tablespoons of the remaining olive oil in a small mixing bowl. Season with salt and pepper to taste and toss to combine. Cover with plastic film and refrigerate for at least 8 hours or overnight.

When ready to serve, remove the octopus, radicchio, and celery-tomato mixture from the refrigerator.

Place the octopus and radicchio in separate strainers and drain off all of the marinade. Do not pat dry.

Heat two sauté pans over medium heat. Add 1 tablespoon of the remaining olive oil to each pan. When very hot, add the octopus to one pan and the radicchio to the other. Sauté each for about 5 minutes, or until they begin to brown on all sides.

Add the celery-tomato mixture to the octopus and sauté for 2 minutes.

Remove the radicchio from the heat and cut each piece in half lengthwise.

Place two pieces of radicchio in the center of each of four plates. Mound equal portions of the octopus on top of the radicchio, garnish with a lemon wedge, and serve immediately.

Serves 4

RIBOLLITA

2002

MARCO CANORA, *Chef/Owner, Hearth*

We first met Marco Canora when he was the chef in Tom Colicchio's ingredient-driven kitchen at Gramercy Tavern. Everyone was bowled over by his ability to deconstruct a recipe for easy translation to the home kitchen. He has since gone on to open his own casual, Italian-inspired, ingredient-driven, restaurant—Hearth, also in New York City.

This recipe is one example of a chef taking a traditional dish and updating it to meet the demands of the sophisticated diner. Marco Canora has taken *ribollita* (Italian for "twice boiled")—originally a Tuscan soup that was no more than leftover minestrone recooked and mixed with bread chunks for a filling next-day's meal—and turned it into a fresh soup accented with beautiful crusty croutons. After tasting this soup we felt *ribollita* ruled!

2 tablespoons extra-virgin olive oil, plus more for drizzling

1 cup diced carrot

1 cup diced celery

1 cup diced onion

1 bunch fresh rosemary, well washed and dried

1 bunch fresh thyme, well washed and dried

1 tablespoon tomato paste

1 head Savoy cabbage, well washed, trimmed, spines removed, and chopped

1 bunch black cabbage or other kale, well washed, trimmed, and chopped (see Note)

Two 32-ounce cans unsalted chicken broth, plus more as needed

One 12-ounce can whole canellini beans, plus another 12-ounce can whole canellini beans, puréed

1 cup ½-inch pieces fresh string beans

1 cup diced seeded zucchini

Coarse salt and freshly ground pepper to taste

Freshly grated Parmigiano-Reggiano cheese for garnish

Croutons (recipe follows)

Heat 2 tablespoons of the olive oil in a large soup pot with a lid over medium heat. Add the carrot, celery, and onion and stir to combine. Cover and allow the vegetables to sweat their liquid for 8 minutes.

Using kitchen twine, tie the rosemary and thyme together.

Uncover the soup pot and stir in the tomato paste. Add the herb bundle and cook, stirring occasionally, for 5 minutes.

Stir in the Savoy and black cabbages, mixing until well combined. Cover and cook for an additional 5 minutes.

Add the chicken broth, bring to a boil, then lower the heat to a simmer. Stir in the whole canellini beans along with the purée, string beans, and zucchini. Season with salt and pepper to taste and simmer for 45 minutes. If the soup gets too thick, add additional broth as needed.

Remove from the heat and serve very hot, sprinkled with freshly grated cheese and freshly ground pepper, drizzled with extra-virgin olive oil and, if desired, garnish with croutons (recipe follows).

Serves 8

CROUTONS

1 loaf peasant-style Italian bread

Approximately ¾ cup extra-virgin olive oil (see Note)

Coarse salt and freshly ground pepper to taste

Preheat the oven to 350°F.

Cut the bread into 1-inch-square pieces. Place the bread cubes in a bowl and toss with the olive oil and salt and pepper to taste.

Transfer the seasoned bread cubes to a baking pan, spreading them out in an even layer. Bake for about 15 minutes, or until golden brown. Remove from the oven and set aside to come to room temperature.

When cool, store, airtight, at room temperature for no more than 2 days.

Note: *Black cabbage, also known as* cavelo nero, *is a dark, almost black kale. Any other kale may be substituted for it.*

The amount of oil required for croutons will depend upon the size of the loaf. You don't want to saturate the bread, only lightly coat it.

POLENTA
WITH SAUTÉED PORCINI MUSHROOMS
2003

SCOTT CONANT, *Chef/Partner, L'Impero, Alto*

Scott Conant, a young and talented American chef, is another one of the new Italian brigade in New York City. He keeps to traditional Italian ingredients but seems to have a knack for preparing them in a unique way. He seemed to explode on the New York restaurant scene in the early days of the twenty-first century, but his talent and charm told us that he was in for the long haul. He quickly became a classroom favorite!

Polenta had become the potatoes of this period. Scott's focus on traditional Italian cooking allowed him to prepare an exquisite example of this traditional home cook's filling dish for us. Everyone who has sampled it says that Scott's polenta is indescribably different from others and the most delicious they have ever eaten.

1 cup heavy cream

1 cup milk

Coarse salt to taste

4 ounces (about 10 tablespoons) polenta

2 tablespoons freshly grated Parmigiano-Reggiano cheese

1 tablespoon unsalted butter

Sautéed Mushrooms (recipe follows)

1 tablespoon chopped fresh chives

Combine the cream and milk in a medium, heavy-bottomed saucepan over medium heat. Cook just until bubbles begin to form around the edges. Add salt to taste and remove from the heat.

Beating constantly with a wooden spoon, slowly add the polenta. Return the pan to low heat and cook, stirring frequently, for about 40 minutes, or until very thick.

Stir the cheese and butter into the polenta. Taste and, if necessary, adjust the seasoning with salt.

Spoon the polenta onto a serving platter. Using a slotted spoon, place the mushrooms over the top of the polenta. Pour the mushroom pan juices over the top and around the edge. Garnish with chives and serve immediately.

Serves 4

SAUTÉED MUSHROOMS

2 tablespoons extra-virgin olive oil

½ shallot, peeled and minced

¼ pound fresh porcini mushrooms, cleaned and chopped

1 cup chicken demi-glace (see Note)

Truffle oil to taste

Coarse salt and freshly ground pepper to taste

Heat the olive oil in a medium sauté pan over medium heat. When very hot but not yet smoking, add the shallot. Cook, stirring constantly, for about 3 minutes, or until the shallot starts to caramelize.

Add the mushrooms and cook, stirring frequently, for about 5 minutes, or until the mushrooms begin to exude their juices. Stir in the chicken demi-glace and bring to a rapid simmer. Simmer for about 12 minutes, or until the liquid has reduced by two-thirds.

Stir in truffle oil and season with salt and pepper to taste. Set aside and keep warm until ready to serve.

Note: Demi-glace is available from fine butchers, specialty food stores, and from D'Artagnan (see page 247).

PEASANT FLOUR SOUP
WITH FLORIDA FROGS' LEGS AND ONION SPROUTS
2003

GABRIEL KREUTHER, *Chef, The Modern*

This recipe is a clear example of the experimentation that flourishes in contemporary American cooking. Peasant soup, elegant frogs' legs, and unusual onion sprouts combine, in the hands of a classically trained Alsatian chef, to make a sublime dish.

6 tablespoons (¾ stick) unsalted butter

3 ounces all-purpose flour

¼ cup olive oil

¼ pound smoked ham, cut into 1- to 2-inch chunks

2 leeks, white part only, well washed and thinly sliced crosswise

2 medium onions, peeled and thinly sliced crosswise

Pinch coarse salt, plus more to taste

1 pound button mushrooms, cleaned and sliced

4 cups hot unsalted, defatted chicken stock

4 cups hot water

Freshly ground pepper to taste

1 pound frogs' legs, deboned (see sidebar)

1 bunch onion sprouts (see Note)

1 tablespoon chopped fresh chives

For years, chefs have recommended the following source for **fresh frogs' legs**, which I pass on to you: Patricia Forino at United—540-885-2552. Sorry! There is no e-commerce in the frog-leg business, but Patricia is very nice to chat with! Jean-Georges Vongerichten gave us this source fifteen years ago.

Preheat the oven to 375°F.

Melt the butter in a small, ovenproof skillet over medium heat. When very hot, add the flour, raise the heat, and cook, stirring constantly, for about a minute, or until the flour is well incorporated.

Transfer the roux to the oven and bake for about 20 minutes, or until very dark brown, watching carefully to prevent burning. If necessary, stir with a wooden spoon occasionally to prevent sticking and burning. Remove from the oven and set aside to cool.

Heat 2 tablespoons of the olive oil in a Dutch oven over medium heat. Add the ham, leeks, onions, and a pinch of salt and cook for about 5 minutes, or until the vegetables sweat their liquid. Stir in the mushrooms and continue to sweat the vegetables, stirring occasionally, for another 5 minutes.

Stir in the stock and water and bring to a boil. Lower the heat, loosely cover, and simmer for 30 minutes.

Carefully whisk in the reserved roux, a bit at a time, and continue to cook for an additional 30 minutes.

Remove from the heat and pass through a fine sieve, pressing on the solids to extract all of the juices, into a clean saucepan.

Return the strained soup to medium heat and bring to a boil. Season with salt and pepper to taste and keep warm until ready to serve.

When ready to serve, season the frogs' legs with salt and pepper to taste.

Heat the remaining 2 tablespoons of olive oil in a large sauté pan over medium heat. Add the seasoned frogs' legs and sauté for about 5 minutes, or until lightly browned and cooked through. Add the sprouts and chives and toss to coat—do not cook the sprouts, just let them wilt slightly.

Spoon equal portions of the frog-leg mixture into the center of each of four shallow soup bowls.

Transfer the soup to a tureen and pass the tureen so that each diner may ladle the desired amount of soup into his or her bowl.

Note: Onion sprouts are available from Melissa's (see page 247) or from other specialty food stores.

Serves 4

FAVA BEAN AND PECORINO SALAD
2004
SARA JENKINS, *Former Chef, 50 Carmine*

Sara Jenkins is at the head of the class of young Italian-inspired chefs using only a few "of-the-moment" ingredients to redefine Italian cooking in America. We have come a very long way from the simple southern Italian home cooking of twenty-five years ago.

Here again, only the best will do. Sara Jenkins has used just a few perfect ingredients to make a salad that sings of Italy. Inspired by her mother, Italian food authority and cookbook author Nancy Harmon Jenkins, Sara has brought many simple, traditional Italian dishes to the restaurant table at 50 Carmine in New York City. She takes no shortcuts—with neither technique, nor ingredients, nor talent! For this class she brought her friend Mark Ladner, chef at the New York restaurant Lupa, as her assistant. We got two great young chefs for the audience's pleasure!

---

2 cups fresh shelled, peeled fava beans

1 cup diced aged Tuscan Pecorino Romano cheese

½ cup mixed chopped fresh herbs, such as flat-leaf parsley, mint, oregano, chervil, tarragon, lovage, fennel greens, celery tops, chives, borage, or sorrel

⅔ cup estate-bottled Italian extra-virgin olive oil

Cracked black pepper to taste

Combine the beans, cheese, and herbs in a bowl. Drizzle in the olive oil and season with cracked pepper. Toss to coat.

Set aside to mellow for 15 minutes before serving.

Serves 6

215

GREEN BEANS WITH PROSCIUTTO
AND CELERY LEAF SALSA VERDE
2002

JUDY RODGERS, *Chef/Owner, Zuni Café, Cookbook Author*

Judy Rodgers' Zuni Café in San Francisco is a destination for every foodie in the world. Judy is most famous for her straightforward approach to food and service, which has inspired hundreds of other chef-restaurateurs. The welcoming atmosphere of the restaurant and the embracing aromas emanating from the wood-burning ovens more than set the tone for the food to come. You will often hear a young chef say, "My dream is to open a Zuni Café."

I had invited Judy Rodgers to come to De Gustibus for about ten years running and always got the same answer: "When my book is finished." Finally, she answered, "The book is finished, count me in." I can assure you that both her class and the book were worth the wait. I hope we can count on repeats on both fronts.

About this recipe, Judy says, "Salsas, especially green ones, are great democratizers in the kitchen. Anyone can make an excellent one, they go with humble as well as fancy dishes, they are crowd pleasers, and they need not be expensive. They are not, of course, forgiving of mediocre ingredients, so make the effort to gather perky, fragrant herbs. Chop them just before you assemble the salsa, and don't do that too far in advance. Time will dull the bright taste and texture."

¾ pound young, tender green beans, stem ends trimmed

Celery Leaf Salsa Verde (recipe follows)

6 ounces thinly sliced prosciutto

Place a gallon of water in a large saucepan over high heat. Add salt to taste—Judy recommends 1 tablespoon per gallon—and bring to a boil. Add the beans and stir once. Return the water to a boil and begin testing the beans for doneness after 30 seconds. Judy says, "They will still be undercooked but how undercooked they are will guide you in judging how much longer they will take."

Taste every 10 seconds until the beans lose their raw crunch. Remove them from the heat and drain them just as they are beginning to lose their grassy taste. Don't overcook or you will miss out on the beans' subtle, sweet flavor and velvety-nutty texture.

Cool slightly under cool, running water—just long enough to stop the cooking. Transfer to a clean kitchen towel and pat dry.

Place the warm, dry beans in a mixing bowl and add just enough of the salsa to coat well. Toss to blend.

Arrange the prosciutto slices, slightly overlapping, on a platter. Pile the beans in a haystack form on top of the prosciutto and drizzle some or all of the remaining salsa over all. Serve immediately.

Serves 4

CELERY LEAF SALSA VERDE

¼ cup tightly packed celery leaves

2 tablespoons tightly packed chopped fresh flat-leaf parsley

2 tablespoons finely diced pale-yellow interior celery ribs

2 tablespoons capers, rinsed, patted dry, and coarsely chopped

1 tablespoon finely diced red onion

1 teaspoon finely diced red jalapeño chili

1 teaspoon finely chopped salt-packed anchovies (optional)

Juice and zest from 1 lemon

½ cup extra-virgin olive oil

Coarse salt and freshly ground pepper to taste

Combine the celery leaves, parsley, celery ribs, capers, onion, chili, and anchovies, if using, in a nonreactive mixing bowl.

Stir in the lemon juice and zest, followed by the olive oil. Season with salt and pepper to taste and set aside for a few minutes to allow the salt to dissolve and the flavors to mingle. Taste and, if necessary, adjust the lemon, oil, and seasonings. Do not refrigerate but keep in a cool spot until ready to serve.

SWEET ONION CREPE WITH WHITE TRUFFLE FONDUE

2002

MARC VETRI, *Chef/Owner, Vetri*

The self-taught Marc Vetri has been able to marry classic Italian cooking with inspiration from many other sources. This recipe is another example of how chefs in the twenty-first century have gone about redefining American cooking: great ingredients, careful experimentation with many cuisines, and a relaxed approach to putting it all together.

6 yellow onions, peeled and cut into julienne

1 tablespoon unsalted butter

1 tablespoon olive oil

Pinch coarse salt, plus more to taste

2 large eggs, at room temperature

½ cup milk

2 tablespoons grapeseed oil

½ cup all-purpose flour

Freshly ground pepper to taste

Freshly grated nutmeg to taste

Approximately 1 tablespoon clarified butter (optional) (see Note page 94)

1½ cups freshly grated Parmigiano-Reggiano cheese

1½ cups heavy cream

Touch of truffle oil or truffle paste (see Note)

Place the onions in a large sauté pan. Add the butter, olive oil, and a pinch of salt. Place over very low heat and cook, stirring occasionally, for about 6 hours, or until the onions are a deep, almost-burned, brown color.

Remove the pan from the heat and place on a wire rack to cool.

While the onions are cooling, prepare the crepes: Whisk the eggs, milk, and grapeseed oil together in a medium bowl. Whisking constantly, beat in the flour along with salt, pepper, and nutmeg to taste.

Heat a nonstick crepe pan over low heat. If using clarified butter, lightly coat the pan with it. Ladle in just enough batter to coat the bottom of the pan evenly. Cook for about 1 minute, or just until the crepe is set and can easily be flipped. Flip and cook the remaining side for 30 seconds. Carefully slide the crepe from the pan and set aside. Continue cooking crepes until you have eight. You might want to make a couple of extras in case one tears.

Preheat the oven to 350°F.

Working with one at a time, lay a crepe out on a flat surface. Spoon a generous amount of the cooled onion over the entire crepe. Roll the crepe up and cut it crosswise into ¾-inch pieces.

Place the crepe pieces, cut side down, on a parchment paper–lined baking sheet. Sprinkle ½ cup of the cheese over the top of the crepe pieces and place in the preheated oven. Bake for about 8 minutes, or until golden brown and crisp.

While the crepes are baking, prepare the sauce: Place the cream in a small saucepan over medium heat. Bring to a boil, then lower the heat and simmer for about 5 minutes, or until slightly thickened. Whisk in the remaining cup of cheese along with the truffle oil (or paste) and cook, whisking constantly, for another minute or two, or just until the sauce thickens.

Remove the crepe pieces from the oven. Spoon equal portions of the sauce on each of four plates. Lay equal portions of the crispy crepes on each plate and serve immediately.

Note: Truffle oil and truffle paste are available from specialty food stores.

Serves 4

GREEN CURRY VEGETABLES

2004

STANLEY WONG, *Chef, Spice Market*

Stanley Wong taught for us when he was at Tan Da in New York City. I was completely fascinated by his Chinese, German, and Jewish heritage, wondering how the mix would translate to the plate. He was a fantastic teacher who brought an enormous enthusiasm to his cooking. He went on to become chef de cuisine at the Jean-Georges Vongerichten–Gray Kunz restaurant, Spice Market, where his talents in culinary exploration can really shine.

This recipe pulls together many of the Asian ingredients that we had been introduced to earlier in this period, plus a couple that we had never heard about. The sauce makes enough for a great many servings, but the vegetables have been portioned for one serving. Obviously, the recipe can be expanded to meet your needs.

1 tablespoon peanut oil

9 fresh bamboo shoots (see Note)

7 snap peas, well washed

3 fresh ears baby corn

3 fresh okra pods, well washed, stems removed

2 fresh asparagus spears, cut crosswise into 1-inch pieces

2 tiny broccoli florets

1 fresh water chestnut, sliced (see Note)

½ Thai eggplant, well washed, trimmed, and cut, lengthwise, into ¼-inch-thick slices

½ red finger chili (see Note)

Green Curry Sauce (recipe follows)

1 tablespoon green peppercorns

1 kaffir lime leaf (see Note)

Nam pla or other fish sauce to taste (see Note)

Coarse salt to taste

Cooked rice (optional)

Heat the oil in a large sauté pan or wok. Add the bamboo shoots, snap peas, corn, okra, asparagus, broccoli, water chestnut, eggplant, and chili and sauté for about 5 minutes, or until crisp-tender.

Stir in enough Green Curry Sauce to coat the vegetables generously. Add the peppercorns, lime leaf, and fish sauce and cook for an additional 5 minutes, or until the flavors have blended. Taste and, if necessary, season with salt to taste.

Remove from the heat and serve immediately with hot rice if desired.

Serves 1

By the end of the nineties, fresh **lemongrass** seemed to be the citrusy scent of choice in all types of cooking in America. It is a subtly fragrant herb that lends just a hint of lemon to a dish. It consists of a woody stalk with coarse, grassy leaves and a small bulb at the stem end. The outer layers of the bulb must be peeled away to reveal the tender, pinkish-fleshed heart. The heart is finely diced or sliced if used raw. If it is to be cooked, the bulb is used along with no more than six inches of the stalk. This tougher part has to be bruised to release the essential oils that will flavor a dish. Fresh lemongrass can now be found in many supermarkets and greenmarkets.

GREEN CURRY SAUCE

4 cups coconut milk

4 cups unsalted, defatted chicken stock

½ cup Green Curry Paste (recipe follows)

½ cup fresh cilantro leaves

Coarse salt to taste

Combine the coconut milk, chicken stock, and curry paste in a heavy-bottomed saucepan over medium heat. Bring to a boil and immediately remove from the heat.

Transfer to a blender, add the cilantro and salt to taste, and process, in batches if necessary, until smooth.

Pour into a container, place the container in an ice-water bath, and set aside to chill.

When chilled, cover and refrigerate until ready to use, or for up to 3 days.

GREEN CURRY PASTE

1 green Thai bird's eye chili, well washed and dried (see Note)

½ pound lemongrass, tender, pale part only (see sidebar)

¼ pound hot green chilies, well washed, stemmed, and chopped

1½ ounces fresh cilantro root (not leaves), well washed and chopped (see Note)

1½ ounces galangal (see sidebar page 182)

¾ cup fresh cilantro leaves

½ cup chopped shallots

¼ cup chopped garlic

1½ tablespoons ground coriander

2¼ teaspoons ground cumin

2¼ teaspoons freshly ground black pepper

Pinch belacan (see Note)

Up to 1 cup water

Place the bird's eye chili, lemongrass, green chilies, cilantro root, galangal, cilantro leaves, shallots, garlic, coriander, cumin, black pepper, and belacan in a blender.

With the motor running, add just enough water to make a smooth paste. Stop the motor from time to time and, using a rubber spatula, push the ingredients down from the sides of the blender jar to ensure that everything is combined.

Transfer to a nonreactive container, cover, and refrigerate until ready to use, or for up to 2 weeks.

Note: Both the sauce and the paste recipe yields are much more than you need for one serving, so you can either increase the amount of vegetables and feed a crowd or store the sauce and paste, covered and refrigerated or frozen, for future use.

Bamboo shoots, fresh water chestnuts, Asian chilies, kaffir lime leaf, nam pla, cilantro root, galangal, and belacan are available at Asian markets.

Belacan is a dark-brown cake made from sun-dried shrimp paste. It has a very strong, sharp aroma and a salty flavor and must be roasted before it can be used to release the flavor and mellow the taste.

221

MACARONI AND CHEESE
WITH VIRGINIA COUNTRY HAM AND WHITE TRUFFLE
2001

PATRICK O'CONNELL, *Chef/Co-Owner and Inn Keeper, The Inn at Little Washington, Cookbook Author*

Patrick O'Connell has always been a terrific inspiration to his De Gustibus classes because he is a self-taught chef who has taken his talents to their highest form. The kitchen is the focal point of Patrick's (and his partner, Reinhardt Lynch's) four-star Relais & Châteaux, The Inn at Little Washington in Virginia, a coveted destination for foodies and seasoned travelers from all over the world. Patrick is known for using local ingredients and traditional recipes, accenting them with luxurious foods and then creating a cuisine all his own.

You don't have to make the Parmesan Tuile Baskets, but if you do Patrick suggests that you use a Silpat-lined cookie sheet to ensure that the tuiles can be easily removed. If you don't have a Silpat sheet, however, a fine-quality nonstick pan will work just fine.

---

3 ounces dried tubular pasta

1 tablespoon olive oil

2 tablespoons unsalted butter

1 tablespoon minced shallot

1 teaspoon minced garlic

1 quart heavy cream

1 cup grated aged Gouda cheese

½ cup freshly grated Parmesan cheese

Coarse salt and freshly ground pepper to taste

Freshly grated nutmeg to taste

4 Parmesan Tuile Baskets (recipe follows)

2 thin slices Virginia country ham, finely julienned

2 teaspoons finely chopped fresh chives

1 small white truffle

Bring a medium pot of salted water to a boil over high heat. Add the pasta and cook until it is al dente, about 2 minutes less than indicated on the package. (The pasta should not be done.) Drain well and transfer to a bowl. Drizzle with the olive oil and toss to keep the pasta from sticking together. (The pasta can be cooked the day before and stored, covered and refrigerated.)

Heat the butter in a medium saucepan over medium heat. Add the shallot and garlic and sauté for about 3 minutes, or until just soft with no color.

Add the cream and bring to a simmer. Lower the heat and simmer, stirring frequently, for about 15 minutes, or until the cream has reduced to 3 cups and coats the back of a metal spoon.

Whisk in the Gouda and Parmesan cheeses and cook, stirring constantly, for about 3 minutes, or until the cheeses have melted into the cream. Season with salt, pepper, and nutmeg to taste.

Remove from the heat and, if desired, strain the sauce through a fine sieve into a clean saucepan. This is done for purely aesthetic reasons, to ensure that there are no lumps; it is not at all necessary. (The sauce can be made and stored, covered and refrigerated, for up to 2 days before using.)

Return the sauce to low heat. Add the reserved pasta and cook, stirring constantly, for about 5 minutes, or until heated through.

Place a tuile basket in the center of each of four dinner plates. Spoon in about ½ cup of the macaroni and cheese. Spoon a bit of the cheese sauce around the edge of the plate. Garnish with the ham and chives.

As you serve, shave some white truffle over the top of each serving so that the diner can be enveloped with the aroma.

Serves 4

PARMESAN TUILE BASKETS

6 ounces freshly grated Parmesan cheese

Preheat the oven to 350°F.

Place a Silpat sheet (see Note) on the cookie sheet.

Spoon 1 teaspoon of the grated cheese into a pile on one corner of the Silpat. Using the back of the spoon, flatten out the cheese until it forms a circle approximately the size of a silver dollar. Continue making circles, leaving about 1 inch between each one, until the sheet is full. You can probably get about fifteen circles on a sheet.

Place the baking sheet in the preheated oven and bake for about 8 minutes, or until the circles have become lacy wafers and are golden brown.

Line up at least six 6-ounce custard dishes upside-down on a work surface.

Remove the pan from the oven and, using a spatula, carefully place a hot tuile on an inverted custard dish so that it flops over and forms a basket shape. As soon as the basket hardens—which should be almost immediately—remove it to a wire rack and continue making baskets. If the tuiles harden before you have had a chance to turn them into baskets, return them to the oven for just a few seconds to soften.

Note: Silpat sheets are reusable sheets made of silicone and fiberglass that are used to line baking sheets to prevent sticking and to facilitate easy removal of the baked product. They are used in place of parchment paper or as a substitute for buttering and flouring. They are found in most kitchen-supply stores.

223

PASTA ALLA MODA RINASCIMENTALE
(PASTA IN THE STYLE OF THE RENAISSANCE)
2002

CESARE CASELLA, *Chef/Owner, Beppe, Maremma, Cookbook Author*

Cesare Casella is the quintessential Tuscan chef. He stays true to his heritage while many others stray from the traditional kitchen. A visit to Beppe is like taking a quick trip to Tuscany. Cesare continues to promote the traditional ingredients of his homeland and has been particularly instrumental in broadening the interest in beans and grains. His company, The Republic of Beans, offers a mail-order source for many varieties of dried beans, grains, and other traditional Italian products.

Taking a class trip with him to Lucca, his birthplace, was like traveling with royalty. He has more friends and family than anyone I have ever met. Each day of the trip, more and more of them joined us to enjoy the humor and fabulous food of this unique man. The twinkle in his eye and the little herb bouquet stuck in the pocket of his chef's jacket signify that he is one of a kind. This is a marvelous traditional Italian recipe and probably the best lasagna that you will ever eat.

1 pound fresh egg pasta sheets

2 tablespoons unsalted butter, at room temperature

1½ recipes *Ragu di Carne* (recipe follows)

Besciamella (recipe follows)

1 cup freshly grated Parmigiano-Reggiano cheese

Note from Cesare: "For almost 300 years, the world has called the popular white sauce of French cuisine *béchamel* after Louis de Béchameil, a butler to Louis XIV. But Béchameil had nothing to do with the invention of this versatile white sauce. According to Italian cookbooks from the Renaissance period, *biancomangiare* or 'white food,' already existed in the 1300s. One recipe from the period calls for combining rice flour with goat, sheep, or almond milk. Legend has it that Caterina de'Medici, when she moved to France to marry Henri II, brought the recipe with her and taught her chef how to make a sauce that she called *Colla-in* (glue) in modern Italian."

Preheat the oven to 375°F.

Bring a large pot of salted water to a boil. Add the pasta sheets and boil for 1 minute. Drain well and transfer to a large bowl of cold water to chill. When chilled, transfer the pasta sheets to a platter. Set aside.

Using the 2 tablespoons of butter, lightly coat the interior of a 9 × 13-inch baking dish.

Spread an even layer of *ragu* over the bottom of the dish. Cover with a layer of pasta. Follow with an even layer of *besciamella*, then another layer of *ragu*. Sprinkle with about ¼ cup of the cheese. Cover the cheese with a layer of pasta, *besciamella*, *ragu*, then another layer of cheese. Repeat twice more, ending with a layer of cheese.

Place the baking dish in the preheated oven and bake for 35 minutes, or until bubbling and lightly browned on the top. Remove from the oven and place on a wire rack to cool for 10 minutes. Cut into squares and serve.

Serves 8 to 10

RAGU DI CARNE

¼ cup olive oil

5 cloves garlic, peeled and minced

3 ribs celery, trimmed, well washed, and chopped

1 medium onion, peeled and chopped

1 medium carrot, peeled, trimmed, and chopped

4 thin slices pancetta (or slab bacon), minced

4 thin slices prosciutto, minced

¾ pound ground pork

¾ pound ground beef

2 cups dry red wine

One 28-ounce can whole Italian tomatoes, well drained

2 cups water

½ teaspoon red pepper flakes

¼ teaspoon freshly ground black pepper

Pinch ground allspice

Pinch freshly grated nutmeg

Pinch ground cloves

Pinch ground cinnamon

Coarse salt to taste

Place the olive oil in a large heavy-bottomed saucepan over medium heat. Stir in the garlic, celery, onion, and carrot and cook, stirring frequently, for about 15 minutes, or until the vegetables are tender.

Add the pancetta, prosciutto, ground pork, and ground beef and cook, stirring frequently, for an additional 10 minutes. Stir in the wine and cook for 5 minutes.

Add the tomatoes and water and bring to a simmer. Cover and simmer for 50 minutes. Add the red pepper flakes, black pepper, allspice, nutmeg, cloves, cinnamon, and salt to taste. Stir to combine and simmer, stirring occasionally, for 90 minutes, or until the sauce is very thick and the flavors have melded.

Check the consistency frequently during the cooking process. If the sauce gets too thick before the cooking time has been reached, add water, about ½ cup at a time, and continue cooking. Taste and, if necessary, add additional salt to taste.

Remove from the heat and allow to come to room temperature. Use immediately or store, covered and refrigerated, for up to 3 days, or frozen for up to 3 months.

BESCIAMELLA

½ cup (1 stick) unsalted butter

½ cup all-purpose flour

4 cups warm milk

Pinch freshly grated nutmeg

Coarse salt and freshly ground white pepper to taste

Melt the butter in a medium heavy-bottomed saucepan over low heat. Stir in the flour and cook, stirring constantly, for 4 minutes.

Increase the heat to medium and, whisking constantly, slowly pour in the milk. Bring to a boil, lower the heat, and simmer, whisking constantly, for 5 minutes.

Season with nutmeg and salt and pepper to taste and remove from the heat.

Use immediately or transfer to a bowl, cover the surface with plastic film (to prevent a skin from forming over the top), and set aside until ready to use. The sauce may also be stored, covered and refrigerated, for up to 2 days. Reheat in a heavy-bottomed saucepan over medium heat before using.

225

BONELESS BARBECUED SPARERIBS
WITH KOHLRABI, PEANUTS, AND BASIL
2003

ANITA LO, *Chef/Owner, Annisa, Rickshaw Dumpling Bar*

Anita Lo is an eclectic chef with a seemingly limitless number of cuisines at her fingertips. She is able to combine the flavors of Asia and the Mediterranean using traditional culinary techniques to create recipes all her own. She is a perfect example of a great chef's ability to take an amalgam of ingredients and create a highly personal, unique, and titillating menu.

5 cloves garlic, peeled

1 stalk lemongrass, tender lower part only, cut into ½-inch pieces (see sidebar page 220)

1 cup sugar

1 cup *nuoc mam, nam pla,* or other Asian fish sauce (see sidebar)

1 side pork spareribs, top cut off at the end of the rib bone

Pork Stuffing (recipe follows)

2 heads kohlrabi, well washed, peeled, and thinly sliced

10 leaves Thai or opal basil

Nuoc Mam Sauce (recipe follows)

Coarse salt and freshly ground pepper to taste

Peanut Sauce (recipe follows)

Fish sauces are the most common flavoring found in Southeast Asia, replacing soy sauce as the defining note in cooking. In Vietnam **fish sauce** is called *nuoc mam;* in the Philippines, *patis;* in Thailand, *nam pla;* and in Cambodia, *tuk trey.* Fish sauce is a thin, extremely strong smelling liquid made from the extract of fermented fish or shellfish. Generally used in fairly small amounts, it lends an aromatic richness to Southeast Asian cuisine. In contemporary American cooking, it is often used to achieve this same richness in non-Asian dishes. It should not be confused with shrimp sauce, which is another pungent sauce used in much the same way.

Combine the garlic, lemongrass, sugar, and fish sauce in the bowl of a food processor fitted with the metal blade and process until well blended.

Transfer the marinade to a glass baking dish. Add the ribs and turn to coat them on all sides. Cover with plastic film and refrigerate for at least 8 hours or overnight.

When ready to bake, preheat the oven to 350°F.

Remove the ribs from the refrigerator and remove and discard the plastic film. Turn the ribs to distribute the marinade evenly. Cover the dish with aluminum foil and place in the preheated oven. Bake for about 1 hour, or until the meat begins to pull away from the bones.

Remove the ribs from the oven, uncover, and transfer to a platter to cool. Reserve the baking dish and leave the oven on.

When the ribs are cool enough to handle, carefully pull out the bones, leaving a hole in the center of each rib.

Place the stuffing in a pastry bag fitted with a wide, round tip. Force the stuffing into the holes in the ribs.

Return the stuffed ribs to the baking dish. Place the dish in the hot oven and bake, uncovered, for 20 minutes, or until the stuffing is cooked through.

While the ribs are finishing, make the salad: Combine the kohlrabi and basil in a mixing bowl. Add just enough of the *Nuoc Mam* Sauce to coat lightly. Season with salt and pepper to taste and toss to coat. Set aside.

Remove the baking dish from the oven. Using a spatula, scrape the excess marinade from the cooked ribs back into the baking dish, and scrape the cooked marinade from the baking dish into a fine sieve. Strain the cooking liquid into a clean dish, discarding the solids.

Cut the ribs into four equal portions and place one portion on each of four dinner plates. Make a ring of Peanut Sauce around the ribs, followed by a drizzle of the strained cooking juices. Mound an equal portion of the kohlrabi mixture on top of the ribs and serve.

Serves 4

PORK STUFFING

½ pound ground pork

½ cup chopped, blanched, shocked glass noodles (see Note)

3 tablespoons rehydrated, cleaned, chopped, dried tree ear mushrooms (see Note)

2 tablespoons grated carrot

2 tablespoons chopped scallion, white and green parts

1 small egg

1½ tablespoons oyster sauce, or to taste (see Note)

½ tablespoon *sriracha* or other Asian hot sauce (see Note)

Sugar to taste (see Note)

Coarse salt and freshly ground pepper to taste

Combine the pork, noodles, mushrooms, carrot, and scallion in a mixing bowl. Add the egg, oyster sauce, and *sriracha* and, using your hands, mix to combine. Season with sugar, salt, and pepper to taste. Either use immediately or cover with plastic film and refrigerate until ready to use, but for no more than a few hours.

NUOC MAM SAUCE

2 Thai bird's eye chilies, minced

1 clove garlic, peeled and mashed

¼ cup *nuoc mam, nam pla,* or other Asian fish sauce (see sidebar)

¼ cup fresh lime juice

¼ cup water

2 tablespoons sugar

2 tablespoons rice wine vinegar (see Note)

Combine all of the ingredients in a small nonreactive container. Stir to combine.

Set aside and let the flavors meld for at least 15 minutes before serving. The sauce may be stored, covered and refrigerated, for up to 3 days.

PEANUT SAUCE

½ cup unsalted chunky peanut butter

6 tablespoons water

1 tablespoon hoisin sauce (see Note)

1 tablespoon *nuoc mam, nam pla,* or other Asian fish sauce (see sidebar)

Combine all of the ingredients in a small bowl, mixing with a wooden spoon to blend well.

Set aside until ready to use. The sauce may be made up to 3 days in advance and stored, covered and refrigerated.

Note: Thai and opal basil, glass noodles, tree ear mushrooms, oyster sauce, sriracha, Thai chilies, rice wine vinegar, and hoisin sauce are all available at Asian markets.

You need just enough sugar in the pork stuffing to balance the heat and help brighten the flavors. You do not want the mixture to be sweet.

PORK BELLY WITH SOYBEAN COULIS AND TURNIPS
2003
WYLIE DUFRESNE, *Chef/Owner, wd~50*

Wylie Dufresne trained at New York City's French Culinary Institute and then took all of the traditional flavors he had absorbed and turned them upside-down. He is at the head of the pack of young, "out-there," cutting-edge chefs taking great risks in the kitchen. Wylie often tests the limits of diners with his avant-garde approach to cooking.

Once he moved from the restaurant line to his own stove at 71 Clinton Fresh Food, Wylie began doing extraordinary things with all kinds of varied—and often unexplored—ingredients, as this recipe so aptly illustrates. This is a very time-consuming recipe to accomplish at home, but the *coulis* and sauce can be made in advance and reheated when ready to serve.

8 cups plus 2 tablespoons water

6 tablespoons coarse salt, plus more to taste

5 tablespoons sugar

2 pounds pork belly

3 tablespoons clarified butter (see Note page 94)

½ tablespoon unsalted butter

2 cups fresh soybeans

1 cup peeled, blanched tiny baby turnips (see Note)

Freshly ground pepper to taste

Soybean *Coulis* (recipe follows)

Pork Belly Sauce (recipe follows)

Combine 2 cups of the water, 6 tablespoons salt, and sugar in a medium saucepan over medium heat. Heat, stirring constantly, for a minute or two, or just until the salt and sugar have dissolved. Remove from the heat and add 6 cups of the remaining water. Set aside until very cool.

Place the pork belly in a nonreactive container large enough to hold it plus the 8 cups of brine. Pour the cooled brine over the pork, cover with plastic film, and refrigerate for 24 hours.

Remove the pork from the brine. Tightly wrap the pork in plastic film to seal it completely.

Bring a medium saucepan of water to 170°F. Add the wrapped pork and poach the pork for 24 hours in water that does not go below 150°F or above 170°F.

When you're ready to finish the dish, preheat the oven to 350°F.

Remove the pork from the poaching liquid and unwrap. Using a sharp knife, carefully trim the skin from the pork and cut the pork into four equal pieces.

Heat the clarified butter in a large, ovenproof sauté pan over medium heat. Add the pork, skin side down, and transfer to the preheated oven. Roast for 8 minutes, or until the fat has crisped and the pork is warm throughout.

While the pork is roasting, prepare the turnips: Place the unsalted butter along with the remaining 2 tablespoons of water in a medium sauté pan over medium heat. Add the soybeans and turnips, season with salt and pepper to taste, and sauté for about 4 minutes, or until the turnips are nicely glazed.

Remove the pork from the oven and, if desired, cut each piece into slices. Spoon equal portions of the Soybean *Coulis* in the center of each of four dinner plates. Arrange one piece of the pork on top of the *coulis* on each plate. Spoon the soybean-turnip garnish alongside the pork and spoon some of the sauce around the edge of the plate. Serve immediately.

Serves 4

SOYBEAN COULIS

1 cup fresh soybeans

1 cup water

Coarse salt to taste

Combine the soybeans, water, and salt to taste in a blender and process to a smooth purée.

Pour the sauce from the blender into a clean container, cover, and set aside until ready to use, or for up to one day.

When ready to use, place in a small saucepan over medium heat and cook until just warmed.

PORK BELLY SAUCE

One 28-ounce can Italian plum tomatoes, well drained

4 cloves garlic, peeled

One 2-ounce piece fresh ginger, peeled and chopped

¼ cup light brown sugar

2 tablespoons *nuoc mam* or other Asian fish sauce (see sidebar page 226)

1½ tablespoons soy sauce

1 tablespoon ground star anise

2 teaspoons ground cinnamon

¼ teaspoon ground cloves

Place the tomatoes in a blender. Add the remaining ingredients and process for 4 minutes.

Pour the sauce from the blender and, if using immediately, transfer to a nonreactive saucepan and place over medium heat. Bring to a simmer, remove from the heat, and serve.

If not using immediately, transfer to a nonreactive container, cover, and refrigerate until ready to use, or for up to 5 days. Reheat in a nonreactive saucepan over medium heat before serving.

Note: Baby turnips are available from specialty produce stores, some supermarkets, and Melissa's (see page 247).

229

BRAISED HANGER STEAK
WITH OLIVE OIL–MASHED SWEET POTATOES
2003
FORTUNATO NICOTRA, *Chef, Felidia*

Fortunato Nicotra is the executive chef at Felidia, Lidia Bastianich's signature restaurant, where he has been able to retain all of the flavors of Lidia's northeastern Italian heritage while combining them with his Piedmontese sensibilities. He remains a steady influence on the popularity of Italian cooking in New York City.

Hanger steak, a classic French bistro steak, was not seen outside France until bistro-inspired restaurants began opening in New York in the eighties. It took a while but by the nineties, hanger steak was found all over the U.S. map. It even made its way into Italian menus.

Although this recipe has sweet potatoes in the title, Fortunato did not bring a recipe for them because he felt they were so simple to prepare. And they are: Roast some sweet potatoes, scrape them from their jackets, and beat enough fruity extra-virgin olive oil into the hot flesh to make it light and fluffy. Season with salt and pepper to taste and voila!

---

3 tablespoons olive oil

1 carrot, peeled, trimmed, and diced

1 onion, peeled and diced

1 rib celery, well washed, trimmed, and diced

2 tablespoons tomato paste

6 cups dry red wine

1 tablespoon honey

4 bay leaves

2 cloves garlic, peeled and crushed

Coarse salt and freshly ground pepper to taste

Two hanger steaks, well trimmed (see sidebar)

Olive Oil–Mashed Sweet Potatoes (optional; see headnote)

Heat 1 tablespoon of the olive oil in a saucepan large enough to accommodate the steaks over medium heat. Add the carrot, onion, and celery and sauté for about 5 minutes, or until the vegetables begin to soften. Stir in the tomato paste and cook for 10 minutes.

Add the wine and honey, raise the heat, and bring to a boil. Add the bay leaves and garlic and season with salt and pepper to taste. Lower the heat to a simmer and simmer for about 1 hour, or until reduced by half.

Preheat the oven to 400°F. Season the steaks with salt and pepper to taste. Place the remaining 2 tablespoons of olive oil in a large skillet over high heat. When very hot but not smoking, add the seasoned steaks and sear, turning once, for about 4 minutes, or until each side is nicely browned.

Using tongs, transfer the steaks to the reduced sauce. Cover and place in the preheated oven to braise for about 1½ hours, or until very tender. If the sauce is not thick enough, remove the steaks, place the sauce on the stovetop over high heat, and simmer until reduced to desired consistency.

Remove from the oven, lift the steaks from the sauce, and cut them crosswise into thick slices. Place equal portions of the meat on each of four plates. Spoon some sauce over the top and serve with Olive Oil–Mashed Sweet Potatoes if desired.

Serves 4

Hanger steak is a delicious cut of meat also known as "butcher's tenderloin" because wily butchers saved this very flavorful but unattractive cut of meat for themselves. It is called "hanger" because it hangs between the loin and rib cages. Virtually all hanger steaks are of the same size and will usually serve two people.

BLACK BASS IN TANGERINE SAUCE
WITH FARRO AND BLACK RICE
2002

SUZANNE GOIN, *Chef/Owner, Lucques, A.O.C, Cookbook Author*

Suzanne Goin is the essence of a modern female chef. Well-schooled and with an enormous passion for food and wine, she has complete respect for all of her ingredients and knows how to marry them well in dishes that you want to eat every day. In this recipe we see two divergent grains brought together in a most unusual, yet delicious, way.

2 cups fresh tangerine juice

Six 6-ounce black sea bass filets, skin on

Zest of 2 tangerines

1 tablespoon fresh thyme leaves

¼ cup extra-virgin olive oil

½ cup bias-cut green garlic (see Note)

Coarse salt and freshly ground pepper to taste

Farro (recipe follows)

Black Rice (recipe follows)

1 *chili de arbol* or other small dried red chili, stemmed and thinly sliced on the bias

1¾ cups reserved farro stock (see Farro recipe)

2½ cups fresh pea tendrils (see Note)

Generous pinch sugar

6 tablespoons (¾ stick) unsalted butter, cut into pieces

3 tangerines, peeled and cut into suprêmes (see Note page 207)

Chili oil for garnish (optional)

Place the tangerine juice in a small nonreactive saucepan over medium-high heat and bring to a boil. Lower the heat and simmer for about 20 minutes, or until reduced by half. Remove from the heat and set aside.

Place the bass in a glass baking dish. Add the tangerine zest and thyme, cover with plastic film, and set aside to marinate for 30 minutes.

Heat 3 tablespoons of the oil in a large sauté pan over medium heat. Add the garlic, season with salt and pepper to taste, and sauté for about 3 minutes, or until just tender but not taking on any color. Add the farro and rice along with the chili and cook, stirring constantly, for about 12 minutes, or until the grains are very hot and beginning to "dance" in the pan. Add 1 cup of the farro stock and cook, stirring frequently, for about 5 minutes, or until the stock is almost absorbed.

Stir in the pea tendrils and remove from the heat so that the pea tendrils just wilt. Keep warm.

Heat the remaining tablespoon of oil in a large sauté pan over high heat. Remove the fish from the baking dish, season with salt and pepper to taste, and place in the hot oil, skin side down. Sear, turning once, for about 6 minutes, or until nicely browned but still rare in the center. Using a slotted spoon, transfer the fish to a warm plate. Tent lightly with aluminum foil to finish cooking.

Pour off any fat remaining in the sauté pan. Add the reduced tangerine juice along with the sugar and place over high heat. Bring to a boil, then immediately add the remaining ¾ cup of farro stock. Return to a boil and whisk in the butter. When the butter is fully incorporated, add the tangerine suprêmes. Taste and, if necessary, adjust the seasoning with salt and pepper to taste.

Spoon equal portions of the farro-rice mixture in the center of each of six dinner plates. Place a piece of fish on top and spoon some of the sauce, including tangerine pieces, over the fish and around the plate. Serve immediately, drizzled with a bit of chili oil if desired.

Serves 6

FARRO

2 tablespoons extra-virgin olive oil

1 medium onion, peeled and cut into quarters, with the root end left intact

1 medium carrot, peeled, trimmed, and cut into chunks

1 rib celery, well washed, trimmed, and cut crosswise into quarters

1½ cups farro (see Note)

½ cup white wine

6 cups water

1 teaspoon coarse salt, or to taste

¼ bunch fresh flat-leaf parsley, well washed

¼ bunch fresh thyme, well washed

Heat the oil in a medium, heavy-bottomed saucepan over medium heat. Add the onion, carrot, and celery and sauté for about 5 minutes, or until the vegetables begin to caramelize. Stir in the farro and, stirring constantly, cook the farro for about 5 minutes, or until aromatic and toasted.

Add the wine and, stirring constantly with a wooden spoon, deglaze the pan. Cook for 1 minute, then add the water and salt.

Using kitchen twine, tie the parsley and thyme together and add them to the farro. Bring the farro to a simmer, lower the heat, and simmer for about 45 minutes, or until the farro is tender.

Remove from the heat and strain through a fine sieve, reserving the cooking liquid and discarding the vegetables and herbs.

Place the farro on a baking pan, spreading it out with a spatula to form an even layer. Allow to cool.

BLACK RICE

2 tablespoons extra-virgin olive oil

1½ cups black rice (see Note)

2 shallots, peeled and diced

1 bay leaf

½ cup dry white wine

4½ cups water

½ teaspoon coarse salt, or to taste

Heat the oil in a medium, heavy-bottomed saucepan over medium heat. Add the rice and sauté for about 4 minutes, or until aromatic and slightly toasted. Add the shallots and bay leaf and cook, stirring constantly, for 1 minute. Add the wine and cook for about 3 minutes, or until reduced slightly.

Add the water and salt and stir to combine. Bring to a simmer, lower the heat, and simmer for an hour, or until the rice is al dente and the liquid has cooked down to form a sauce that coats the rice. If the water evaporates before the rice is done, add water, no more than ¼ cup at a time. When the rice is done, there should be no liquid remaining in the pan.

Place the rice on a baking pan, spreading it out with a spatula to form an even layer. Allow to cool.

Note: Green or immature garlic is available from Asian markets, specialty food stores, and Melissa's (see page 247). Fresh pea tendrils are also available from Asian markets as well as some specialty produce stores.

Farro is a traditional Italian grain, often called Tuscan couscous, that is available from Italian markets and some specialty and health-food stores.

Black rice is an unpolished, long-grain rice with a slightly sweet, earthy flavor and chewy texture when cooked. It is available from Southeast Asian markets and some specialty food stores.

233

ARCTIC CHAR AND ORGANIC BEET STEW
WITH SOYBEANS AND PINE NUTS
2001

DAN BARBER, *Chef/Owner, with* MICHAEL ANTHONY, *Chef, Blue Hill, Blue Hill at Stone Barns*

"Organic" became the culinary key word at the turn of the twenty-first century, and Dan Barber at his restaurant Blue Hill in New York City's Greenwich Village was saying it the loudest. It is a wonderfully romantic restaurant where you dine superbly, eating the most delicious—and often unusual—dishes that use absolutely pristine ingredients.

Dan has taken the organic experience to a totally new level at Blue Hill at Stone Barns, a restaurant on the Rockefeller property at Pocantico Hills, New York, where much of what is served comes from the restaurant's own gardens and greenhouses. Along with Michael Anthony, chef-in-residence there, Dan has made his dream a reality.

8 medium organic beets, well washed

3 cloves organic garlic, peeled

1 sprig fresh lemon thyme

Coarse salt and freshly ground pepper to taste

1 cup olive oil

2 cups freshly squeezed orange juice, preferably from organic oranges

1 grapefruit suprême, chopped (see Note page 207)

1 tablespoon fresh soybeans, blanched and peeled

1 tablespoon toasted pine nuts

1 teaspoon honey

1 teaspoon minced mixed fresh organic herbs (parsley, thyme, chives, tarragon, or whatever mix you like)

1 teaspoon white balsamic vinegar (see Note)

4 pounds arctic char filet

Preheat the oven to 350°F.

Place the beets on a large piece of heavy-duty aluminum foil. Add the garlic, lemon thyme, and salt and pepper to taste. Drizzle with the olive oil and toss to coat. Pull the foil up and around the beets to seal tightly. Place the packet in a baking pan in the preheated oven and roast for about 1 hour, or until the beets are tender when pierced with the point of a small, sharp knife.

Remove from the oven, unwrap, and set aside to cool.

Place the orange juice in a small nonreactive saucepan over medium heat and bring to a boil. Lower the heat and simmer for about 30 minutes, or until reduced by half. Remove from the heat and set aside.

Preheat the oven to 275°F.

Peel and trim the cooled beets and cut them into ¼-inch dice, setting the trimmings aside.

Place the trimmings in a blender or food processor and process to a smooth purée.

Combine the diced beets, grapefruit, soybeans, pine nuts, honey, and herbs in a small saucepan. Add the balsamic vinegar, beet purée, and the reduced orange juice and place over low heat. Taste and, if desired, season with salt and pepper to taste.

Season the char with salt and pepper to taste. Place the char on a lightly oiled baking dish in the preheated oven and roast for 10 minutes, or until just barely warmed through.

Spoon the beet stew on a platter. Lay the char on top and serve.

Note: White balsamic vinegar is available at Italian markets and some specialty food stores.

Serves 8

FLUKE WITH SEA BEANS AND RADISH
2001
DAVID PASTERNAK, *Chef/Partner, Esca, Bistro Du Vent*

David Pasternak is one of New York's fish mavens, practicing his art at the acclaimed restaurant, Esca. He demands that we use only the freshest, most beautiful seafood. Unfortunately, we are not all privy to David's suppliers, so some of his dishes are impossible to prepare at home. For this dish you do need absolutely pristine fluke, so be first in line when the boat comes in at the dock!

Crudo is the defining word for David. At a time when seviche (also known as ceviche or cebiche) had become "old hat," chefs, led by David, began to serve *crudo* (Italian for "raw food"). The term is primarily used for appetizer portions of pristine, uncooked meat or fish served thinly sliced and beautifully garnished with exquisite oils or complementary herbs or vegetables. Vegetables are also served in this same fashion.

David always has a newly discovered olive oil that he introduces to each class. His latest loves have been oils from Sicily and Liguria. To finish this dish, you will need a very light, fruity, extra-virgin olive oil.

---

4 ounces sea beans (see Note)

4 ounces red radish, well washed and cut crosswise into thin slices

Coarse sea salt to taste

Fresh lime juice to taste

8 ounces sushi-grade fluke, cleaned, with the blood line removed

Freshly ground pepper to taste

Extra-virgin olive oil for drizzling

Chill four luncheon plates in the freezer.

Gently toss the sea beans and radish together in a small bowl. Season with a bit of sea salt and a squeeze of lime juice.

Using a very sharp knife, cut the fluke into paper-thin slices.

Remove the plates from the freezer. Arrange equal portions of the fluke, with slices overlapping slightly, on each plate. Season the fluke with a bit of sea salt, pepper, and a squeeze of lime juice. Place a small mound of the sea-bean salad on each plate. Drizzle a bit of olive oil over each plate and serve immediately.

Note: Also called samphire, glasswort, and sea pickle, sea beans are a type of beach plant that grows along both the Pacific and Atlantic coasts. The plant rather resembles a cactus without needles. Both the leaves and stems are edible, quite crisp with a taste of the sea. They are available fresh during the summer and early fall at specialty food markets and some fish markets. Although called samphire, sea beans are a different species than European samphire (see sidebar page 24).

Serves 4

CHOCOLATE TART
2000

FRANÇOIS PAYARD, *Pastry Chef/Owner, Payard Patisserie & Bistro, Cookbook Author*

I first met François Payard when he was pastry chef for Daniel Boulud. He subsequently opened what is, to me, the most beautiful patisserie and restaurant in Manhattan, serving food equal to the romantic setting. When you walk in, you feel as though you are in Paris. François's pastries are quintessentially French, and it is rather nice to feel that no matter how much has changed in the contemporary kitchen, some things have remained the same. We salute the constancy of the classic French kitchen!

In all our years François has been the only teacher to tell the class, "Be quiet and listen to me because I have more to say—if you want to learn, you have to listen!" I can tell you that no one, including me, makes a sound while he is teaching. We all feel as though we are in the hands of a master, and you know what, we are!

---

1 pound fine-quality bittersweet chocolate, finely chopped

1¾ cups heavy cream

¾ cup milk

3 large eggs

2 Tart Shells (recipe follows)

Preheat the oven to 350°F.

Place the chocolate in a stainless-steel or other heatproof bowl. Set aside.

Combine the cream and milk in a medium saucepan over medium heat and bring to a boil, watching carefully to ensure that the mixture doesn't boil over or scorch. Immediately remove from the heat and, stirring slowly, pour the hot liquid over the chocolate until the mixture has blended completely and the chocolate is melted.

Whisk the eggs together in a heatproof bowl. Whisking constantly, add about a third of the hot chocolate mixture to the eggs to temper them. When blended, gently whisk the egg mixture into the hot chocolate mixture.

Pour an equal portion of the chocolate into each of the baked tart shells, filling each shell almost to the top. Place in the preheated oven and bake for about 15 minutes or until the centers are set.

Remove from the oven and place on wire racks to cool before serving.

Makes two 9-inch tarts

TART SHELLS

1 pound, 1.6 ounces (about 3 cups plus 1½ tablespoons) all-purpose flour, plus more for the work surface

½ pound (2 cups) confectioners' sugar

Seeds from 1 vanilla bean

½ pound (1 cup or 2 sticks) unsalted butter, cut into small pieces and chilled

3 large eggs

Combine the flour and sugar in the bowl of a heavy-duty electric mixer fitted with the paddle attachment. Mix in the vanilla seeds.

Add the chilled butter and mix on low speed for about 3 minutes, or until the dough looks crumbly and the butter is in small particles.

With the motor running, add the eggs one at a time, mixing just until the eggs are incorporated.

Scrape the dough from the bowl and form into a neat ball. Wrap with plastic film and refrigerate for 1 hour.

Preheat the oven to 350°F. Lightly flour a work surface.

Remove the dough from the refrigerator and unwrap. Divide the dough into two equal pieces.

Using a rolling pin, roll each piece of dough out to an ⅛-inch-thick circle about 11 inches in diameter.

Lightly coat two 9-inch tart pans with removable bottoms with vegetable spray. Fit a dough circle into each of the prepared pans, carefully pinching off any dough hanging over the edges. Using a dinner fork, prick the dough all over.

Cut a piece of parchment paper to fit the bottom of each tart shell. Place the parchment paper into each shell, then cover it with pie weights or dried beans.

Place the pans in the preheated oven and bake for 10 minutes. Remove the weights and parchment paper and bake the shells for an additional 5 minutes, or until cooked through and light brown.

Remove from the oven and set aside to cool.

237

CHOCOLATE CREPES SUZETTE
WITH MEYER LEMON CONFIT
2003

JOHNNY IUZZINI, *Pastry Chef, Jean Georges*

Johnny Iuzzini is another great pastry chef whom I first encountered when he was in the kitchen of Restaurant Daniel. He was somewhat "different" in that he had blue hair and a very carefree style. But when it came to baking, Johnny was demanding and precise, but with all the imagination that his blue hair indicated. Although steeped in the French classics, Johnny loves to take them out on a limb. He is a prime example of the future of the American chef in the dessert kitchen.

1½ cups all-purpose flour

¼ cup plus 2 teaspoons cocoa powder

¼ cup sugar

1 teaspoon salt

8 large eggs, at room temperature

¼ cup plus 1½ tablespoons brown butter (see Note)

2 tablespoons plus 1 teaspoon rum

2 tablespoons plus 1 teaspoon Grand Marnier

2 cups milk

1 cup heavy cream

Suzette Sauce (recipe follows)

Meyer Lemon Curd (recipe follows)

48 Meyer lemon suprêmes (see Note page 207)

Meyer Lemon Confit (recipe follows)

Fleur de sel for garnish

To make the crepe batter, combine the flour, cocoa powder, sugar, and salt in the bowl of a heavy-duty electric mixer fitter with the whisk attachment. With the motor running on low, beat in the eggs.

When the eggs are incorporated, scrape down the sides of the bowl and beat in the brown butter. Add the rum and Grand Marnier and beat to blend.

Beat in the milk and then the cream, mixing just enough to barely incorporate.

Transfer to a container with a lid, cover, and refrigerate for at least 8 hours or overnight.

When ready to serve, preheat the oven to 350°F.

Heat a nonstick crepe pan over medium-low heat. Ladle in just enough batter to coat the bottom of the pan evenly (about 2 tablespoons). Cook for about 1 minute, or until the crepe is just set and can easily be flipped. Flip and cook the remaining side for 30 seconds. Carefully slide the crepe from the pan and set aside. Continue cooking crepes until you have 24. You might want to make a couple of extras in case one tears.

Using a pastry brush on one crepe at a time, lightly coat half of each crepe with some Suzette Sauce. Place a tablespoon of lemon curd in the center and top with a suprême. Fold the crepe over the filling to make a half-moon shape. Using a pastry brush, lightly coat the top with Suzette Sauce.

Transfer the finished crepes to a baking sheet and place in the preheated oven for about 3 minutes, or until warmed through.

Remove from the oven and serve, two per person, garnished with a spoonful of confit and a sprinkle of *fleur de sel*.

Serves 12

238

SUZETTE SAUCE

1 cup sugar

¾ cup plus 2½ tablespoons freshly squeezed Meyer lemon juice

¾ cup freshly squeezed orange juice

1½ cups (3 sticks) salted butter, cut into pieces

Zest of 1 orange

Zest of 1 Meyer lemon

Place the sugar in a medium, heavy-bottomed saucepan over medium heat and cook, stirring frequently, for about 6 minutes, or until the sugar has caramelized.

Carefully pour in ¾ cup of the lemon juice along with the orange juice and stir with a wooden spoon to deglaze the pan.

Add the butter and stir to combine. Bring to a boil, then immediately remove from the heat.

Beat in the remaining lemon juice along with the orange and lemon zests. Keep warm until ready to use.

MEYER LEMON CURD

1 cup sugar

½ cup freshly squeezed Meyer lemon juice

5 large eggs, at room temperature

½ cup (1 stick) plus 2½ tablespoons unsalted butter, at room temperature

1½ sheets gelatin, softened in a bowl of cool water

Zest of 1 Meyer lemon

Combine the sugar and lemon juice in a medium, heavy-bottomed saucepan. Stir in the eggs and butter and place over medium heat. Cook, whisking constantly, for about 5 minutes, or until the mixture comes to a low boil.

Remove from the heat and whisk in the gelatin.

Pass through a fine sieve into a clean container. Stir in the zest and immediately place in an ice-water bath to cool.

When cool, cover with plastic film and refrigerate until ready to use, or for up to 5 days.

MEYER LEMON CONFIT

½ pound Meyer lemons, preferably organic, well washed and cut crosswise into ⅛-inch-thick slices, seeds removed

Sugar to equal half the weight of the sliced lemons

Weigh the lemon slices. Then weigh enough sugar to equal half the weight of the lemons.

Sprinkle a thin layer of sugar in the bottom of a heavy-bottomed Dutch oven–type pan. Add a single layer of lemon slices and cover with sugar. Continue making layers until all of the lemons and sugar have been used. Add just enough water to barely cover. Place a piece of parchment paper cut to fit the top of the pan over the lemons. Place over very low heat and cook for about 3 hours, or until the lemon slices are almost transparent.

Remove from the heat and place the pan in an ice-water bath to cool.

When cool, carefully remove the confit to a shallow container and store, covered and refrigerated, until ready to use, or for up to 1 month.

Note: Brown butter, also known as beurre noisette, is butter, either salted or unsalted, that has been cooked slowly until it has a light-brown color and a nutty aroma and taste.

239

CHOCOLATE CREAM
WITH COCONUT BAILEYS SOUP
AND CHOCOLATE-FLAVORED PUFFED-RICE CEREAL
2004

JEHANGIR MEHTA, *Pastry Chef, AIX*

Jehangir Mehta has made his mark on the New York restaurant scene with very exotic combinations of flavors and ingredients. He is currently wowing diners at AIX, a wonderful French-inspired restaurant on New York City's Upper West Side. Although his desserts are often conceptually unusual, the flavors, textures, and ingredients all seem to come together with absolutely delicious results. Jehangir represents the extremes to which the contemporary American pastry kitchen has gone. He is fearless!

2 cups finely chopped fine-quality bittersweet chocolate

½ cup (about 6 large) egg yolks

½ cup sugar

2 cups heavy cream

Coconut Baileys Soup (recipe follows)

Chocolate-Covered Cocoa Puffs (recipe follows)

To make the chocolate cream, place the chocolate in a stainless-steel or other heatproof bowl. Set aside.

Place the egg yolks and ¼ cup of the sugar in another stainless-steel (or other heatproof) bowl and whisk to combine. Set aside.

Combine the cream with the remaining ¼ cup of the sugar in a medium, heavy-bottomed saucepan over high heat and bring to a boil. Immediately remove from the heat and, whisking constantly, pour the hot cream into the egg-yolk mixture.

When well combined, transfer the mixture back to the saucepan in which you heated the cream and place over medium heat. Cook, whisking constantly, for 2 minutes, or until the mixture easily coats the back of a spoon.

Remove the cream mixture from the heat and, whisking constantly, pour it over the chocolate. When well blended, cover with plastic film and refrigerate for about an hour, or until the texture of the mixture resembles ice cream.

When ready to serve, place an ice cream scoop of the chocolate cream in the center of each of six shallow soup bowls (you will have leftovers—yummy!). Pour equal portions of the soup into each bowl, taking care not to disturb the chocolate cream. Sprinkle with Chocolate-Covered Cocoa Puffs and serve immediately.

Serves 6

240

COCONUT BAILEYS SOUP

2 cups frozen coconut purée, thawed
(see Note)

¾ cup Baileys Irish Cream liqueur

Combine the coconut purée and liqueur in a mixing bowl, whisking to combine well.

Pass through a fine sieve into a clean container to remove any lumps. Cover and refrigerate for about 2 hours, or until ready to use. (If making ahead of time, the soup can be stored, covered and refrigerated, for up to 2 days.)

Serve well chilled.

CHOCOLATE-FLAVORED PUFFED-RICE CEREAL

½ cup sugar

2 cups chocolate-flavored puffed-rice
cereal

Line a baking pan with parchment paper. Set aside.

Place the sugar in a medium, heavy-bottomed saucepan over medium heat and cook, stirring occasionally, for about 7 minutes, or until the sugar has caramelized.

Stir in the cereal until coated with the hot syrup.

Transfer the hot mixture to the parchment-lined baking pan, spreading it out as much as possible without breaking up the mix too much. Set aside until cool enough to handle.

When cool enough, break the cereal into small pieces. Store, tightly covered, until ready to use, or for up to 5 days.

Note: Frozen coconut purée is available from East Indian markets and some specialty food stores.

241

IN THE
DE GUSTIBUS
CLASSROOM

Hands-On Classes

ON LOCATION

*In the late nineties, we took
De Gustibus out of the Macy's
classroom and into the restaurant
kitchen as we began a series of what
we called Hands-On Classes. In these
classes the students went into restaurant kitchens to prepare menus devised
by working chefs. We found that these
classes gave home cooks not only the
opportunity to see how restaurant
kitchens work on a daily basis, but also
the feeling (if only for a couple of
hours) that they could truly
"stand the heat."*

*In a typical Hands-On Class, the
chef and cooks all pitch in to make
the kitchen time as professional (and
fun) as possible. The class's morning
activities are topped off by the thrills
of joining the chef for lunch, and
dining on food that they have
jointly prepared.*

PROVENCE, FRANCE

Class Trips

LUCCA, ITALY

CONVERSION CHARTS

WEIGHT EQUIVALENTS

The metric weights given in this chart are not exact equivalents, but have been rounded up or down slightly to make measuring easier.

AVOIRDUPOIS	METRIC
¼ oz	7 g
½ oz	15 g
1 oz	30 g
2 oz	60 g
3 oz	90 g
4 oz	115 g
5 oz	150 g
6 oz	175 g
7 oz	200 g
8 oz (½ lb)	225 g
9 oz	250 g
10 oz	300 g
11 oz	325 g
12 oz	350 g
13 oz	375 g
14 oz	400 g
15 oz	425 g
16 oz (1 lb)	450 g
1½ lb	750 g
2 lb	900 g
2¼ lb	1 kg
3 lb	1.4 kg
4 lb	1.8 kg

VOLUME EQUIVALENTS

These are not exact equivalents for American cups and spoons, but have been rounded up or down slightly to make measuring easier.

AMERICAN	METRIC	IMPERIAL
¼ t	1.2 ml	
½ t	2.5 ml	
1 t	5.0 ml	
½ T (1.5 t)	7.5 ml	
1 T (3 t)	15 ml	
¼ cup (4 T)	60 ml	2 fl oz
⅓ cup (5 T)	75 ml	2½ fl oz
½ cup (8 T)	125 ml	4 fl oz
⅔ cup (10 T)	150 ml	5 fl oz
¾ cup (12 T)	175 ml	6 fl oz
1 cup (16 T)	250 ml	8 fl oz
1¼ cups	300 ml	10 fl oz (½ pt)
1½ cups	350 ml	12 fl oz
2 cups (1 pint)	500 ml	16 fl oz
2½ cups	625 ml	20 fl oz (1 pint)
1 quart	1 liter	32 fl oz

OVEN TEMPERATURE EQUIVALENTS

OVEN MARK	F	C	GAS
Very cool	250–275	130–140	½ –1
Cool	300	150	2
Warm	325	170	3
Moderate	350	180	4
Moderately hot	375	190	5
	400	200	6
Hot	425	220	7
	450	230	8
Very hot	475	250	9

SOURCES

CHEESES

The Artisanal Cheese Center
www.artisanalcheese.com;
877-797-1200

Coach Farm
www.coachfarm.com;
800-999-4628

CHILIES, SPICES, AND HERBS

Adriana's Caravan
www.adrianascaravan.com;
800-316-0820

Kalustyan's
www.kalustyan.com;
212-685-3451

Melissa's
www.melissas.com; 800-588-0151

Penzey's Spices
www.penzeys.com; 800-741-7787

FISH AND SHELLFISH

Browne Trading Company
www.browne-trading.com;
800-944-7848

Ducktrap River Fish Farm
www.ducktrap.com; 800-828-3825

Paramont Caviar
www.paramountcaviar.com

KITCHEN EQUIPMENT

Macy's
www.macys.com; 212-695-4400

Bridge Kitchenware
www.bridgekitchenware.com;
212-688-4220

Broadway Panhandler
www.broadwaypanhandler.com;
866-COOKWARE

J. B. Prince Company, Inc.
www.jbprince.com; 800-473-0577

Korin Japanese Trading
www.korin.com; 800-626-6235

Sur La Table
www.surlatable.com;
800-243-0852

Williams-Sonoma
www.williams-sonoma.com;
877-812-6235

MEAT, GAME, AND POULTRY

D'Artagnan
www.dartagnan.com;
800-327-8246

Hudson Valley Foie Gras
www.hudsonvalleyfoiegras.com;
845-292-2500

Niman Ranch
www.nimanranch.com;
866-808-0340

Jamison Farm
www.jamisonfarm.com;
800-237-5262

Salumeria Biellese
212-736-7376

SPECIALTY FOOD STORES & WEB SITES

American Spoon Foods
www.spoon.com; 800-222-5866

Asia Market
212-962-2028

Buon Italia
www.buonitalia.com;
212-633-9909

Citarella
www.citarella.com; 212-874-0383

Dean and Deluca
www.deandeluca.com;
800-221-7714

Katagiri
www.katagiri.com; 212-755-3566

The Kitchen Market
(for Mexican/Southwest ingredients)
www.kitchenmarket.com;
212-243-4433

Kosher Depot
www.kosherdepot.biz;
718-479-3206

La Tienda
(for Spanish ingredients)
www.latienda.com; 888-472-1022

Zabar's
www.zabars.com; 800-697-6301

Zingerman's
www.zingermans.com;
888-636-8162

TRUFFLES AND WILD MUSHROOMS

Urbani Truffles
www.urbani.com; 800-281-2330

Marché aux Delices
www.auxdelices.com;
888-547-5471

WINE INFORMATION

Kobrand Corporation
www.kobrandwine.com;
212-490-9300

INDEX OF CHEFS

Page numbers in *italic* refer to photographs.

249

INDEX OF RECIPES AND INGREDIENTS

250

252

253

255

Thank you very much to Arlene, Bobbi and Florence for you help who made this demonstration attractive and fun! Keep the calories away from now on!

[signature]

Arlene —
wow, was that some experience! want you to know how grateful i am that you considered me to give a class. i enjoyed every minute (then collapsed on my bed as soon as i got home!). i really loved working with — and was so impressed by — your staff.

The best place to be in New York ... ...with Arlene

[signature]

To the Great Crew at De Gustibus. You are the Best! Not My hands down

To Dear Arlene and to all the girls that made it so easy.
Thank you
Con affetto
Nidia

Dear Arlene,
I just wanted to thank you again for inviting me on the De Gustibus program. Your arrangements & organisation were excellent and it was a great pleasure to work with you.
Please do drop by any time you are in Paris
All best wishes for the continuing success of the series

[signature]

Dear Arlene —
Just a note to thank you for your assistance with the Cooking Class. Daughters was without a doubt our best experience with the New York Trip. Your team is tops and you run a great operation
Best Cathy.

DEAR all —
Thanks for treating us so well! You have spoiled us for all our other Classes
Emmy, Mark, Parke

What a Wonderful Evening
I enjoyed the Evening to no ends
Sincerely
Edna Lewis

Arlene,
Thanks for having me at De Gustibus. Your staff was fantastic; so helpful + friendly and it was amazing to see + experience what you've worked so hard to build + grow. The place feels of 1,000 good times.

I'll be back hopefully on a book tour w/ books in hand?!!

Happy Holidays!

Ana Sofia

It was nice to be here!
Seggi

Arlene ~
Thank you for having me at De Gustibus. You are always so wonderful to speak to—you instill such energy and creativity in your classes. We enjoyed it very much—and the knives are fabulous!

David Page and Barbara Shinn
Home Restaurant

To the Wonderful Staff at De Gustibus,
My Many Thanks For Such a Wonderful Team Effort. You Made It so Easy to Have Fun And Enjoy My Class At Your School.

All My Best For a Wonderful Holiday!
James Barrett

Dear Arlene,
Had a wonderful and challenging time at De Gustibus. Thanks for all your help and support. Your staff was great.

Best—
Jan

Best Wishes to all my new friends.

Wow, what an extraordinary time. I can't thank everyone enough for all the support and hard work. It was wonderful working and with a team such as De Gustibus. Congratulations again on being one as well.

Sincerely,
Scott Brehm @ Elis

P.S. Looking forward to seeing everyone @ Elis

Dear Arlene—
A belated but sincere thanks for having Joe and me at De Gustibus. My highest compliments to you and your terrific staff. We felt very welcome and your efforts on behalf of our book were greatly appreciated. Any time you want us back, we'll be there?!. And thanks so much for accomodating my mother and her friends — very generous.

All Best,
David Lynch